The Atlantic Slave Trade
Second Edition

This survey is a synthesis of the economic, social, cultural, and political history of the Atlantic slave trade, providing the general reader with a basic understanding of the current state of scholarly knowledge of forced African migration and compares this knowledge to popular beliefs. *The Atlantic Slave Trade* examines the four hundred years of Atlantic slave trade, covering the West and East African experiences, as well as all the American colonies and republics that obtained slaves from Africa. It outlines both the common features of this trade and the local differences that developed. It discusses the slave trade's economics, politics, demographic impact, and cultural implications in relationship to Africa as well as America. Finally, it places the slave trade in the context of world trade and examines the role it played in the growing relationship between Asia, Africa, Europe, and America. This new edition incorporates the latest findings of the last decade in slave trade studies carried out in Europe and America. It also includes new data on the slave trade voyages that have just recently been made available to the public.

Herbert S. Klein is the author of 22 books and 155 articles in several languages on Latin America and comparative themes in social and economic history. Among these books are *The Middle Passage: Comparative Studies in the Atlantic Slave Trade* (1978) and four studies of slavery, the most recent of which are *Slavery and the Economy of São Paulo, 1750–1850* (co-author, 2003); *African Slavery in Latin America and the Caribbean* (co-author, 2008), and *Slavery in Brazil* (co-author, 2009), as well as four books on Bolivian history, including *A Concise History of Bolivia* (2003). He has also published books on such diverse themes as *The American Finances of the Spanish Empire, 1680–1809* (1998) and *A Population History of the United States* (2004).

New Approaches to the Americas

Edited by Stuart Schwartz, *Yale University*

Also published in the series

THE ATLANTIC
SLAVE TRADE

SECOND EDITION

HERBERT S. KLEIN

Stanford University

CAMBRIDGE
UNIVERSITY PRESS

CAMBRIDGE UNIVERSITY PRESS
Cambridge, New York, Melbourne, Madrid, Cape Town,
Singapore, São Paulo, Delhi, Mexico City

Cambridge University Press
32 Avenue of the Americas, New York, NY 10013-2473, USA

www.cambridge.org
Information on this title: www.cambridge.org/9780521182508

First published 2010
Reprinted 2011 (twice), 2012, 2013

A catalog record for this publication is available from the British Library.

Library of Congress Cataloging in Publication Data

Klein, Herbert S.
The Atlantic slave trade / Herbert S. Klein. – 2nd ed.
    p.   cm. – (New approaches to the Americas)
Includes bibliographical references and index.
ISBN 978-0-521-18250-8 (pbk.)
1. Slave trade – Africa.   2. Slave trade – Europe.   3. Slave trade – America.
I. Title. II. Series.
HT1322.K54 2010
306.3´6209–dc22   2010002320

ISBN 978-0-521-76630-2 Hardback
ISBN 978-0-521-18250-8 Paperback

CONTENTS

List of Maps, Figures, and Tables

Maps

Figures

Tables

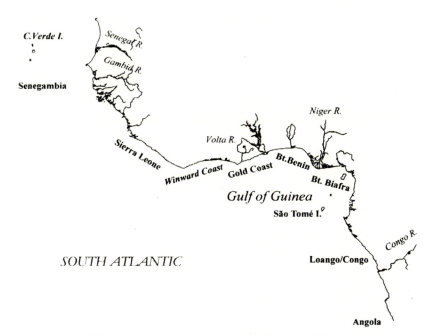

Map 1. Major slave-trading zones of western Africa.

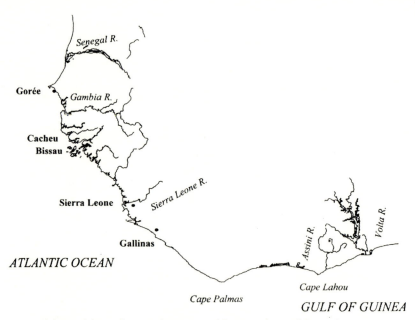

Map 2. Major slave-trading ports of Senegambia and Sierra Leone.

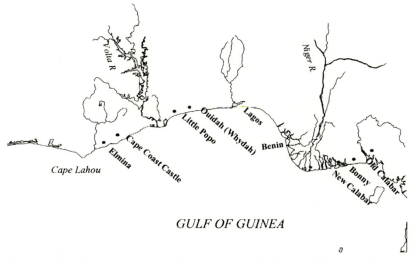

GULF OF GUINEA

Map 3. Major slaving ports of the Gold Coast and the Bights of Benin and Biafra.

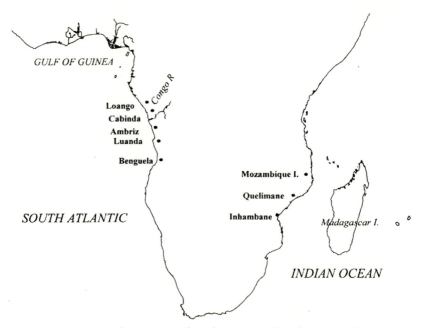

Map 4. Major slaving ports of southwestern and southeastern Africa.

Introduction

Despite its central importance in the economic and social history of Western expansion, its fundamental role in the history of America, and its profound impact on African society, the Atlantic slave trade remained one of the least studied areas in modern Western historiography until the past quarter century. This late start was not due to any lack of sources, for the materials available for its study were abundant from the very beginning. Rather, it was ignored because of its close association with European imperialism and a resulting lack of interest in a morally difficult problem, and because of a lack of tools with which to analyze the complex quantitative data.

Even today, despite a quarter century of sophisticated multinational studies, the gap between popular understanding and scholarly knowledge remains as profound as when the trade was first under discussion in literate European circles in the eighteenth century. For a variety of political and intellectual reasons having a great deal to do with the nature of contemporary North American politics, the scholarly research is largely ignored as a society riven by racial conflict finds the trade a topic too difficult to treat in a rational manner. Yet, in the heat of the debate it is this rationality that is most needed.

Not only has there been a failure in the dialogue between the academic and general literate world, but there is a surprising ignorance even within the scholarly world at large about the nature of the trade. There exist few coherent summaries of the recent literature on the slave trade for the general or scholarly public, and this failure to communicate the recent scholarly research has allowed the general discussion about the trade to become so politicized and emotional that most academics and intellectuals refuse to confront the trade with anything approaching a rational analysis. It is for all these reasons that I have undertaken this survey of the current knowledge of the Atlantic slave trade. Though much is still unknown about the trade, there is already a surprising consensus among scholars as to its general shape and its economic arrangements. There is even some fundamental scholarly, if not popular, agreement about the numbers involved. This consensus crosses academic areas and national boundaries, and as much as possible I have tried to incorporate the latest findings from all the relevant disciplines and international literature.

In many ways the delay in providing a survey such as this is due to the very depth and complexity of the materials. To understand the trade one must be literate in demographic history and quantitative analysis, have a good grounding in economics, and read several languages. This is aside from having a detailed knowledge of the history of Africa and the Americas in this period. Even these tools are insufficient, as some basic anthropological understanding is also required. While any one scholar can only approximate these requirements, I hope that I have laid enough of a foundation so that scholars more prepared than I in any one of these areas can build on the work I have provided.

Before examining the trade in detail, it is worth exploring the historiography on this subject, which goes back to the eighteenth century. The first studies of the Atlantic slave trade began in the 1750s at the very height of its momentum, when some 75,000 slaves were arriving in the ports of America each year. In an attempt to build a case against the forced migration of African slaves, English abolitionists tried to determine the basic dimensions of the trade, the patterns of mortality of slaves and crew, and the relative economic impact of the trade on the African and American economies. Though the aim was to provide useful propaganda for their anti–slave trade campaign the abolitionists did engage in some serious research. When the English Parliament began to impose the first formal constraints on the traders in the 1780s and 1790s, it initiated the systematic collection of statistical materials on the trade by British government agencies, a service that the government would continue until the middle of the nineteenth century.

Along with these published sources, almost all European slaving nations kept detailed statistical records on the trade for tax purposes. A good many private company records found their way into the national archives of Europe and America in the nineteenth century. Finally, in the late eighteenth and early nineteenth centuries, commercial newspapers kept detailed records of African slave ship arrivals and departures.

From all these published and documentary sources, something like half or more of the slaving voyages ever undertaken have left a written record.

Yet after the 1810s, there was little interest in analyzing the trade. The British abolitionists had convinced their own government to terminate the trade, and then proceeded to use force and persuasion to abolish the trade in other nations. At the same time, the termination of the Atlantic slave trade in the middle decades of the nineteenth century coincided with the European conquest and colonization of Africa, as well as the growing domination of imperialist and racist ideology in metropolitan thought. In this context there was little interest in discussing the slave trade, which was deemed by most writers to have been a necessary evil at worst, if not a positive benefit to the world through its supposedly "civilizing" efforts.

It was not until the crisis of World War I that European intellectuals began to question the basic assumptions behind imperialism. In this debate, the Atlantic slave trade became one of the "crimes" of Western imperialism and could only be denigrated. It was from this perspective of paternalism that writers began to restudy European contact with the rest of the world. The result was a narrative filled with stories of violence and exploitation, based on a minimum of research and an ignorance of the archival sources. This literature created a series of myths about the African participation, the costs of the trade, the pattern of shipping slaves across the Atlantic, the mortality they suffered, and the ultimate gains and benefits to the Europeans. "Tight packing," "astronomic" mortality rates of 50 percent or more, "cheap slaves" bought for supposedly worthless beads and costless rum and the so-called triangular trade all were added to the crimes list.

Despite the dominance of this uncritical literature, which still survives in many of the history texts for secondary- and university-level courses, critical studies began to appear as early as the second decade of the twentieth century. The first modern scholarly studies were the work of a small group of dedicated French and North American scholars. Gaston-Martin and Padre Rinchon in France and Elizabeth Donnan in the United States were the first to begin the systematic study of the trade, gathering together much of the archival material available in French and English archives. These scholars published a series of pathbreaking studies in the 1920s and 1930s. These included several collections of documents, plus the impressive initial survey of the French trade by Gaston-Martin, all of which laid the foundations for the modem study of the slave trade in the post–World War II period.

It was the growth of the new field of African history as well as the awakening of interest in Afro-American history in the 1950s and 1960s that finally opened up a major research effort in this area. Though many scholars were beginning to work on various aspects of the trade from the African, European, and American perspective, the work of Philip Curtin provided a major new impetus to slave trade studies. In 1969 he published *The Atlantic Slave Trade: A Census*, which was an attempt to estimate the volume of the trade from the available secondary literature. An original contribution to historical methodology as well as to the field of slave trade studies, Curtin's work provided an estimate of the total volume of the African slave trade to Europe, the Atlantic islands, and America from the 1440s until the 1860s. This involved a careful scrutiny of all the published estimates and a reconstruction of the numbers by zone and period based on explicit demographic and economic models. Though concentrating on the theme of the numbers of Africans shipped, Curtin was required to survey all of the issues that would eventually become basic themes in this latest period of research. The demographic evolution of the American slave populations was a fundamental concern of Curtin, as was the mortality suffered in the Atlantic crossing, since these primary factors permitted estimates of the numbers of Africans transported when no known figures were available. He also touched on the problems of African population growth and European economic interests in the trade.

But it was his estimate of some 9.5 million arrivals and 11 million Africans transported over the course of the trade that caused the most immediate response among scholars. The resulting debate generated a major search among the unpublished sources for new numbers and new sources to challenge or refine the numbers he provided. It was this international search of the European, American, and African archives for all the extant data on slave ship crossings that led to a major new period of research and analysis of the Atlantic slave trade, Once this new body of materials was made available, many older debates could be directly addressed and new and more sophisticated questions raised about the economic, social, and even political history of this major transoceanic human migration. This new scholarship resulted in a surprisingly large international output of publications, which have made this field one of the more active and productive in modern historical scholarship.

The questions that have been addressed by this recent scholarship can be grouped around a series of interrelated themes, and it is these issues and the debates they generated that I would like to analyze in this book. These questions concern the origins of the trade; its basic economic structure; its demographic, social, and economic impact; and, finally, the causes and consequences of its abolition.

In writing this book I have had the encouragement and support of a number of friends and colleagues. Frank Smith, my editor at Cambridge University Press, encouraged me to undertake this book in the first place, and without his support it would never have been written. I am equally indebted to Philip D. Curtin, who provided me with the earliest help in dealing with these complex records and encouraged me to publish my results. Stanley Engerman was always willing to lend a hand in helping me to analyze these voyages, and we often published the results together, and David Eltis aided me greatly with his own encyclopedic knowledge and kept me abreast of the latest from the slave voyages project. My old friend Charles Garland generously took the time to explain the workings of his ships. Jean Boudriot kindly allowed me to use his drawings, based on the construction notebooks of Mathias Penevert, of the slave ship *L'Aurore* built in Nantes in 1784, which appear as illustrations in this book. I am also grateful for the careful reading both David Eltis and Stanley Engerman gave to this manuscript.

INTRODUCTION TO THE SECOND EDITION

I have decided to do this second edition for several reasons. The first edition, now almost ten years old, has gone through 10 printings and has been well received not only in the English-speaking world but it has also been translated into and much cited in other languages. Secondly, and more importantly, slave trade studies have continued their robust development after this book was published and there is important new research on both traditional topics and newer themes of study. Even in terms of raw data collection, much new material has just recently become available. Under the aegis of David Eltis, the reconstruction of the extant voyages has continued since the publication of our first CD on the trade. This year, a first complete second edition of the slave voyage listing has been made freely available on the Internet, and both the data on the minority of voyages with complete information and the new estimates for all voyages provided by this Emory University–based project now allow a far more refined analysis of the timing, the origins, and the destination of the African transatlantic migration. At the same time, the continued production of European scholars, particularly the French and the Dutch, has led to new and more profound analysis of traditional slaving communities. Brazilian scholars have systematically surveyed the merchant participants for the first time, and they have even produced new detailed studies of the internal movement of newly arrived Africans from the coast to the interior. Nor have African scholars paused in their ongoing evaluation of the impact of the trade on Africa. Finally, the French in their traditional way have also produced new surveys of the trade, which have been useful to compare with my own readings of these materials. I myself have also undertaken new research on the earlier and later aspects of the trade, which has refined my own understanding of these periods. Most of my own primary research on the trade has appeared in a number of books and articles, and for those scholars who wish to examine and critique my scholarly sources, my published studies and these bibliographies will provide direction.

For this second edition I was aided by the suggestions for changes made by Olivier Pétré-Grenouilleau and Francisco Vidal Luna. Finally, this book is dedicated to Judy, who has made such a profound difference in my life.

CHAPTER 1

SLAVERY IN WESTERN DEVELOPMENT

Why were Africans enslaved and transported to the New World? This is the fundamental question that faces anyone studying the Atlantic slave trade. Why were Africans the only ones enslaved and why did the American colonies need this type of labor? Could not America have been developed without slaves? In this chapter, I suggest answers to the first question, while in the following chapter I examine the nature of the American labor market in the fifteenth to the nineteenth century to answer the query about why slavery was the adopted solution to the perceived shortage of labor in America.

Though of limited importance, slavery still existed in Europe in 1492. Like almost all complex societies in world history until that time, the states of Europe had known slaves from their earliest foundations, and slavery in earlier centuries had been a fundamental labor institution. As in most such societies this had involved what was called domestic slavery, in which the labor power of the household was extended through the use of these workers. But slaves in Europe at various times and places had performed all known tasks and had even formed separate classes and groups beyond the household level. Few European or other peoples escaped slavery themselves and almost all societies treated their slaves as outsiders, rootless and ahistorical individuals who were ultimately held against their will by the threat of force. In all societies where they existed, slaves were also the most mobile labor force available.

Slaves, of course, were not unique in either the work they performed or in their lack of control over their own lives. Peasants, serfs, even clansmen and kinsmen were often in temporary conditions of servitude. With peasants tied to the land, obligated to the nonagricultural elites for corvée (nonpaid labor), and often severely restricted in terms of age gradations and rules within their own kin groups, there was often little to distinguish slaves from other workers in terms of the labor they performed or the rights that were immediately available to them. But where slavery came to be a recognized and important institution, it was the lack of ties to the family, to kin, and to the community that finally distinguished slaves from all other workers. In fact, their lack of kin, community, and land made slaves especially desirable in the preindustrial world. True slaves were persons without the bindings and linkages common to even the lowest free persons, and were thus completely dependent on the will of their masters. Masters could use their slaves at far less cost in reciprocal obligations than with any other labor group in their societies.

Although many pre-fifteenth-century societies held slaves, in most cases such slaves were only a minor part of the labor force and were not crucial producers of goods and services for others. Most complex societies rested on the labor of settled village agriculturalists, and part-time artisanal specialists in manufactures who equally shared the peasant status. These two groups were the primary producers, and slaves were relegated to very specialized work for the elite, domestic service in the better households, and sometimes very hazardous state enterprises such as mining to which even obligated peasants could not be assigned to work. Sometimes, conquered warriors were enslaved and used in special public works activities, but in most societies it was the peasants who performed most of this labor.

Thus, while slavery was an institution known to many complex societies, slavery as a system of industrial or market production was a much more restricted phenomenon. Most scholars now date its origins for Western society in the centuries immediately prior to the Christian era in the Greek city-states and the emerging Roman Empire of the period and argue that, for slavery to become a dominant factor in society, it was essential that an important market economy at the local and international level be developed, that a significant share of the agricultural production for that market come from nonpeasant producers, and that slave labor become the major factor in that production. All these conditions, it is now assumed, were only met within our historical memory in the two centuries before the Christian era under the Romans.

With large artisanal shops using slave labor and producing goods for an international market, the classical Greek economy of the sixth and fifth centuries b.c. was distinguished by the utilization of slave labor, which historians would later define as an original development of the institution. But the concentration of slaves in urban areas, their limited use in rural production, and other constraints on slave production meant that Greek slavery would not be as fully elaborated an economic institution as that which developed in the Roman Empire.

The Roman conquest of a greater proportion of the Eurasian land mass than any other previously known empire, created a major market economy. Market economies obviously existed before, just as previous conquest states created large number of slaves as booty for the conquering armies, but the Romans carried all of these factors to another level of intensity. Their enormous armies absorbed as much as 10 percent of the male peasant work force in Italy at the same time as their elite began to purchase large tracts of land with their earnings from conquest and subsequent taxation of the conquered. In a time of economic expansion and limited supplies of free labor, and an initially cheap supply of conquered slaves, it was natural to turn toward slave labor. Although slaves became more expensive as conquests slowed, they were always less costly an alternative than paying wages high enough to attract peasants away from subsistence agriculture. It is this traditional problem of expanding markets and limited labor supplies that creates a condition ideal for slave or other servile labor arrangements if the political power exists to enserf and enslave given populations.

The Roman case is unusual among documented preindustrial historical societies in the size and importance of both major urban centers and long-distance markets. Up to 30 percent of the Italian peninsula's population may have been urban at the height of the empire, with another 10 percent being urbanized within the empire beyond. To feed these nonagriculturalists required supplies more abundant than could be produced by traditional peasant agricultural arrangements. Thus, the growth of large landed estates manned by slaves, and supervised by overseers for absentee landlords, became a major force in the supply of foodstuffs for market consumption. The high degree of specialization of labor and the demands of the market for mass-produced goods to satisfy international as well as interregional consumption also provided an incentive for slave artisanal labor.

Finally, the sheer size of the slave labor force was unusual in premodern times. While all such figures are extremely speculative, it has been estimated that at the height of the Roman Empire, the population of Italy contained some 2 to 3 million slaves, who represented between 35 to 40 percent of the total population. While peasant agriculture was still the predominant form of rural labor, the size of the slave population meant that it played a vital role in most of the productive enterprises. Slave gangs were a common feature of rural agriculture, and slaves could be found in all parts of the empire and were owned by most classes in the society. It was also evident that slaves were often a large element in many local populations and well-developed slave communities appear to have been common. This is especially evident at times of major slave rebellions, where there existed a community of interests expressed among the slaves despite their diverse origins.

All this does not mean that Romans did not have household servants and domestic slaves, or that elites did not use slaves for highly specialized tasks, roles common to all societies where slaves were held. But in terms of the production of goods and services for the market, the Romans can be said to have created a modern slave system that would be similar to those established in the Western Hemisphere from the sixteenth to the end of the nineteenth century. It is for this reason, as much as its historic role in the origins of modern western European institutions, that Roman law and custom in regard to slave labor would prove to be so important to post-1500 slave regimes.

In their definition of the legal status of slaves, the Romans also profoundly influenced such legal precepts for American slave societies. It was the primary aim of Roman law to guarantee the total rights of property for the master. All slaves were absolutely denied the legal right to personal liberty. But beyond this, the society for its own purposes could put restraints on masters and their power over their slaves. Other fundamental aspects to legal personality, such as the rights to personal property and security, were not totally denied to the slaves. So long as these rights did not deter the mobility of the slave labor force, they could be partially or fully accepted. This more "humane" attitude often sprang from the self-interest of the master class, whose desire was for a stable labor force. This stability might result in the qualification of the master's absolute rights in the name of greater efficiency and social peace.

Roman slavery was a thriving institution so long as the Roman Empire survived. Although slaves did not disappear from Europe until well into the modern period, slavery as a major economic institution collapsed with the barbarian invasions from the fifth to the eighth century a.d. The same reasons that gave rise to the importance of the slave regime earlier explain its collapse at the end of the imperial era. The decline of urban markets, the breakdown of long-distance trade, and the increasing self-sufficiency of agriculture all created a situation in which slave labor was no longer efficient, and peasant agricultural labor again predominated. More and more, slavery was reduced to the level of household and domestic tasks. In the early Middle Ages, the retrenchment of the international market and the stress on defense and security led to the rise of a new semiservile labor force with the creation of the serfs, peasants who sacrificed part of their freedom in return for protection by the local elite. Serfs soon became the predominant labor force, easily displacing the last vestiges of slave labor in agricultural production in Europe.

At no time during this period of retrenchment and enserfment, did slavery itself disappear from Europe. Among the Germanic peoples on the northern frontiers, it remained important as warfare continued to create a supply of slaves. In the non-Christian world of the Mediterranean, of course, slavery actually experienced a renaissance between the eighth and the thirteenth centuries. The Muslim invasions of the Mediterranean islands and especially of Spain brought the increasing use of slaves in agriculture and industry. Moreover, the existence of Islamic slave markets encouraged a lively trade in Christians.

It was the revival of European long-distance trade as a result of the first Crusades, which again brought Christian Europeans more actively into the slave trade and into slave production. From the tenth to the thirteenth century, the expansion of the Genoese and Venetians into Palestine, Syria, the Black Sea, and the Balkans, along with their possessions in the eastern Mediterranean islands of Crete and Cyprus, all created a new impetus to slavery. A lively market in Slavic peoples developed in this period, which gave rise to the use of the term slave to define this status. Slavs, of course, were not the only peoples to be enslaved. On the islands of the eastern Mediterranean, for example, black slaves could be found in the early fourteenth century, along with all types of Muslims from North Africa and Asia Minor, Christians from Greece and the Balkans, and northern Europeans.

Along with slavery, plantation agriculture and sugar production were also common to parts of the Mediterranean world after the eighth century. Sugar was introduced from Asia to Europe during the Islamic invasions, but it was the First Crusade at the end of the eleventh century that gave the Christians a chance to become sugar producers in their own right. In the twelfth and thirteenth centuries, Christian estates in Palestine began to produce sugar with a mixed labor force made up of slaves, villeins, and free workers. After the fall of these lands to the Turks at the end of the thirteenth century, the center of sugar production moved to Cyprus. Here Italian merchants and local rulers used slave and free labor to produce sugar. Cyprus in turn was soon replaced by the Venetian colony of Crete and then by Sicily, which had been producing sugar for the European market since the late eleventh century. With the fall of Palestine and Syrian centers to the Turks, Sicilian production became preeminent. The Mediterranean coast of Islamic Spain in the late thirteenth and early fourteenth centuries became another important production center for northern and western Europe. The westernmost advance of European sugar production reached the southern Portuguese Atlantic province of the Algarve at the beginning of the fifteenth century. In not all these cases was sugar produced by slaves, nor were they the exclusive labor force in any particular area. But the identification of slavery with sugar was well established long before the conquest of America. The techniques of sugar production and slave plantation agriculture that developed on the Atlantic islands and later in the New World had their origins in the eastern Mediterranean in the early Middle Ages.

After the eighth century, slavery in mainland Christian Europe was reduced to a minor labor arrangement almost exclusively confined to domestic activities. Slaves no longer played the vital role within European agriculture that they had under the Romans. The slow revival of commerce and activities after the tenth century led to increases in land utilization and colonization and a subsequent growth of the peasant population, which proved more than sufficient to maintain the slowly developing market economies. In such a situation, slave labor was too costly.

Only in the more advanced Islamic Mediterranean world could slaves be purchased in large quantities and the institution of slavery be revived as a major factor in production. The sole European state in this period to provide an important market for slaves was therefore Islamic Spain, which was a significant importer of Christian slaves from the eighth to the tenth century. But the decline of the Iberian Islamic states led to the closure of this market. The subsequent conquest of these states by the northern Iberian Christians resulted more in enserfment than slavery for the captured Muslim peasants and artisans. The experience of the Egyptian rulers who imported 10,000 Christian male slaves per annum in the late thirteenth and early fourteenth centuries, was not typical of Christian Europe at this time.

By the end of the Middle Ages, several varieties of slave regimes existed in Europe, the most important of which were found in the Mediterranean region. No European state was without a few slaves, but the use of slave labor in agriculture and manufacturing on a large scale had long disappeared. The emerging power of the European economy was now fed by an expanding peasant labor force. Although the legal structures originating in Roman law were still intact in Christian Europe, the institution of slavery was not a major force by the time the first Portuguese caravels arrived on the Guinean coast at the beginning of the fifteenth century.

Slavery also existed in the African continent from recorded times. But like medieval Christian Europe, it was a relatively minor institution in the period before the opening up of the Atlantic slave trade. Slavery could be found as a domestic institution in most of the region's more complex societies, and a few exceptional states may have developed more industrial forms of slave production. But African slaves were to be found outside the region as well. With no all-embracing religious or political unity, the numerous states of Africa were free to buy and sell slaves and even to export them to North African areas. Caravan routes across the Sahara had existed from recorded times, and slaves formed a part of Africa's export trade to the Mediterranean from pre-Roman to modern times. But a new dimension to that trade occurred with the expansion of Islam in the eighth century. As the Islamic world spread into India and the eastern Mediterranean, Islamic merchants came to play an ever more important part in the African slave trade. The frontier zones of the sub-Saharan savannas, the Red Sea region, and the east coast ports on the Indian Ocean in turn became major centers for the expansion of Muslim influence. From the ninth to the fifteenth century, a rather steady international slave trade occurred, with the majority of forced migrants being women and children. Some six major and often interlocking caravan routes and another two major coastal regions may have accounted for as many as 5,000 to 10,000 slaves per annum in the period from a.d. 800 to 1600. The primary route remained North Africa, followed in order of importance by the Red Sea and the East African trades.

The majority of African nations continued to experience slavery as a minor institution within largely kin- and lineage-based social systems. In these societies, slaves performed largely domestic and even religious functions, serving as everything from concubines to sacrificial victims, and performed all types of service from those of warrior or administrator to agricultural laborer. But as in most societies where slaves were to be found, they were not crucial to the production process, which remained largely in the hands of other classes. In these societies, moreover, the status of slaves was not as precisely fixed as in regimes in which slaves played a more vital role in production. Children of free fathers and slave mothers would often become free members of the kin group; second-generation acculturated slaves would become less subject to sale and to totally arbitrary control and assume far more rights and privileges.

There were, however, a few exceptional societies where slavery was clearly a fundamental institution, playing a dominant role in either the economic, social, or political life of the local state. In many of the sub-Saharan Islamicized borderland regimes, slaves were used extensively as soldiers, and also in agricultural labor on a major scale. Several of the Wolof states had agricultural slaves who produced for local consumption as well as for export. The most famous of these agriculturally based slave systems was that developed in the Niger River valley in the Empire of Songhay in the fifteenth century. Irrigated plantations with up to several thousand slaves produced wheat, rice, and other commercial food crops, which not only supported the army of the local empire but also were sold to the caravans crossing the Sahara. Slaves were also used in western Sudanese gold mines and in the Saharan salt works. In East Africa among the commercial towns of the coast, some plantation slaves could also be found near Malindi and Mombasa in the north and on the island of Madagascar. (See Maps 1–4.)

But these major commercial uses of slaves were more the exception than the rule, and the shifting nature of trade, warfare, and ecology on the Saharan border meant that most of the western African Islamic savanna states were relatively unstable. They were subject to attack by non-African border states, which was the fate of the Songhay Empire, destroyed by Moroccan invaders in the 1590s. They were also often located in unstable ecological zones, and severe periods of drought usually led to the destruction of local economies and states. Major slave regimes in Africa, especially in the west, were thus relatively few and of limited longevity in the period prior to the arrival of the Christian Europeans.

Although large-scale commercial use of slaves was limited, the use of slaves within most African societies was widespread. The existence of this large number of slaves meant that a lively internal slave market and intracontinental slave trade existed. Thus, a dual slave trade came into existence well before the opening of the West African–Atlantic routes. Through the north and to the east, slaves were being shipped outside Africa in steady numbers for at least some six centuries prior to the arrival of the Portuguese. In this period preceding the Atlantic slave trade, anywhere from 3.5 to 10 million Africans left their home-lands. These streams of forced migrants tended to contain far more women and children than would the migrants later participating in the Atlantic slave trade, and they also came from regions that would only moderately be affected by the Atlantic movements. Along with this international slave trade, there was also a thriving internal slave trade that satisfied the needs of local African states. Given the overwhelming use of slaves for domestic and social purposes, the stress in this trade was even more biased toward women. For both these long-term trades, the whole complex of enslavement practices from full-scale warfare and raiding of enemies to judicial enslavement and taxation of dependent peoples had come into use and would easily be adjusted to the needs of the Atlantic slave trade when this came into existence in the early fifteenth century.

These pre-Atlantic trades, however, did differ in important respects from the European trade. Aside from the far greater participation of women and children, and their concentration on northern and eastern African peoples, they were less intense and had a slighter impact on local conditions. Although the number of persons who were forcibly trans-ported was impressive, these pre-1500 northern and eastern African slave trades still fit in with a level of production and social and politi-cal organization in which slave trading remained an incidental part of statecraft and economic organization. There is even some question as to whether the internal trade was more important than the external trade in this pre-Atlantic period.

The arrival of the Portuguese explorers and traders on the sub-Saharan African coast in the early 1400s would ultimately represent a major new development in the history of the slave trade in Africa in terms of the intensity of its development, the sources of its slaves, and the uses to which these slaves would be put. But initially there was little to distinguish the Portuguese traders from the Muslim traders of North Africa and the sub-Saharan regions. Portuguese interest was primarily directed toward controlling the North African Saharan routes by opening up a route from the sea. Their prime interest was gold, with slaves, pepper, ivory, and other products as only secondary concerns. Even when they began shipping slaves in 1444, they were mainly sent to Europe to serve as domestic servants. Africans had already arrived at these destinations via the overland Muslim-controlled caravan routes, and thus the new trade was primarily an extension of the older pat-terns. The Portuguese even carried out extensive slave trading along the African coast primarily to supply the internal African slave market in exchange for gold, which they then exported to Europe. Their concentration on gold as opposed to slaves was based on the growing scarcity of precious metals in Europe. An expanding European economy was running an increasingly negative balance of trade with Asia, and the direct European access to the sub-Saharan goldfields helped pay for that trade. It was only with the introduction of sugar production to the Atlantic islands and the opening up of the Western Hemisphere to European conquest at the end of the fifteenth century that a new and important use was found for slaves. As once again slaves became a major factor in agricultural production within the European context, Portuguese interest in its African trade slowly shifted from a concern with gold and ivory to one primarily stressing slaves.

As long as the Portuguese concentrated their efforts in the regions of Mauritania, Senegambia, and the Gold Coast, they essentially integrated themselves into the existing network of Muslim traders. The Muslims had brought these coasts into their own trade networks, and the Portuguese tapped into them through navigable rivers that went into the interior, especially the Senegal and Gambia Rivers, or through the establishment of coastal or offshore trading posts: Arguin Island off the Mauritania coast, the Cape Verde Islands off the Senegambia coast, and the Guinean Gulf islands of São Tomé and Principé. Even their establishment of São Jorge da Mina (Elmina) on the Gold Coast in 1481 fit into these developments. Although Portuguese slave trading started slowly at about 800 slaves taken per annum in the 1450s and 1460s, it grew close to 1,500 in the next two decades and to over 2,000 per annum in the 1480s and 1490s, about a third of whom were sold to Africans themselves in exchange for gold. But a major structural change occurred after 1500, with a combination of the effective settlement of the island depot and plantation center of São Tomé in the Gulf of Guinea and the beginning of intense trade relations with the Kingdom of the Kongo after 1512, which brought West Central Africa into the Atlantic slave trade in a major way for the first time.

The Kongolese were located by the Congo River and were unconnected to the Muslim trade before the arrival of the Portuguese. The Kongo Kingdom also sought close relations with the Portuguese and tried to work out government control of the trade. The Portuguese sent priests and advisers to the court of the Kongolese king, and his representatives were placed on São Tomé. These changes occurred just as the Spanish conquest of the Caribbean islands and the Portuguese settlement of the Brazilian subcontinent was getting underway and thus opened the American market for African slaves. The decimation of the native Arawak and Carib peoples in the Caribbean islands, the first major zone of European settlement, encouraged the early experimentation with African slave labor initially brought from São Tomé by occasional Portuguese and Genoese merchants to the West Indian islands as early as the 1520s.

All these changes found immediate response in the tremendous growth of the Portuguese slave trade. Averaging just over a thousand per annum in the 1490s, by the 1510s the volume of the trade passed 3,000 slaves per annum, and after the 1530s these slaves were shipped directly to America from the entrepôt island of São Tomé just off the African coast. This latter development marked a major shift in sources for African slaves for America. The acculturated and Christianized blacks from the Iberian Peninsula had been the first Africans forced to cross the Atlantic. Now it was non-Christian and non-Romance language speakers taken directly from Africa, the so-called *bozales*, who made up the overwhelming majority of slaves coming to America.

Another major change came about in the 1560s as a result of internal African developments. Hostile African invasions of the Kingdom of the Kongo led to direct Portuguese military support for the regime and finally in 1576 to their establishment of a full-time settlement at the southern edge of the kingdom at the port of Luanda. With the development of Luanda came a decline in São Tomé as an entrepôt, for now slaves were shipped directly to America from the mainland coast and from a region that was to provide America with the most slaves of any area of Africa over the next three centuries. By 1600, the Atlantic slave trade was finally to pass the northern and eastern African export trades in total volume, though it was not until after 1700 that slaves finally surpassed in value all other exports from Africa.

Just as the beginnings of the Portuguese slave trade had complemented a traditional trading system, the first use of Atlantic-slave-trade Africans by Europeans was in traditional activities. For the first half century, the European slave ships that cruised the Atlantic shoreline of Africa carried their slaves to the Iberian Peninsula. The ports of Lisbon and Seville were the centers for a thriving trade in African slaves, and from these centers slaves were distributed rather widely through the western Mediterranean. Though Africans quickly became the dominant group within the polyglot slave communities in the major cities of the region, they never became the dominant labor force in the local economies. Even in the southern coastal cities of Portugal where they were most numerous, they never represented more than 15 percent of the population at the maximum, while in other Portuguese and Castilian port cities they usually numbered less than 10 percent. Coming into communities where slavery was an already functioning institution and where free peasants were numerous, Africans were used no differently than the Moorish slaves who preceded and coexisted with them. African slaves and freedmen were to be found primarily in urban centers and worked mostly in domestic service. Though not in significant numbers, African slaves could also be found in most major skilled and unskilled occupations. There were even some new and unusual occupations for African slaves, such as being sailors aboard both slave and nonslave ships trading with Africa, an occupation that persisted down into the nineteenth century. But these activities were not of fundamental importance to the local European economies.

Even the wealthiest European masters owned only a few slaves, and an owner who held fifteen African slaves in sixteenth-century Portugal was considered very unusual. Although slave owners were wealthy aristocrats, institutions, and professionals, many of whom were also major landowners, they infrequently used their slaves in agriculture. Slaves were sometimes to be found in rural occupations but never as a significant element in the local agricultural labor force. Given their high costs, and the availability of cheap peasant labor, African slaves in continental Europe would not play a significant role in the production of basic staples, and a slave system, as defined by the classical Roman model, did not develop inside continental Europe in the fifteenth and sixteenth centuries.

The African slavery that evolved in early modern Europe blended into an already existing slave system, and even adapted traditional Christian institutions to the non-Christian and non-Islamic Africans. As Moors and other groups died out and Africans became the predominant slaves, local institutions such as religious brotherhoods began to stress a more African orientation to the slave community. Special festive days were given over to African Catholic lay organizations in the city of Seville, and they could be found in all European towns where blacks were a significant group. There even developed by the end of the sixteenth century a free colored population. The city of Lisbon by the 1630s had an estimated 15,000 slaves and an established community of some 2,000 free colored.

Because of their relatively easy integration into an already functioning system, and because they were held in small groups and were never a majority of the local population, African slaves readily adopted the culture, language, and religion of their masters. So rapidly did they integrate into the dominant society, that they came to be called *ladinos* or "Europeanized" African slaves to distinguish them from the *bozales*, or non-Europeanized Africans. It was these ladino slaves who accompanied their masters on voyages of discovery and conquest to the Atlantic Islands and the New World, and were the first black inhabitants of America.

But despite their early migration and the important role they played in establishing the legal, social, and cultural norms for the Africans who followed them, the Europeanized African slaves were not the ones who were used to establish the new economic role for European slave labor. It was Africans brought directly to the previously unpopulated Atlantic islands beginning in the first half of the fifteenth century, who were to define the new plantation model of Afro-American slave labor. The use by Europeans of African slaves in plantations evolved not in continental Europe with its ladino slaves, but in these Atlantic islands.

Just as Portugal was opening up the African coast to European penetration, its explorers and sailors were competing with the Spaniards in colonizing the eastern Atlantic islands. By the 1450s, the Portuguese were developing the unpopulated Azores, Madeira, the Cape Verde Islands, and São Tomé, while the Spaniards were conquering the previously inhabited Canary Islands by the last decade of the century. Some of these islands proved ideal for sugar cultivation and Italian merchants were not slow in introducing the latest in Mediterranean sugar production techniques. After much experimentation, the most important sugar-producing islands turned out to be Madeira, the Canaries, and São Tomé. Sugar became the prime output on Madeira Island by the middle of the fifteenth century, and by the end of the century Madeira had become Europe's largest producer. The Portuguese imported Guanches, the native Canarians, as slaves along with Africans, and by the end of the 1450s Madeira sugar was being sold on the London and continental markets. By the 1490s, production for export was reaching its maximum of almost 1,500 tons of sugar per annum. Given the terraced nature of the sugar estates, production units were relatively small, and the labor force was mixed African slaves and free wage workers, while the mills were still using traditional Mediterranean technology. In all this was still a relatively small-scale operation compared to what would develop in America in the next century.

By the 1530s, Madeira was in decline and was outdistanced by competition from the other islands. The Canary Islands came into production in the 1480s and probably surpassed Madeira by the 1540s. Here, as in Madeira, Guanche natives along with Spanish Moors and Africans were used as slaves, and a mixed slave and free labor force evolved on the plantations and in the mills. As on Madeira, high startup costs for milling meant that there were more sugar producers than millowners, and an intermediate group of small-scale planters evolved who worked for larger and richer millowners.

The final Atlantic island that developed sugar and the one that most completely relied on slave labor was the island of São Tomé, in the Gulf of Guinea. In terms of plantation size, the universality of slave labor, and production techniques, this was the Atlantic island closest to what would become the American norm. By the 1550s, there were some sixty mills in operation on the island producing over 2,000 tons per annum and some 5,000 to 6,000 plantation slaves, all of whom were Africans. Eventually American competition, Dutch invasions, and a series of major African slave revolts destroyed the local sugar industry. But the island continued its increasingly important role as a transfer and slave trade provisioning entrepôt. One estimate suggests there were on average some 5,000 to 6,000 Africans being held in slave pens for transport to Europe and America by the middle of the sixteenth century.

Thus, all the sugar islands went through a rather intense cycle of boom and bust that rarely lasted more than a century. But they both opened up a major market for sugar consumption in Europe and provided many of the labor patterns and technical organization that would be introduced into the New World. Non-Christian and non-Europeanized Africans directly imported from the African coast were brought to work the rural estates on these islands. Urban and domestic slavery were minor occupations and slaves – above all, in São Tomé – were held in extremely large holdings by the standards of the period. Most of the trappings of the New World plantation system were well established, with the small number of wealthy millowners at the top of the hierarchy holding the most lands and the most slaves or workers, followed by an intermediate layer of European planters who owned slaves and sugar fields but were too poor to actually be millowners in their own right. A poor European peasant population hardly existed, with only skilled administrative and mill operations opened to nonslave-owning whites.

The lowest layer consisted of the mass of black slaves who made up both the majority of the labor force as well as of the population as a whole. Thus, well before the massive transplantation of Africans across the Atlantic, the American slave plantation system had been born.

But even if slavery was associated with sugar and Africans were now the most common of Europe's slaves, why could not the colonies have been settled by other types of laborers coming from the colonizing nations? The answer to this query rests on an analysis of the labor market within Europe itself. The late fifteenth and early sixteenth centuries comprised a period of rapid economic growth for western Europe, whose population was still increasing relatively slowly since the end of the Black Death in the fourteenth century. Thus most states perceived their populations were still too few to develop their economies and rising wages reflected the increasing tightness of local labor markets. Peasants only recently freed from serfdom were still just entering urban life, as well as settling many of the open internal frontiers of Europe, where land was still relatively cheap. Moreover, the decline of the eastern Mediterranean states and the rise of the Atlantic and western Mediterranean commercial communities all provided unprecedented economic and social opportunities in Europe itself. Finally, the growth of large professional military establishments as a result of the long-term warfare with the Islamic states in the Mediterranean as well as increasing warfare in Europe as a result of the emergence of the schismatic Protestant movement within western European Christianity also provided a drain on local labor. Added to these local attractions and constraints were the high costs and insecurity of travel to the New World. Even with the unique attraction of abundant precious metals, Castilians were as much attracted to European destinations as to American ones, and most in fact stayed home. Relatively few Castilians and even fewer Portuguese traveled to the New World.

Thus, for all intents and purposes the costs of attracting European workers to America were too high to be able to get major settlement going in the empty lands available to most of the European colonizing powers, especially those who came after Spain and Portugal. Even for the Iberians, slaves were considered essential for the development of their urban centers and Africans quickly made up half or more of their urban populations. With free workers too costly, then an alternative imported labor, if it was cheap enough, could take its place. In the context of late fifteenth-century Africa and Europe, it was Africans who could be purchased and transported at a cost that was within the capacity of the

American colonizing powers to pay and still make a profit out of their colonies.

There did, of course, exist the possibility of using American Indian workers to produce the crops and other exportable goods that would pay for the effective colonization of the Americas. But, as I will show in the following chapter, there was a series of constraints and limitations to the use of this ever-declining native population that kept the Americas in a constant state of labor shortage. Increasing European consumption of ever more popular American products, and a desperate scramble by all Europeans to take advantage of that demand by colonizing the open American frontier, guaranteed a massive importation of African slaves as the only long-term viable and consistent source of labor for Europe's American colonies.

CHAPTER 2

AMERICAN LABOR DEMAND

The European conquest of the American hemisphere did not automatically guarantee the expansion of African slave labor to the New World. Africans within Europe and the Atlantic islands were still a relatively minor part of the European labor force, and even sugar production was not totally in the hands of black slaves. At the same time, the existence of at least some 20 to 25 million conquered American Indians presupposed that the Europeans would have an abundant supply of labor available for the exploitation of their new colonies. Europe itself was experiencing major population growth in the sixteenth century, and could probably rely on migrations of its poorer peasants and urban dwellers for its American labor needs. Yet despite these alternative labor supplies, America became the great market for some 9 to 10 million African slaves in the course of the next five centuries, and it was in the New World that African slavery most flourished under European rule.

Before examining the history of the forced African migration to the Americas, it is therefore essential to understand why Europeans turned to Africans to populate their mines, factories, and farms in such numbers. Much has been written of the relative "otherness" of Africans to northern Europeans or the alienness of African culture. But the longterm contact of the Mediterranean with Africans from at least the time of Egyptian civilization onward makes one doubt the importance of this phenomenon. Also, the extensive history of Europeans enslaving each other would suggest that there was nothing special about the Africans and slavery in the European mind at the end of the fifteenth century. Finally, no special need for such Africans within the European economy existed as a driving force behind the purchase of enslaved Africans on the South Atlantic African coast. Without question, American labor market conditions most influenced the growth of the Atlantic slave trade.

Initially it appeared as if the few thousand Iberian conquistadors would turn toward Indian slavery as the major form of labor in America. Already using the enslaved labor of Africans, Muslims, and Guanches (natives of the Canary Islands) in Europe and the Atlantic islands, the first Spaniards and Portuguese immediately went about enslaving all the American Indians they could find and keep. But for a series of political, cultural, and religious reasons, the government of Spain eventually decided against permanently enslaving the American Indians. Spain had just finished with enserfment and other forms of semifree labor arrangements, and was committed to the principle of free wage labor.

The Spaniards also found in Mesoamerica and the Andes powerful peasant-based empires that could be effectively exploited without the need to destroy their political and social systems. Using traditional Indian nobility to control Indian peasant labor and preconquest labor taxes and corvée labor arrangements to force them into the market proved an efficient way to exploit local Amerindian labor along with the usual mechanism of wages. Finally, the commitment to an evangelical mission and doubts about the legitimacy of enslaving Christians all pushed the Spanish Crown toward acceptance of American Indian autonomy and the principles of a free labor market.

In the case of the Portuguese, there was less metropolitan constraint in enslaving Indians. Also, the weakness of the political systems of the Tupi-Guarani Indian groups they conquered on the Brazilian coastline, and their inexperience with systematic peasant labor, made them less easy to exploit through noncoercive labor arrangements. Although the Portuguese initially had a large pool of Indians to exploit and wholeheartedly adapted to Indian slave labor, such labor would eventually prove too unreliable and costly to guarantee the necessary agricultural labor force they needed to maintain the economic viability of their American colony.

Thus, for a multiplicity of economic, political, and even religious reasons, the Iberians eventually abandoned the possibility of Indian slavery. But what was to prevent them from exploiting their own peasantry and urban poor? After all, Spain had a population of over 7 million persons in the 1540s, and it added another million persons to that number by 1600. But this population grew in a period of major economic and political expansion. Spain's control over a vast European and American empire saw a tremendous growth of its cities, with Seville doubling its population to over 110,000, and such new urban centers as Madrid being constructed. Agriculture also flourished in this imperial century, all maintained by a free wage labor force. Finally, the establishment of full-time professional Spanish armies in other European states guaranteed a final major area of employment. All this created a large demand for Spanish labor within Spain and its very extensive European possessions. Thus, wages for Spanish workers in Europe were high enough to make mass migration to America too costly an operation.

The situation for the Portuguese was even more stringent. With under 1 million in population, Portugal was straining its resources to staff the vast African and Asian trading empire it had just established. Demand for labor was so high and wages so remunerative that no pool of cheap Iberian labor could be tapped for the initially quite poor lands of Brazil. With dyewoods as the only important export, compared with the gold, slaves, ivory, and spices from Africa and Asia, Portuguese America was a very uninteresting proposition in the European labor markets.

This left the Europeans with only the free Indian peasant masses of America as a potential labor force. In Mesoamerica and the southern Andes of the Pacific coast, the existence of centuries-old established peasant societies initially gave the Spaniards the ability to exploit local labor for all its needs. With precious metals being the first successful export, and with mining technology being well developed in Amerindian society, it was relatively easy to create a native American mining labor force. Through wage labor incentives and discriminatory taxation, large numbers of Indian laborers were attracted to the rich silver mines in Mexico and Peru. To supply food for the mines and for the developing Spanish cities, the Spaniards were also able to use a blend of corvée labor, along with market incentives and discriminatory taxes, to force through a major reorganization of Amerindian agriculture. The Spanish adapted many of the American foods to their own diet, but they also succeeded in having the Indians produce wheat and other traditional European crops for their needs.

In the central provinces of the Spanish American empire the need for European or African laborers was relatively limited. But even in this best of all possible situations for the Europeans, there was a slow realization that alternative labor was needed. European diseases were especially virulent among the Indians of the coastal zones, which were soon depopulated, and also severely affected the peasant highland areas.

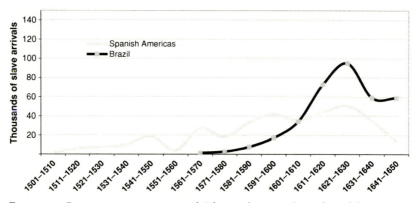

Figure 2.1. Comparative movement of African slaves to Spanish and Portuguese American ports, by decade, 1501–1650. *Source:* Emory database, estimates accessed Sept. 14, 2009.

Also regions outside of the main peasant areas were soon depopulated of their hunting-and-gathering Indians nor could the establishment of church missions in these areas acculturate a sufficient labor force for developing major exportable crops. With an excellent supply of precious metals, and a positive trade balance with Europe, the Spaniards of America could afford to experiment with the importation of African slaves to fill in the regions abandoned by Amerindian laborers. They could also use the African slaves to make up for the lack of an urban poor labor force among the Spaniards in the new imperial cities of America. They found African slaves useful for the very reasons that they were kinless and totally mobile laborers. Indians could be exploited systematically but they could not be moved from their lands on a permanent basis. Being the dominant cultural group, they were also relatively impervious to Spanish and European norms of behavior. The Africans, in contrast, came from multiple linguistic groups and had only the European languages in common and were therefore forced to adapt themselves to the European norms. African slaves, in lieu of a cheap pool of European laborers, thus added important strength to the small European urban society that dominated the American Indian peasant masses.

Thus, the Atlantic slave trade to America until the first decades of the seventeenth century would be primarily a trade to the Spanish colonies in the New World. It is estimated that until the 1620s, African slave arrivals went predominantly to Spanish America (see Figure 2.1 and Table A.2, in the Appendix). These arrivals to the colonies of

Spanish American represented an estimated 76 percent of the 270,000 or so Africans who had come to America by 1609.

The Portuguese experience with their American Indian workers was less successful. The few hundred thousand Indians conquered by the Portuguese in coastal Brazil were nowhere near the millions of Indians controlled by the Spaniards. They were less adaptable to systematic agricultural labor and were even more highly susceptible to European diseases. As the local economy expanded, their numbers declined and their relative efficiency with it. Since the Portuguese had already had extensive experience with African slaves in their Atlantic islands and had ready access to African labor markets, once the decision was made to exploit fully their American colony, their turn toward African workers was only conditioned by availability of capital for importations. By 1600 the northeastern plantations initially based on Indian slave labor were producing enough income to begin a massive importation of slaves. Thus, by the first decade of the century African slave arrivals to Brazil equaled the number arriving to Spanish America, and by the 1610s had surpassed this later zone in importance. By 1650, Brazil absorbed an estimated 350,000 slaves. Although Brazil predominated as the region of arrival for African slaves it never achieved more than 65 percent of all American arrivals (and that in the 1620s) since Spanish America continued a steady absorption of such immigrants. Thus, the whole first half of the seventeenth century saw Brazil as the dominant zone of arrivals; in total, Spanish America still absorbed an estimated 349,000 African slaves by 1650.

The northern Europeans who followed the Iberians to America within a few decades of the discovery had even fewer Indians to exploit than the Portuguese and were unable to develop an extensive Indian slave labor force, let alone the complex arrangements for free Indian labor developed by the Spaniards. Nor did they have access to precious metals to pay for imported slave labor. But, unlike the Iberians of the sixteenth century, they did have a cheaper and more willing pool of European laborers to exploit, especially in the crisis period of the seventeenth century.

But even with this European labor available, peasants and the urban poor could not afford the passage to America and paying for that passage through selling of one's labor to American employers in indentured contracts became the major form of colonization in the first half century of northern European settlement in America. The English and the French were the primary users of indentured labor, and they were helped by a pool of workers faced by low wages within the European economy. But the end of the seventeenth-century crisis in Europe, and especially the rapid growth of the English economy in the last quarter of the century, brought a thriving labor market in Europe and a consequent increase in the costs of indentured laborers. With their European indentured laborers becoming too costly, and with no access to American Indian workers or slaves, it was inevitable that the English and the French would also turn to African slaves, especially as they discovered that sugar was one of the few crops that could profitably be exported to the European market on a mass scale.

Thus, despite their initially higher cost, African slaves finally became the most desired labor force for the Europeans to develop their American export industries. That Africans were the cheapest available slaves at this time was due to the opening up of the West African coast by the Portuguese. Given the steady export of West African gold and ivory, and the development of Portugal's enormous Asiatic trading empire, the commercial relations between western Africa and Europe now became common and cheap. Western Africans brought by sea had already replaced all other ethnic and religious groups in the European slave markets by the sixteenth century. Although Iberians initially enslaved Canary Islanders, these were later freed as were the few Indians who were brought from America. The Muslims who had been enslaved for centuries were no longer significant as they disappeared from the Iberian Peninsula itself and became powerfully united under Turkish control of North Africa. The dominance of the Turks in the eastern Mediterranean also closed off traditional Slavic and Balkan sources for slaves. Given the growing efficiency of the Atlantic slave traders, the dependability of African slave supply and the stability of prices, then it would be Africans who would come to be defined almost exclusively as the available slave labor of the sixteenth century.

Although importations to Brazil and Spanish America remained steady until well into the eighteenth century, it was the new French and English island and mainland colonies that began to take the bulk of the arriving slaves. By the 1720s, the Iberian colonies were absorbing less than half of all the slave arrivals, while the North European colonies were by then accounting for an estimated 58 percent of all Africans arriving in America (see Figure 2.2).

With their rapid conquest of the American heartland and the enormous wealth that was generated, the Spaniards became the first Europeans to have the capital necessary to import slaves, and the earliest years

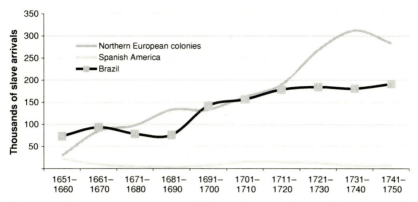

Figure 2.2. Comparative movement of African slaves to Spanish, Portuguese, and northern European colonial American ports, by decade, 1651–1750. *Source:* Emory database, estimates accessed Sept. 14, 2009.

of the Atlantic slave trade drew Africans primarily toward Mexico and Peru. Although the relative importance of African slaves was reduced within Spanish America in the sixteenth and seventeenth centuries, African migrations to these regions was not insignificant and began with the first conquests. Cortes and his various armies held several hundred slaves when they conquered Mexico in the 1520s, while close to 2,000 slaves appeared in the armies of Pizarro and Almargo in their conquest of Peru in the 1530s, and in their subsequent civil wars in the 1540s. Although Indians dominated rural life everywhere, Spaniards found their need for slaves constantly increasing. This was especially true in Peru, which was initially both richer and lost a progressively higher proportion of its coastal populations to European diseases in areas that were ideal for such European crops as sugar and grapes. Already by the mid-1550s there were some 3,000 African slaves in the Peruvian viceroyalty, with half of them in the city of Lima. This same balance between urban and rural residence, in fact, marked slaves along with Spaniards as the most urban elements in Spanish American society.

The needs for slaves within the Peruvian viceroyalty increased dramatically in the second half of the sixteenth century as Potosí silver production came into full development, making Peru and its premier city of Lima the wealthiest zone of the New World. To meet this demand for Africans a major slave trade developed, especially after the unification of the Portuguese and Spanish Crowns from 1580 to 1640 gave the Portuguese access to Spanish American markets. Initially, most of the Africans came from the Senegambia region between the Senegal and Niger Rivers, but after the development of Portuguese Luanda in the 1570s, important contingents of slaves from the Congo and Angola began arriving.

The slave trade to Peru was probably the longest and most unusual of any of the American slave trades, for it involved two distinct stages. Africans shipped across the Atlantic were first landed at the port of Cartagena on the Caribbean coast of South America. They were then transshipped a short distance to the port of Portobello on the Caribbean side of the Isthmus of Panama, taken by land across to the Pacific, and then shipped to Callao which was the entry port for Lima. This second phase on average took some four to five months, which more than doubled the normal trip from Africa to America and probably more than doubled the voyage mortality of the slaves as well.

Once reaching Lima, the slaves were then sold throughout the viceroyalty, from Upper Peru (Bolivia) and Chile in the south, to Quito in the north. Initially, African slaves tended to be heavily grouped in urban areas, but new economic roles opened up for them at the margins of the Indian rural society. Although Indian free and conscripted labor was used to mine the silver and mercury throughout Peru, gold was a different matter. Most gold was found in alluvial deposits in tropical lowlands far from Indian populations. Thus, as early as the 1540s, Africans in gangs of ten to fifteen slaves were working gold deposits in the tropical eastern cordillera region of Carabaya in the southern Andes. While these local goldfields were quickly depleted, the precedent was set, and in both Portuguese and Spanish America gold mining tended to be an industry using African slaves.

Though a major component of urban population and the dominant workers in gold mining, African slaves were also used in agriculture. To serve such new cities as Lima, Spaniards developed major food producing farms in the outskirts of the city, which were worked by small families of slaves. Even more ambitious agricultural activity occurred up and down the coast in both specialized sugar estates and vineyards and more mixed agricultural enterprises. In contrast to the West Indian and Brazilian experience, the slave plantations of Peru were likely to be mixed-crop producers. On average, the plantations of the irrigated coastal valleys, especially those to the south of Lima, had around 40 slaves per unit. The major wine- and sugar-producing zones of the seventeenth century, such as Pisco, the Condor, and Ica Valleys, contained some 20,000 slaves. In the interior, there were also several tropical valleys were slave estates specializing in sugar could be found. These interior plantations, like

those of the coast, were relatively small, and given that production was
for the Peruvian and relatively limited Pacific coast trade, the dominant
characteristic of commercial plantation agriculture was its mix of products. Finally, cattle ranching was also a specialty of the African slave
population. Slaves also played a vital role in parts of the viceroyalty's
communications infrastructure, being especially prominent as muleteers
on the interior routes and as seamen in both private and royal vessels.

But it was in all the cities of the Spanish continental empire that
the slaves played their most active economic role. In the skilled trades
they predominated in metalworking, clothing, and construction and
supplies, and were well represented in all the crafts except the most
exclusive, such as silversmithing and printing. In semiskilled labor, they
were heavily involved in coastal fishing, as porters and vendors, and in
food handling and processing, and were even found as armed watchmen
in the local Lima police force. Every major construction site found
skilled and unskilled slaves working alongside white masters and free
blacks of all categories as well as Indian laborers. In a few trades by
the middle decades of the seventeenth century, free and slave Africans
and Afro-Americans were dominant and could exercise master status
without opposition, and in most trades they were well represented in
the lower statuses of apprentice and journeyman. Sometimes opposition
in areas where they were fewer in number was quite bitter, but the
lack of a powerful American guild organization permitted blacks, free
and slave, to participate freely in most crafts. They also predominated
in the semiskilled and unskilled urban occupations, from employment
in tanning works, slaughterhouses, and even hat factories to being the
dominant servant classes. All government and religious institutions,
charities, hospitals, and monasteries had their contingent of half a dozen
or more slaves who were the basic maintenance workers for these large
establishments.

As the city of Lima grew, so did its slave population and by 1640
there were some 20,000 slaves. This growth was initially faster than the
white and Indian participation in the city and by the last decade of
the sixteenth century Lima was half black and would stay that way for
most of the seventeenth century. Equally, all the northern and central
Andean coastal and interior cities had black populations that by 1600
accounted for half of their total populations. As one moved further south
into the more densely populated Indian areas, their relative percentage
dropped, though black slaves could be found in the thousands in Cuzco,
and even the interior city of Potosí, which was dominated by Indian

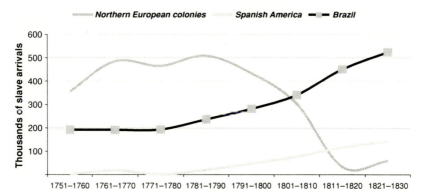

Figure 2.3. Comparative movement of African slaves to Spanish, Portuguese, and northern European colonial American ports, by decade, 1751–1830. *Source:* Emory database, estimates accessed Sept. 14, 2009.

workers, was estimated to have some 6,000 blacks and mulattoes, both slave and free, in 1611.

In a pattern common to the rest of Spanish and Portuguese America, free blacks and mulattoes appeared from the very beginning of the conquest and colonization period, some of them even coming from Spain itself. Often discriminated against on racial grounds by whites competing for the better jobs, they nevertheless were to be found at all levels of society from unskilled to master positions. In some cases they were paid wages equal to white workers, in others they were paid less even than the rental wages of the slaves. In some occupations they could not break into the elite classes, but in construction and shipping, where blacks were well represented, they became shipmasters, architects, and master carpenters and builders. In all cases, their numbers grew. By 1600, in most cities the free colored had reached 10 to 15 percent of the local black and mulatto population, and a century later they usually represented half of their numbers. Neither especially favoring manumission nor opposing it in any systematic way, Iberian society allowed the normal operations of the market to lead to manumission through self-purchase by the slaves themselves, pious individuals emancipating their slaves, or free fathers manumitting their children.

African slaves in the viceroyalty of Mexico were also to be found from the first moments in the armies, farms, and houses of the Spanish conquerors. As in Peru, the first generation of slaves probably numbered close to the total number of whites. They were also drawn heavily into the local sugar and European commercial crop production in the warmer lowland regions, which were widely scattered in the central zone of the viceroyalty. Also, given the initial discovery of silver in the northern regions of the viceroyalty where there were few settled Indians, Africans were initially even used in silver mining. In a mine census of 1570, 45 percent of the laboring population comprised some 3,700 Africans slaves, double the number of Spaniards, and just a few hundred less than the Indians. But the increasing availability of free Indian wage labor lessened the need for more expensive African slave labor, and they disappeared from the mines by the end of the century. Given the more extensive Indian population in Mexico, Africans were used less than in Peru and their relative importance declined over time. Though slaves performed many of the same urban tasks in Mexico City as they did in Lima, the former was essentially an Indian and mestizo town, and slaves never achieved the same importance in the labor force.

The relative significance of Mexican slavery was well reflected in the growth of its slave population, which peaked at some 35,000 slaves by 1646, when they represented less than 2 percent of the viceregal population. In contrast, the number of slaves in this same period within the Peruvian region had reached close to 100,000, where they accounted for between 10 and 15 percent of the population. Though the Peruvian slave population would stagnate in the next century, it would not go into the severe decline shown by the Mexican slave population in the eighteenth century. By the last decade of that century, Peru had close to 90,000 slaves, while Mexico had only 6,000 left. The Mexican experience clearly demonstrated the importance of the relative weight of the much larger Mesoamerican Indian population on the labor market. In both regions, however, the 1650s marked the end of their great period of massive slave importations. By 1650, Spanish America, primarily Peru and Mexico, had succeeded in importing from the earliest days of the conquest some 250,000 to 300,000 slaves, a record that would not be repeated in the next century of colonial growth.

The major demand for African slaves after 1650 came from Portuguese America and the marginal lands that the Spaniards had previously neglected, above all, those in the Caribbean. In these areas there were no stable Indian peasant populations to exploit and few alternative exports in the form of precious metals. Successful colonization and development of these new lands required the export of products that Europe could consume, and this would eventually lead to sugar production and the massive use of African slave labor. The first of the European powers to develop this system and the model for all later developments throughout the Americas were the Portuguese, who took possession of the eastern coastline of South America in the early sixteenth century on their expeditions to Asia.

The Portuguese initially had little interest in the settlement of Brazil. With the riches of the Pacific being exploited as the Portuguese opened up a water route to the Spice Islands and then to India, there was little demand for development of Brazil. The first commercial exports in fact were woods logged by local Indians from which were extracted dyes. But this relative neglect ended when Portugal was suddenly confronted by European rivals who were willing to contest its control over this American territory. French and British merchants began to send their own ships into Brazilian waters to pick up the profitable dyewoods, and soon used the coast as a base for attacking the Portuguese East Indies fleets that cruised the South Atlantic. The French and British even went so far as to set up permanent settlements at both the Amazonian estuary in the Northeast and in Guanabara Bay in the South. This convinced the Portuguese of the necessity of fullscale colonization.

Portugal's experience in the Azores, Madeira, and São Tomé Islands showed that sugar was the ideal crop to guarantee the existence of a profitable colony. This decision was greatly aided by the fact that the Portuguese still dominated the Atlantic slave trade and could easily and cheaply deliver slaves to America. Thus, by the 1550s was born the first plantation system in the New World, a system that very rapidly dominated the sugar markets of Europe and effectively ended the importance of the Atlantic islands producers.

Brazil was not the first American zone to produce sugar, since Columbus had already brought sugar to Santo Domingo as early as 1493. But it was the first to develop a major export industry to Europe and the northeastern Brazilian regions of Pernambuco and Bahia became the center of the world's most important sugar zone by the end of the sixteenth century. With the Portuguese merchant class supplying the slaves, it was the Dutch who carried Brazilian sugar to Europe and turned Antwerp into Europe's sugar-marketing center. The northeastern mills of Brazil soon evolved into far larger operations than their Atlantic island predecessor. Between the use of better soils and newer milling techniques, Brazilian mills were producing six times the output per annum than the Atlantic island engenhos (mills). What had been settled in a marginal way and with little interest from the Crown now took on a central role in Portugal's vast empire, with sugar being the crucial link between Portugal, Africa, and Brazil.

Given the insatiable demand of the mills for unskilled agricultural labor, the Brazilians would experiment with many of the forms of labor organization that later colonists would attempt, exempting only indentured European workers. They imported African slaves from the very beginning, but they also sought to enslave the local American Indian populations and turn them into a stable agricultural labor force. From 1540 to 1570, Indian slaves were the primary producers of sugar in Brazil, and accounted for at least four-fifths of the labor force in the Northeast and almost all the labor component in the southern sugar mills developing in the Rio de Janeiro region. Owners obtained these slaves both through purchase from other Indian tribes or through direct raiding on their own.

Although Portuguese efforts in this area showed that an enslaved and indebted Indian labor force could be created out of the Tupi-Guarani Indians of the coast, despite an open frontier and constant warfare with Indian groups, the institution of Indian slavery, which now claimed tens of thousands of Indians, was doomed to failure. The most important factor undermining its importance was the endemic diseases that the Europeans brought with them and which became epidemic when they affected the Indians. In the 1560s, at the height of Indian slavery, a major smallpox epidemic broke out among the Indians with massive deaths resulting in these previously unexposed populations. It was estimated that 30,000 Indians under Portuguese control, either on plantations or in Jesuit mission villages, died of the disease. This susceptibility to disease resulted in lower prices for Indian than for African slaves. When combined with increasing Crown hostility toward enslavement, especially after the unification of the Portuguese Crown with that of Spain after 1580, Indian slavery was made less secure and more difficult to maintain.

Whereas the Northeast had few Africans before 1570, by the mid-1580s Pernambuco alone reported 2,000 African slaves, comprising one-third of the captaincy's sugar labor force. With each succeeding decade the percentage of Africans in the slave population increased. By 1630 some 170,000 Africans had arrived in the colony and sugar was now predominantly a black slave crop. The early decades of the seventeenth century would prove to be the peak years of Brazil's dominance on the European sugar market, with exports reaching to well over 20,000 metric tons per annum. No other sugar-producing area rivaled Brazil at this point, but this very sugar production monopoly excited the envy of other European powers and led to the rise of alternative production centers.

Crucial to this new plantation movement would be the Dutch, who initially provided Brazil's major commercial link with northern Europe. The long Dutch struggle for independence against Spanish domination, from the 1590s to the 1640s, profoundly affected Portugal, Africa, and Brazil. The incorporation of Portugal into the Spanish Empire from 1580 to 1640 brought Portugal into direct confrontation with the rebellious Dutch. As early as 1602 the Dutch had established their East India Company to seize control of Portugal's Asian spice trade, followed in 1621 by the West India Company organized to take Portugal's African and American possessions. The Dutch West India Company sent the first of many war fleets into the South Atlantic in 1624. Defeated in their initial attempts to seize either the province of Bahia or Pernambuco, the two wealthiest sugar and slave zones in Brazil, the Dutch finally captured and held Recife and its interior province of Pernambuco in 1630. With this base in sugar production, the Dutch were now direct competitors of their former Brazilian partners. Their next step was to capture Portugal's African possessions, which resulted in the Dutch becoming a dominant power in the Atlantic slave trading system as well. First, the fortress of Elmina (Ghana) on the Gold Coast was captured in 1638 and then Luanda and most of the Angolan region was taken in 1641.

The temporary Dutch seizure of Pernambuco and the Portuguese African settlements profoundly affected the subsequent history of sugar production and African slavery in America. For Brazil, the Dutch occupation resulted in Bahia replacing Pernambuco as the leading slave and sugar province; in the reemergence of Indian slavery to replace the African slaves lost to the Dutch; and in the ensuing Indian slave trade opening up the interior regions of Brazil to exploitation and settlement. For the rest of America, Dutch Brazil would became the source for many of the tools, techniques, credit, and slaves that would carry the sugar revolution and its slave labor system into the West Indies, thereby terminating Brazil's monopoly position in European markets and leading to the creation of wealthy new American colonies for France and England.

Constant rebellion and increasing Portuguese attacks finally led to the decline of Dutch Pernambuco by the 1640s. In need of furnishing their Amsterdam refineries with American sugar, the Dutch began to bring slaves and the latest milling equipment to the struggling British and French settlers in the Caribbean and carried their West Indian–produced sugar into the European market. In the 1640s, Dutch planters with Pernambuco experience arrived in Barbados as well as Martinique

and Guadeloupe to at Olinda finally fell to the Portuguese troops introduce modern milling and production techniques. Dutch slave ships
soon followed, providing the credit to the local planters to buy African
slaves. Finally, Dutch West Indian freighters hauled the finished sugar to
the refineries in Amsterdam. Even more dramatically came actual mass
migration of Dutch planters and their slaves to these islands in 1654
when Pernambuco and their capital. In Guadeloupe, several hundred
Dutchmen and their slaves arrived in this period, and an equal number
landed in Martinique and Barbados. While many of these new colonists
eventually returned to the Netherlands, enough remained in America
so that their coming gave a major new boost to the Caribbean sugar
industry in the 1650s.

The opening up of the Lesser Antillean islands and the northeastern
coast of South America to northern European colonization represented
the first systematic challenge to Iberian control of the New World.
French and English settlers began to take over lands never fully settled by the Portuguese or the Spanish, from the Amazonian estuary to
the lands north of Florida. The most successful of these new settlements
were those planted by the English, French, and Dutch in the abandoned
islands of the Lesser Antilles from the 1620s to the 1640s. Using every
style of settlement practice from private companies to fiefdoms, the
English and French attempted to settle these uninhabited islands with
white European laborers, who mostly came as indentured (or engagé)
workers. Fighting off attacks of local Carib Indians, the Europeans immediately began to plant tobacco, which was the first successful commercial crop. Indigo for European textile dyes was also produced and finally
came the turn toward sugar, which was the costliest commercial crop to
produce.

In this race for settlement, the English initially made far more head-
way than the French. By 1640, for example, the English had 52,000
whites on their islands of Barbados, Nevis, and St. Kitts (compared with
22,000 in the settlements of New England), while the French islands
of Martinique and Guadeloupe still had no more than 2,000 white settlers. But in the next two decades growth was steady and by the end of
the 1650s, there were some 15,000 white Frenchmen in these islands.
At midcentury, tobacco and indigo were the primary exports in all
the islands, and though slaves were present from the beginning, their
numbers were few and they were still outnumbered by the whites. The
arrival of the Dutch finally made sugar a far more viable proposition,
especially as the opening up of Virginia tobacco production led to a crisis

in European tobacco prices. Sugar had been planted on all the islands from the beginning, but few could get commercially viable processing accomplished until the Dutch came. They brought the needed credit to import the expensive machinery to get the mills into successful operation. They also supplied African slaves on credit from their factories in El Mina and Luanda.

The transformation that sugar created in the West Indies was truly impressive. The experience of Barbados, the first of the big production islands, was typical. On the eve of the introduction of sugar in 1645, over 60 percent of the 18,300 white males were property owners, and there were only 5,680 slaves. Tobacco was the primary crop and the average producing unit was less than ten acres. By 1680, there were over 38,000 slaves on the island, almost all of whom were African-born, and some 350 sugar estates. Of the indentured whites, only some 2,000 remained and their numbers were falling. Already local society was dominated by the new elite of large planters, and the 175 Barbados planters who owned 60 slaves or more controlled over half the land and slaves on the island. The median size of these large plantations consisted of 100 slaves and 220 acres of land. At this point in time Barbados was both the most populous and the wealthiest of England's American colonies and averaged some 265 slaves per square mile, compared with less than 2 slaves per square mile in the recently captured island of Jamaica. The slave ships were bringing in over 1,300 Africans per annum to Barbados and by the end of the century this tiny island contained over 50,000 slaves. This Barbados model was quickly followed by the British possessions on the Leeward Islands of Nevis, Antigua, Montserrat, and St. Kitts, which by 1700 had reached half of Barbados's sugar export output (or 30 percent of the total British American sugar produced) and contained some 20,000 African slaves. Like Barbados, over three-quarters of the total population on these small Leeward Islands were black slaves. By then, these small British islands and the slowly developing island of Jamaica had imported well over 260,000 Africans and were approaching an average of 8,000 African slave arrivals per annum.

The experience of the French islands was similar to that of Barbados, though the changes occurred at a slower rate. In the major island of Martinique as well as the smaller center at Guadeloupe, the free white labor force was more deeply entrenched and small farm units were still important until the end of the century. Nevertheless, sugar relentlessly began to absorb the best lands and the flow of slaves continued unabated. By 1670, Martinique, Guadeloupe, and St. Christopher had some

300 sugar estates exporting a third of the 29,000 tons produced by all Brazilian regions in that year, just fifteen years after the Dutch had established the first successful French mill. Growth also continued for the French in terms of adding new lands, and in the late 1660s the French settled the abandoned western half of the island of Santo Domingo, which they termed Saint Domingue. With extremely rich and abundant level virgin soils, this region began a slow and steady growth. By the early 1680s, it had 2,000 African slaves and double that number of whites; while all the French islands now contained over 18,000 slaves, with only some 14,000 whites, few of whom were still indentured.

By the end of the seventeenth century, then, a whole new sugar and slave complex had emerged in the French and British West Indies. Whereas Brazil had absorbed a migration of some 500,000 to 600,000 slaves from Africa up to 1700, the non-Iberian Caribbean now took second place in the slave trade and received over 450,000 Africans in the same period. This left Spanish America as the third major area of importation with some 350,000 to 400,000 slaves arriving in these two centuries. The struggling English and French colonies of North America were still relatively small importers of slaves, probably accounting for less than 30,000 before 1700.

The West Indian plantation regime began on islands like Martinique and Barbados, which because of soil quality and hilly terrains had difficulty developing very large units. Though the tendency was to move toward ever larger estates, the West Indian plantations in the late seventeenth century still looked in terms of acreage and size of work force much like those in Brazil. Fifty or so slaves per plantation was the norm. But in the early days of the eighteenth century, a whole new system began to emerge of truly giant estates, as sugar moved into the more open areas of Jamaica and Saint Domingue. Seized from the Spanish in 1655, Jamaica by the 1730s replaced Barbados, just as by the 1740s Saint Domingue replaced Martinique, as the largest sugar producer in their respective colonial empires. Now the average estate reached over 200 acres, and the number of slaves per plantation was passing 100. This increasing size of acreage and population, which was becoming typical for major Caribbean sugar plantations in the eighteenth and nineteenth centuries, whether French, British, or later Spanish, was unique by the standards of the other slave societies in the Americas.

The movement of African slaves into these larger islands was impressive. By 1720, when the slave population of Jamaica had climbed to 74,000 persons, the island had become the most populous slave colony in the British West Indies. By 1760 the island's slave population reached 173,000, and they accounted for just under half of the 365,000 Africans resident in the British West Indies. At the same time Jamaica's white population numbered only some 10,000, so that the relation of blacks to whites had passed the 10 to 1 ratio. Like its predecessor islands, Jamaican slaves were 95 percent rural, and 75 percent of them were engaged in sugar production. By the 1770s, an average estate held 204 slaves and contained well over 1,000 acres. In this prototypical Caribbean plantation society, urban slavery of the kind developed in eighteenth-century Spanish and Portuguese America, with their twenty-one cities of 50,000 to 100,000 persons, was of minor importance. Also, diversified commercial foodstuff production for local consumption, which was a major occupation of Peruvian blacks, hardly existed in societies that were so dependent on foreign imports or slave subsistence production for all their basic food supplies.

Saint Domingue demonstrated many of the patterns of growth set by Jamaica. It took Saint Domingue something like eighty years from its definitive settlement to overtake Martinique. By 1740 its 117,000 slaves represented close to half of the 250,000 African and Afro-American slaves now found in the French West Indies. Growth of the white population continued, but as in the case of the English islands, it slowed considerably as the black population began increasing at impressive rates. Unlike the British West Indies, Saint Domingue also developed a powerful, if small, class of free colored persons who made up almost half of the 26,000 free population on the island.

By the middle of the eighteeth century, it was clear that Saint Domingue was the dominant island in the Caribbean. It was the greatest sugar-producing colony in America, it now held the largest West Indian slave population, and it was also quickly becoming the world's largest producer of coffee, which had only been introduced into the island in 1723. By the late 1780s Saint Domingue planters were recognized as the most efficient and productive sugar producers in the world. The slave population stood at 460,000 people, which was not only the largest of any island but represented close to half of the 1 million slaves then being held in all the Caribbean colonies. The exports of the island represented two-thirds of the total value of all French West Indian exports, and alone were greater than the combined exports from the British and Spanish Antilles. In any one year, well over 600 vessels visited the ports of the island to carry its sugar, coffee, cotton, indigo, and cacao to European consumers.

The rise of the French and British sugar colonies had been aided by the intervention of the Dutch in the first half of the seventeenth century. But the growing power of France and England led to their emergence as major imperial powers in Asia against the Dutch and the Portuguese and as direct competitors in the African slave trade to America as well. By the end of the seventeenth century, British and French slave traders had replaced the Dutch as the primary suppliers of slaves to their American colonies and had seized a major share of the western African slave trade. In the period from 1700 to 1808, the British slavers would move 3.1 million Africans to America, while the French would bring just over 1 million. Most of these African slaves were brought to the West Indies sugar islands. Moreover, the imperial wars would also result in the English obtaining a greater share of the sugar islands. In the early 1760s, France was forced to cede the islands of Grenada, St. Vincent, Dominica, and Tobago to Great Britain, which together brought in another 70,000 slaves into the British West Indies and a significant new group of sugar producers.

An increasing share of the Africans arriving in America in the eighteenth century were absorbed into the sugar plantation system. Such work by the middle of the century occupied something like 1.4 million slaves, both African- and American-born. This was at a minimum some 40 percent of the 3.5 million African and Afro-American slaves to be found in America at this time and represented the single largest occupation in which the slaves were employed. The plantation system was in place in Brazil and the Caribbean, and it dominated slavery in America. The plantation zones of dense black and mulatto populations ruled over by a few whites became the norm for the Caribbean islands as well as the mainland colonies. Although the Jamaican ratio of 10 Africans or Afro-Americans for every 1 white was the extreme, it was most common for blacks and mulattoes to be in the majority wherever the plantations were to be found.

Despite its importance, plantation agriculture was not the only use to which African slaves would be put. In the eighteenth century, there developed a major new use of Africans in the American labor market. In Brazil the relatively stagnant sugar industry was counterbalanced by a thriving gold and diamond mining industry based on slave labor. Indian slave-raiding expeditions opened up these mining districts in the interior of central Brazil and provided slaves to mine these metals. Discovered in the 1690s, these mining zones held some 50,000 African slaves by the early 1720s and over 100,000 by the mid-1730s. In the

1720s diamonds were also discovered in this region of Minas Gerais and nearby Goias, Bahia, and Mato Grosso. This eighteenth-century diamond boom, which started and peaked later than gold, tended to use fewer slaves in far more scattered holdings than in the gold-washing operations, and probably absorbed no more than a third of the 225,000 or so slaves involved in Brazilian mining in the second half of the eighteenth century.

Given the chaotic nature of these new minefields and the crucial role of slave labor, it was inevitable that Minas Gerais would become a major center of emancipated slaves as well. Probably in no other slave region of America did the free colored grow as rapidly, or become as important an element so early in the settlement process. By 1786, when there were some 174,000 slaves in the province, the number of free colored had already passed the 123,000 level. Their growth now continued even more dramatically than that of the slave population. By the first decade of the nineteenth century, freedmen finally outnumbered slaves and had become the largest single group in this fast growing provincial population. That growth would continue into the nineteenth century despite the continued expansion of the slave population. In fact, it was only in the Spanish and Portuguese colonies that freedmen grew to such importance before the abolition of African slavery. Common to the French and British colonies was the lack of a significant class of freedmen among the slaves. In the late eighteenth century, free colored were at most 8 percent of the total slave population in the French and British colonies. There were only 13,000 free colored compared with 467,000 slaves in the British West Indies in the 1780s, and only 59,000 free colored alongside the 698,000 slaves in the British continental colonies of North America at the end of the decade. They also numbered just 32,000 compared with 603,000 slaves in the French islands. In contrast, the free colored in the late eighteenth century were already an important part of the plantation world and its environs in the Spanish and Portuguese colonies. By 1780, Brazil, for example, was residence for 406,000 freed persons of slave descent, and they represented over a quarter of the slave population. By this time in all the Spanish American colonies, the 819,000 free colored were over two and a half times larger than the slave labor force.

The Brazilian gold-mining economy also gave rise to an important regional urban culture. By the second half of the century Minas Gerais had a dozen cities in the 10,000 to 20,000 range that supported a highly developed urban life-style based heavily on both skilled and unskilled slave labor. Thus, the interior mining slavery of central Brazil, unlike what would occur in the gold-mining zones of northwestern Spanish America in the same period, gave rise to a sophisticated urban civilization. In towns like Ouro Preto, which reached 20,000 population by the 1740s, there developed a surprisingly rich baroque culture, which was expressed in a rather sumptuous display of the plastic arts and of music, much of which derived from the hands of black craftsmen, artists, and musicians.

The mining boom in central Brazil would also have a profound impact on the subsequent growth of slavery and black populations in other parts of Brazil. The port of Rio de Janeiro became the primary city for the mines of the central interior provinces and, when it was made the capital of the colony in 1763, its 100,000 persons were twice the number of those in Salvador de Bahia, the second largest city. Another benefactor of the new slave mining economy were the central and southern highlands around São Paulo, which began producing animals and foodstuffs for the Minas Gerais market on small free and slave-based farms. Also a major grazing industry to supply beef, hides, and the crucial mules for the mines was fostered in the open plains of Rio Grande do Sul and as far south as the eastern bank of the Plata River, and this cattle industry was heavily dependent on African slave labor. By the end of the eighteenth century, Rio Grando do Sul had some 21,000 slaves and 5,000 free colored in a population of 71,000. While Africans were a minority of the cowboys on the cattle ranches of Rio Grande do Sul, the salting and beef-drying establishments were run with slave labor. Jerked or dried beef (called charque) was produced in special factories (charqueadas), which usually contained between 60 to 90 slaves. By the early nineteenth century, these charqueadas of the Rio Grande do Sul region employed some 5,000 slaves and their production went mostly to feed the slaves on the sugar plantations and at the mines to the north. In the southern Paulista area known as the Campos Gerais area around the city of Curitiba, it was primarily slaves who were the cowboys and an average Curitiba ranch of 5,000 head of cattle had six gauchos (cowboys) and one overseer, all slaves. The southern provinces even used slaves in fishing. From Cape Frio south to Santa Catarina, whaling became a major industry from the second half of the eighteenth century until the first decades of the next century. The costly and elaborate cutting and boiling factories were run mostly with slave labor, with the typical factory employing between 50 and 100 slave workers. Though a highly seasonal occupation, the factories could employ as many as 2,000 to 3,000 slaves in a good season.

Nor was this the only use of slaves in seaborne trades. Slave sailors were an important part of Brazil's coastal shipping, and it was estimated that by the end of the eighteenth century some 2,000 coastal ships employed some 10,000 slave sailors. Brazil was also rather unusual in its use of slave sailors in international shipping as well, especially so in its Atlantic slave trade routes. Because of its direct trading relations with Africa, in which no triangular linkages existed with Portugal, Brazil early developed a very powerful merchant marine. Hundreds of Brazilian-owned ships plied the South Atlantic taking Brazilian rum, gunpowder, tobacco, and European and American manufactured goods to Angolan and Mozambican ports, and exchanging them for slaves, which were then brought to Brazil. Brazilian-owned vessels also controlled most of the carrying trade to Europe. Given the crucial role slaves played in all aspects of the Brazilian economy, it was no accident that even on slavers, there were typically Brazilian-owned slaves listed as members of the crew. In 147 of the 350 slave ships that arrived in the port of Rio de Janeiro between 1795 and 1811, Brazilian-owned slaves were listed as crew members, numbering 2,058 out of the 12,250 sailors engaged in the trade.

In the late eighteenth century, direct government subsidies also helped foster new slave imports into Brazil's northern colonies of Pernambuco and Maranhão. At approximately the same time as cotton was developing in the British colonies with the aid of slave labor, it was also becoming a major staple export of these two previously neglected zones. The typical cotton plantation in these two states contained 50 slaves per unit, not too different from what would be the average size of a cotton plantation in the southern states of the United States in the nineteenth century. By the early 1790s Brazil accounted for 30 percent of British raw cotton imports, and over 30,000 slaves were involved in cotton production a decade later. The cotton plantation system continued to expand for two decades more until ginned U.S. cotton production wiped out Brazil's comparative advantage and brought a long-term decline to the industry.

The final major development in the Brazilian slave economy was the massive use of slaves for production in the internal market in the province of Minas Gerais. Declining mining output by the first decade of the nineteenth century meant that slave miners represented only

10 percent of the province's 150,000 slaves. The majority of Minas's African and Afro-Brazilian slaves were now employed in producing foodstuffs and rough textiles for the national market – a very unusual use of such a large number of slaves in any zone in America. Despite that fact that the free colored population was now employed everywhere and was greater in number than the slaves, direct African slave arrivals continued at a steady pace right through the nineteenth century and by the time of abolition at the end of the century, the slave population had more than doubled. This meant that at both the beginning and the end of the nineteenth century, Minas Gerais had the largest slave population of any province in Brazil.

As of 1800, Brazil held close to 1 million slaves. It thus had the largest single concentration of African and creole slaves in any one colony in America at this time and also accounted for probably the most diverse economic usage of slaves to be found in the Western Hemisphere. Brazil with its half million free colored was also the largest center of the new class of black and mulatto freedmen in America. Although sugar, gold, diamonds, and other export products went through the classic colonial boom-bust cycles, the vitality of the Brazilian economy was such that new products were developed, new regions opened up, and a lively internal market was created. All this guaranteed that the flow of slaves would not cease. In the last decade of the century, 23,000 African slaves per annum were arriving in the ports of Brazil, and this pace would continue until reaching over 43,000 Africans by the third decade of the new century.

The slave trade to the Spanish American colonies was also encouraged in the late eighteenth century as Spain began to open up all its New World colonies to freer trade. At the beginning of the century it had allowed the English to take over the asiento (or monopoly contract) for slave trading to Spanish America. The English brought some 75,000 Africans into Spanish American ports over a twenty-five-year period. The newly opened port of Buenos Aires obtained some 16,000 Africans, most of whom were shipped to Upper Peru and the interior, while the traditional ports of the Panamanian isthmus and Cartagena got the rest. As others took over the British asiento after 1739, the patterns developed in this first third of the century were accentuated. Slaves flowed steadily into the Caribbean corner of the Isthmus of Panama, the north coast of South America, and the Rio de la Plata region. But the major new center for slave arrivals would be the Spanish West Indies. Especially after the temporary capture of Cuba by the

British in the 1760s, the Crown decided to open the islands to full-scale commercial development and permitted the free trade in slaves for all nations to the Spanish American possessions in 1789. The result of this free-slave-trade policy was the growth of new slave centers in northern South America (above all, in what is today Colombia and Venezuela), and the islands of Puerto Rico and Cuba. Cuba ultimately proved to be the largest slave colony ever created in Spanish America.

To develop the new gold mines of the New Granada, the cacao plantations of Venezuela, and the sugar plantations of its Caribbean islands, the Spaniards imported African slaves on a major scale. In the early eighteenth century the gold region of the Choco district of the viceroyalty of New Granada (in what is today the coastal lowlands of northeastern Colombia) was opened in a lightly populated area. By the 1780s there were over 7,000 African slaves in the region, who accounted for over 13 percent of the viceroyalty's total slave population. The cacao plantations of Venezuela had started with Indian labor late in the sixteenth century and by the middle of the seventeenth century had established dominance over the Mexican and Spanish markets. In this expansion, African slaves played a crucial part. They totally replaced Indian labor by the end of the eighteenth century when some 60 percent of the colony's 64,000 slaves were engaged in cocoa production, with the typical cacao plantation averaging some 30 African slaves.

The last major area of new slave labor development in Spanish America was the island of Cuba, which was to have an explosive growth in the last quarter of the eighteenth century. From a base of about 10,000 slaves at the beginning of the century, the African labor force had reached the 65,000 figure by the end of the 1780s, over a third of whom were already employed in the making of sugar. Coffee production also had begun, and Cuba was entering the world market as a significant producer. On the eve of the Haitian rebellion of 1791, Cuba was already well on its way to emerging as the major slave island in the Caribbean.

Just as the fall of Dutch Pernambuco had changed the map of slave distribution in America in the seventeenth century, the Haitian rebellion would have the same impact in the nineteenth century. In 1789, the revolution that swept through France had its profound impact on a bitterly divided elite in Saint Domingue. The world's largest, most dynamic, and efficient sugar plantation society would tear itself apart, first with an armed conflict between its white and free colored master class and finally in August of 1791 with a full-scale slave revolt. The end result of this only successful slave rebellion in America was the establishment of an independent Haitian government by 1804, and the abolition of slavery on the island. In 1804, sugar production fell to a third of its 1791 levels, and by the next decade Haiti dropped out of the sugar market altogether. Even coffee production, which survived the destruction of the plantations, would only be maintained at half the 1791 output in the first decade of the nineteenth century.

The elimination of the producer of 30 percent of total world production created an expanded market and rising sugar prices for planters from Cuba and Jamaica to Bahia and Rio de Janeiro. At the same time the incipient coffee plantation economies in Jamaica, Rio de Janeiro, Puerto Rico, and Cuba were given a major boost when the world's largest coffee producer lost half its production in this same decade. In the decade after the Haitian Revolution, Jamaica, Brazil, Cuba, and Puerto Rico more than doubled their sugar output. But it was Cuba that was eventually to replace Saint Domingue as the world's primary cane producer by the middle decades of the nineteenth century. It also became a major coffee producer, and by the 1830s the island's coffee plantations employed some 50,000 slaves, a number roughly equal to those in sugar.

The steady expansion of sugar and the spectacular growth of coffee had a direct impact on Cuban population growth. As was to be expected, there would be a dramatic increase in both slave immigrants and total slave population. But in contrast to the traditional Caribbean experience up to this time, all other sectors of the population would grow as well. From a strong eighteenth-century base, the free white population expanded at almost the same rate as did the slave population, and there was also a slower but constant increase of free colored persons. The slaves increased to 324,000 in the mid-1840s, and by the 1860s they peaked at 370,000. Cuba was also unusual by West Indian standards in having a large urban population, which contained about 20 percent of its slave labor force. It also differed in its use of indentured labor alongside slave labor. Despite the continuation of the slave trade to 1867, the demand for labor became so intense that by the 1840s planters brought in hundreds of enslaved rebel Mayan Indians from Yucatan and also attracted the first of the more than 100,000 Chinese coolies who would be carried to Cuba in the next twenty years. These Indians and Chinese laborers were immediately put to work in the cane fields alongside the African and creole black slaves, and by the 1860s there was evolving a mixed slave and indentured labor force on the larger sugar estates. In 1862, when 34,000 Chinese and 700 Yucatan Indians were working in the ingenios (sugar mills), the average estate held 126 African slaves and the island's sugar plantations contained 173,000 slaves.

The growth of Spain's second major Caribbean production center, Puerto Rico, was to follow much the same pattern experienced by Cuba. But the existence of a large and growing free peasant population and a limited range of soils appropriate for sugar constrained the size of the plantations. By the 1830s the island reached its maximum slave population of 42,000 Africans and the local sugar estates were averaging 40 slaves per unit. While a slave population of this size ranked Puerto Rico as a relatively small slave society by Caribbean standards, the concentration of slaves in sugar was unusual. The existence of a large free population of 317,000 persons (of whom two-fifths were free colored) meant that many of the tasks performed in Cuba or the French West Indies by slaves were performed by free wage laborers in Puerto Rico. This meant that an extraordinarily high ratio of the slaves, or two-thirds to three-quarters, worked in sugar.

The progress of slavery and sugar on the remaining French controlled islands of Martinique and Guadeloupe were not that dissimilar from what had occurred in Cuba and Puerto Rico. In 1789 the two islands and their dependencies had a total of almost 170,000 slaves, which climbed to 180,000 when the French slave trade was finally abolished. Equally, the elimination of Saint Domingue production gave a major boost to Jamaica, and to British Caribbean slavery. In the last decade of the eighteenth century, British slavers were already bringing in some 19,000 Africans per annum to these colonies, of which two-thirds went to Jamaica. The slave population of the British West Indies was approaching the 600,000 size of the slave population of the French West Indies colonies at their height in 1790, and would surpass that in the early nineteenth century. The African and Afro-American slaves on Jamaica alone had reached over 350,000 persons by 1810 and it was now the world's largest producer of sugar and seems to have continued to dominate the world market until slavery was abolished in the 1830s.

Brazil was also profoundly affected by the shock of the 1791 Haitian rebellion. Not only did it take over from Saint Domingue and Cuba the role of America's coffee production center, but its sugar industry revived in both the Northeast and in the south central provinces of Rio de Janeiro and São Paulo. By the 1820s Bahia doubled its sugar mills and increased its slave population to nearly 150,000 persons. Pernambuco followed suit with an expansion of its sugar production and by the

1850s, at the closing of Brazil's international slave trade, it had 145,000 resident slaves. Big sugar estates also developed in Rio de Janeiro, and by the early 1820s there were over 170,000 slaves in the province, some 20,000 of whom were to be found on the sugar estates of the region.

But coffee was to be Brazil's big nineteenth-century slave crop. Although coffee had been produced in Brazil since the early eighteenth century, the collapse of Saint Domingue provided a space for the expansion of Brazilian coffee production. From Rio de Janeiro coffee spread south toward São Paulo and west toward Minas Gerais. In 1831 coffee exports finally surpassed sugar exports, and Brazil was then producing double the combined output of Cuba and Puerto Rico and was the world's largest producer. From the beginning coffee was produced on plantations by slave labor. Large coffee plantations could contain as many as 400,000 to 500,000 trees and a workforce of 300 to 400 slaves. More typical, however, was the plantation of 70 to 100 slaves, which was still double the size of the average West Indian coffee estate even in the nineteenth century.

Rio de Janeiro was initially the leading coffee producer and by the 1860s an estimated 100,000 of the province's 250,000 slaves were in coffee production, and that figure rose to 129,000 in the next decade. An intense African slave trade kept the coffee fazendas supplied with slaves until the 1850s – reaching a high of 43,000 African arrivals per annum in the 1820s. In the 1840s coffee finally passed sugar in importance in São Paulo and some 25,000 slaves were working in the province's coffee fazendas. Coffee also developed in the southern Minas Gerais region, known as the Zona de Mata. But it was not until the 1850s that coffee finally became the major export in terms of total value. The slave population on the province's coffee fazendas probably reached a maximum of 42,000 out of a total provincial slave population of 382,000 by the early 1870s. In all, by this decade something like 245,000 slaves were working in coffee in the three states of Rio de Janeiro, São Paulo, and Minas Gerais.

The three remaining slave colonies on the mainland coast of South America – Cayenne, Surinam, and British Guiana – would all pass through stages of growth and change similar to what had occurred in both the West Indies and Brazil. All three colonies were directly influenced by the Haitian Revolution. French Guiana had a relatively small slave population of 10,000 by the 1780s but it revived in the nineteenth century and by the 1840s there were 19,000 slaves, of whom 3,000 were owned by the very large free colored population. An attempt to retain a dynamic export sector with imported indentured laborers from India after abolition was largely a failure and the region went into a long period of decline. As early as the 1670s the colony of Surinam had 30,000 slaves and their number peaked at 75,000 in the 1790s. British Guiana experienced the same pattern of development as Surinam, but on a larger scale. Through a system of dikes and other hydraulic works, the below-sea-level coastal plain was made into a rich plantation zone producing sugar, coffee, cotton, and cacao. Responding quickly to the post-Haitian boom in prices of slave-produced commodities, the colony's plantations expanded dramatically. In the 1790s its slave population probably numbered close to 120,000 and even as that labor force declined in the next decades, it still numbered close to 110,000 by 1810, which made it the second largest slave colony of British America.

The last major slave-importing region to be considered is, of course, the United States. Although slaves had been introduced into Virginia by the Dutch in 1619, until the late seventeenth century the primary labor force was indentured English servants. But the increasing cost of indentured laborers after the 1670s and the growth of an English slaving fleet in this period impelled the British continental colonies toward the use of African slaves as they had in their West Indian possessions. Although slaves were imported into every continental colony, there were only two really major centers of slave labor. The first region was the tidewater zone of the Chesapeake Bay, which included the colonies of Virginia, Maryland, and parts of North Carolina; and a second region further south centered on South Carolina and Georgia. The first zone was primarily a tobacco producer and was unusual by New World standards, in that it was a crop primarily produced by slaves. In Cuba and the rest of the Americas, tobacco was usually produced by small freehold farmers with few slave workers in these fields.

The Chesapeake became the primary tobacco producer for the world, exporting some 38 million pounds by 1700 and effectively liquidating English West Indian production. It was also the most important slave zone in continental North America, holding some 145,000 slaves (or 60 percent of the total in the thirteen colonies) by 1750. The Georgia–South Carolina region became a major rice producer on coastal plantations, with some slave-produced indigo in the backland areas. These slave-based rice plantations absorbed 40,000 slaves by midcentury. By 1790 there were an impressive 698,000 slaves in what was now the United States, 94 percent of whom were in the so-called southern states from Maryland south. Although slavery existed in every state at that time, in the northern region this slavery was mostly domestic, while in the south it was intimately tied to the export of primary crops to Europe.

But rice and tobacco would soon pale in significance to the production of cotton. Although long- and short-staple cotton had been grown in the southern region for some time, as it was in the West Indies and South America, only the introduction of mechanical cleaning of the short-staple and heavily seeded cotton in the 1790s with the cotton gin permitted cotton planting to penetrate into the interior of the country and also to become a competitive crop on the world market. Starting in the rice regions, cotton spread inland quickly, and as early as the 1830s half of the cotton was being produced in the newly settled regions of Alabama, Mississippi, and Louisiana (which became part of the United States in 1803). By the middle of the nineteenth century this was the largest single export from the United States, more valuable than all other exports combined, and it was an overwhelmingly slave-produced crop. Moreover, U.S. cotton dominated the world market and reduced cotton production for export in most of the other American regions. But most of the slaves for these plantations came from internal growth and interregional continental migration rather than the Atlantic trade. The slave trade delivered over half a million slaves until the trade was formally abolished in 1808. Another million slaves, however, were moved to the new planting regions through the internal slave trade that brought slaves from the Upper South and the coast toward the "Deep South."

A slave trade that brought in half a million Africans up to 1808 would not have resulted in a slave population of 1.2 million persons in 1810 under normal conditions of growth and migrations due to the African trade in the rest of the Americas. In most regions of America, the age and sex biases among the arriving slaves guaranteed that the resident American slave population could not reproduce itself, at least during the period of heaviest African migrations. In some few zones, where the trade brought a smaller stream of Africans over a long period, the creole (or American-born) slaves were able to influence total slave growth through their own positive growth rates. While this occurred in parts of Brazil and Spanish America, nowhere was it so positive as in the United States. By the last quarter of the eighteenth century, even before the end of the Atlantic slave trade, the resident creole slave populations had achieved high positive rates of growth and were causing solid increase in the total resident slave population. Just after the end of the slave trade in 1808 there were some 1.2 million slaves, and they grew to almost 4 million by 1860 without the assistance of African migration. All of this growth came from native-born slaves, who by the 1810s already accounted for 85 percent of the total slave population.

Defined as a slave society because of its dependence on slave labor for the production of export crops, the United States nevertheless had a high percentage of free persons. In this it was similar to Brazil where roughly two-thirds of the population were free. But the contrast was in the free population. This was overwhelmingly colored in Brazil and overwhelmingly white in the United States, given North America's low level of manumission and the slow growth of a free black population. The United States was also similar to Brazil in its relative distribution of slave ownership, with only a third of the free southern population being owners. They both thus differed from the West Indies with its high ratios of slaves to free and high ratio of slave owners within the free population. They also differed from the West Indies in the average size of their slave plantations. Whereas Louisiana sugar plantations averaged 175 slaves per unit and approached West Indian levels, the typical southern cotton plantation was on the order of 32 slaves. This figure was close to the norm for a typical coffee or mixed farming plantation in Brazil.

Given the transformations of the American slave economies at the end of the eighteenth century and the tremendous growth of new zones of exportation, it is no accident that the last decades of the century recorded the highest levels of African arrivals in the history of the Atlantic slave trade. The two decades of the 1760s and 1770s brought in 1.3 million slaves for an average of close to 66,000 Africans per annum. By the 1780s, probably the peak decade of the trade, the arrivals reached 75,000 per annum. International wars and the Haitian Revolution temporarily slowed the pace of the trade, with average arrivals only reaching 69,000 per annum in the 1790s. So impressive was this movement of slaves that the period from 1700 to 1808 saw the arrival of over 6 million Africans in the Americas, which represented two-thirds of the total number of Africans who were ever sent to America (see Table A.2, in the Appendix). It has been estimated that if the United States and Great Britain had not closed the trade in 1808, the total volume of annual arrivals would have gone to 160,000 – or double the peak 1780s figure – by the 1830s.

The trade to the United States though initially small was to prove an important component of this eighteenth- and early nineteenth century movement. Volume had reached 5,000 per annum early in the century and was at close to 16,000 per annum in the first decade of the nineteenth century. In just two years, 1805 and 1806, Rhode Island slavers alone imported on average 6,400 slaves per annum, and this was only one source of Africans for the U.S. market. It has been estimated that the 156,000 slaves who arrived in the United States in the period from 1801 to 1808 represented 26 percent of the total Africans landing in the Americas in the last epoch of unrestricted trade. Nevertheless, the 500,000 Africans who arrived in the United States in the entire history of the trade were still a minor part of the 10 million who came to the Americas during that time period.

Though the United States and the English colonies had closed the slave trade by 1808, Cuba, Puerto Rico, Brazil, and parts of the non-English Caribbean still kept up a steady stream of slave labor imports. Though international war and partial abolition seriously affected slave movements, the return of peace soon had decade figures averaging close to 60,000 Africans per annum by the 1820s. Nor did they drop below the 50,000 range until the 1840s, and even then 43,000 Africans were still arriving every year up to midcentury. Though by then only Cuba and Brazil were still actively purchasing African slaves, their demand and that of the French earlier had succeeded in adding another 2.3 million Africans after 1808 to the 6 million who had already come from 1701 to 1808. It was only the forced termination of the Brazilian trade at midcentury that finally diminished this extraordinary volume of forced migrations. Though Cuba still kept bringing in Africans in the next two decades, the trade had diminished to just 14,000 per annum in the 1850s and slowly petered out in the next decade. As I will show later in this work, this diminution and eventual termination of the Atlantic slave trade were due to external forces and not to any lessening of demand for African labor by the American markets. On the contrary, had not Spain and Brazil been forced to terminate their participation in the Atlantic slave trade, the trade might well have continued well into the twentieth century.

As this survey of the use and growth of African slavery in the Americas has suggested, export agriculture and effective colonization would not have occurred on the scale it did if enslaved Africans had not been brought to the New World. Except for precious metals, almost all major American exports to Europe were produced by Africans. There is also little question that the West Indies and most of Brazil would not have been effectively settled without the use of these African slaves. Given the wealth generated by these colonies for the respective metropolitan powers, there was no willingness to forgo the use of African slave labor in the name of a still inarticulate call to equality for all peoples, a theme that would only emerge within European and American thought late in the eighteenth century. Until that time the slave plantations of the small West Indian islands were worth more to London and Paris than continents filled with free-labor settlers.

CHAPTER 3

AFRICA AT THE TIME OF THE ATLANTIC
SLAVE TRADE

The political, economic, and social structures of sub-Saharan Africa were well developed when the Europeans opened up the West African coast to international trade at the beginning of the fifteenth century. Advanced civilizations existed throughout the continent, most regions to the Cape had been settled, and the basic plants and animals had been domesticated for several centuries. Throughout the continent, advanced mining and industrial activity existed alongside agriculture and herding. Gold had been exported to the European and Middle Eastern markets for centuries, and iron was smelted from local ores throughout the continent. A large part of this region had already been in direct contact with North Africa and the Mediterranean world since the classic civilizations of Egypt, Greece, and Rome. Even before 1400 its eastern coast had been in contact with India and the Pacific islands. Finally, along the southern fringes of the Sahara from coast to coast it was a basic part of the Islamic world order.

Sub-Saharan society and economy developed later than North Africa. Complex societies, urban centers, and the spread of plants, animals, and technology to all regions from the savannas of the Sudan to the Cape of Good Hope were not achieved until the post-Christian era. It took from 200 b.c. to a.d. 500 for advanced agricultural, grazing, and mining culture to reach all of central and southern Africa. By then there were complex stratified societies based on settled village agriculture everywhere in Africa. Moreover, not until the end of the great Bantu migrations by around a.d. 700 did the linguistic map of Africa finally become firmly established in its broadest aspects. Although increasingly sophisticated markets introduced ever wider regions into contact with each other after this date, migrations tended to be local, except for the slave trade and some modest movement of pastoralists responding to ecological change, and the map of population distributions remained fairly stable.

Most of the eastern and western Sudan above the equator, the best known regions to the Mediterranean world, were in contact with that culture from the earliest times. Even prior to the final desiccation of the Sahara around 2000 b.c., the Sudan was tied to North African developments, and the closing of this frontier did not end contact between these two worlds. Iron smelting, for example, which begins in North Africa with the rise of Carthage circa 1000 b.c., reached as far south as West Central Africa by 300 b.c., the same time as copper smelting arrives in this region. Thus, despite the sand barrier of the Sahara, the movement of ideas, people, and commodities continued at a slow but steady pace.

From 200 b.c. to around a.d. 500, the integration of societies and economies in the various ecological zones of savanna, tropical forest, coast, and dry lands had fully evolved. Moreover, many of these complex societies and economies were to be found in both central and southern Africa even before the final great migrations of the Bantu speakers from the north spread a more unified culture throughout Africa. Agriculture, grazing, mining, and settled village life were common to all Africa by the end of the first century a.d.

Though economic and social development in the post-Christian era brought with it the rise of complex stratified societies everywhere in Africa, only the political history of the Sudan area is well known because of its contacts with the Mediterranean world. Here the developments are familiar to the world north of the Sahara from at least the first century a.d. The western Sudan in the Christian era was intimately tied to the fate of the region of western North Africa known as the Maghreb. The domestication of the camel was crucial in making that relationship even more intense. Camel caravans finally became the norm after a.d. 300 and revolutionized the trans-Saharan trade. Camels could carry heavier loads than mules and do so over longer distances without water. They could also graze on more arid lands than was usable by goats. Horses and cattle were also soon an important part of the savanna culture north of the equator and south of the desert. An entire transhumance grazing culture developed from the western to the eastern Sudan region and as far south as the equator and the tsetse fly frontier – a line beyond which all cattle and horses died.

In the western Sudan, gold production at Bambuk, a site on the upper Senegal River near the Falémé River, was the first well-known export center from West Africa northward. Gold from Bambuk reached Roman imperial markets as early as a.d. 300. Several major empires developed here in the savanna interior near the upper reaches of the Senegal and Niger Rivers, all based on two factors – their dominance over gold exports and control over the southern cities of the caravan routes. The most famous of these early recorded empires was that of Ghana, which controlled both the Bambuk goldfields and the most western of the caravan routes that ended in Morocco. Given its intimate relationship with North Africa, it was inevitable that Ghana and its succeeding empires of the whole Sudan area would be influenced by the explosive expansion of the Islamic religion after its foundation in the seventh century a.d. All the empires that traded north were converted to Islam between the tenth and twelfth centuries a.d. In turn, these newly Islamicized traders brought Islam even further south toward the Lower Guinean Coast in the next centuries.

So intimate was the relationship between North Africa and the western Sudan that the seizure of the crucial trading city of Awdaghust, the southern terminus of the western caravan route, by the Almoravides Berbers in the 1050s marked the end of the Ghana Empire, which had controlled that city. Two centuries later the Mande peoples were able to establish a new imperial state in the western Sudan based on both the original Bambuk goldfields, as well as the newly opened ones in Buré on the Upper Niger and in the Akan region of present-day Ghana. The Mali Empire, which lasted from circa a.d. 1250 to 1350, was much more extensive than the Ghana Empire had been and stretched from the Gambia River on the Atlantic to the Upper Niger in the east and the Lower Guinean Coast in the south. Its center was the city of Timbuktu, which became the principal "desert port" of the western Sudan. It was also unusual in having a powerful bureaucracy, which was able to control the dynasty and maintain stability for a long period of time, while it developed a complex trading economy based on gold, textiles, salt, and a large number of products exported to both local and long-distance markets.

The Mali Empire slowly collapsed in the late fourteenth century and in turn was replaced by the empire that the Songhai peoples created around 1450. The Songhai Empire had its capital at Goa, but continued to use Timbuktu as its commercial center. This region of West Africa was thus well organized and well integrated into the Mediterranean world at the time of the arrival of the Portuguese. And it was this region that would first participate in the Atlantic slave trade.

In fact, the opening up of western Africa to the Atlantic world was intimately related to the developments in the Christian and Islamic Mediterranean worlds. The long conflict between Christianity and Islam would mark the history not only of Europe and the Mediterranean but also of sub-Saharan Africa. The most important development in this respect was the reorganization of the Islamic world under the dynamic Ottoman Turks, which began in the fourteenth century. Coming from Central Asia, the Turks created the Ottoman dynasty at Baghdad in the 1300s, and slowly expanded westward. By 1453 they captured Constantinople and renamed it Istanbul, thus destroying the last of the eastern Christian empire. The Ottoman Turks then pushed by land and sea toward the west and encountered the expanding Christian Europeans head on. Not only did the Turks pick up much of the Balkans, but they even besieged Vienna and attempted to conquer Italy and Mediterranean Europe by sea. They also moved into North Africa and took Egypt in 1517.

In the meantime, the two leading powers of the expanding world of Europe also moved into North Africa. The kingdoms of Spain and Portugal, with their long-term contacts with Islam, decided to expand into North Africa. In 1415 Portugal took the North African town of Ceuta just south of the Iberian Peninsula, and soon followed with the capture of Tangiers. It then slowly moved down the northwestern coast of Africa from the 1470s to the early 1500s, reaching as far south as the city of Agadir. All this was at the expense of the independent Kingdom of Morocco. In turn, Castile expanded not only into Sicily and the Italian peninsula in the early sixteenth century, but from 1590 to 1610 systematically seized many of the Maghrib cities to the east from Melilla to Tripoli. But local Berber and Arab groups allied with either Morocco or the Ottoman Turks eventually took the majority of these cities back from the Europeans. During their hold over these North African centers, however, the Portuguese especially came into intimate contact with the Saharan caravan routes and their sub-Saharan participants.

Given their longtime experience in the Atlantic fisheries and the recent stabilization of their society, which gave the merchant classes a major role in the state, the Portuguese were the first of the western European states to expand beyond the Atlantic and Mediterranean heartland. With footholds in their ports in North Africa and in the eastern Atlantic islands of the Azores and Madeira, the Portuguese now moved their famous caravels into the South Atlantic. From 1430 to 1490 they would explore the West African coast from Agadir to the Cape of Good Hope. In the early 1440s the first Portuguese sailors returned from sailing beyond the Sahara. Sometime before the 1470s they had learned to sail offshore into the South Atlantic to pick up the northwestern trade winds, which brought them up to the Azores and made the return voyages viable for far southern exploration. By the end of the 1480s they had reached the Cape of Good Hope.

Thus was West Africa opened up to direct European contact and the previously closed Atlantic shore suddenly emerged as an alternative trade route for African societies. The Portuguese were quick to exploit this new trading zone. In the 1450s they obtained exclusive Christian rights for dealing with Africa south of Cape Bojador from the pope. In 1466 they settled the island of Santiago in the Cape Verde Islands; in 1482 they built the fort of São Jorge da Mina (Elmina in current-day Ghana); by 1483 they were in contact with the Kingdom of the Kongo just south of the Congo (Zaire) River in Central Africa; in 1493 they had definitely settled the island of São Tomé in the Gulf of Guinea, and by 1505 they had constructed the fort of Sofala on the Mozambique coast of East Africa.

Initially, the Portuguese treated their African contacts as they had the North Africans they encountered. They raided and attempted to forcibly take slaves and plunder along the coast they visited. Thus, when they landed at Rio de Oro just south of Cape Bojador in 1441, they seized several Berbers along with one of their black slaves. In 1443 a caravel returned to the same Idzãgen Berbers to exchange two aristocratic members of the group for gold and 10 black slaves. In 1444 and 1445 merchants and nobles of the Algarve outfitted two major expeditions against the Idzãgen and the first brought back 235 Berber and black slaves who were sold in Lagos. Thus began the Atlantic slave trade.

But not only did the second and later expedition encounter serious hostility from the now prepared Berbers, but attempts to seize slaves directly from the black states on the Windward Coast ended in military defeat for the Portuguese. The result was that the Portuguese moved from a raiding style to peaceful trade, which was welcomed by Berber and African alike. In 1445 came the first peaceful trade with the Idzãgen Berbers at Rio Oro in which European goods were exchanged for African slaves. Trade with the Idzãgen led to the settlement of a trading post (called a "factory") at Arguim Island off the Mauritanian coast; and after 1448 direct trade began for slaves and gold with the West African states.

Quickly the Portuguese moved to control the uninhabited coastal and delta islands and erect local settlements and forts. They also traveled inland to explore their new markets. Well before 1500 they were familiar with West African geography and Portuguese travelers had already visited West Africa's three leading goldfields. Gold was the primary article the Portuguese sought in their trade with Africa, and they took slaves and other local products as secondary trading items. They built their first major continental fort, São Jorge da Mina (Elmina), on the Ghana coast just east of the Cape of Three Points on land at the edge of the rain forest and with direct access as well to open savanna lands. This fort, along with that of Axem settled in 1500 just east of the cape and also in Ghana, was built in the heart of what would become known to Europeans as the Gold Coast on the Gulf of Guinea. The Portuguese by the first two decades of the sixteenth century were purchasing over 400 kilograms per annum from inland traders, which was roughly one-fourth of West African gold production in that period. Portuguese ships even engaged in an active coastal trade, moving goods and slaves between other African states to these gold-exporting nations as well as shipping in products from Europe, Asia, and North Africa. In their desire for African gold, which had a major impact on royal finances in Europe, the Portuguese were willing to satisfy local demands for any goods desired, procuring them everywhere, even from North Africa and Benin. Most of the goods imported by the Portuguese had already been brought by overland routes to these coastal and interior peoples before the arrival of the Europeans. Major imports in the early Portuguese trade to the Gold Coast were North African dyed cloths and copper ingots and bracelets, all items that local consumers and smiths were used to purchasing from Muslim sources. It was the volume of these goods that was new to these West African markets, not the goods themselves. Thus, the major impact of the coming of the Europeans to Africa was the addition of new trading routes rather than strange or exotic products. Whereas the Niger River flowing mostly north toward the Sahara had been the great connecting link for the peoples of West Africa until then, now the Senegal, Gambia, and other local rivers running west and south toward the Atlantic coasts became the major links to the outside world. So intense and widespread did this trading become over most of West Africa, that the Portuguese language quickly became the basis of a trading patois that was spoken throughout the region.

In opening up the African Atlantic coast, it was the Europeans who provided the initiative and the communications with the outside world, however openly local peoples accepted this new trading possibility and reoriented their inland markets. The question worth exploring at this point is why Europe expanded at this time. After all western Europe in the fifteenth century was a relatively poor zone by world standards. China, India, and Asia Minor were all richer than Europe. Nor were the Europeans the only ones coming to Africa. Already Islamic traders had been shipping goods off the East African coast, and in this century as well a Chinese fleet had reached the same coast.

In the whole process of the so-called expansion of the West, which would make Europe the dominant region on the world stage from the fifteenth to the twentieth century, it was not the exploring or first contacts that were so important as much as the maintenance of that contact. The whole opening up of Africa, which was the first major thrust of Europe overseas and the beginning of the age of Western domination, colonialism, and imperialism, exhibited many of the characteristics that defined that expansion and help to explain the extraordinary dynamism of the European response. Once opening up a market, the Portuguese could mobilize large quantities of capital and labor to outfit subsequent expeditions to exploit these newly discovered markets. After the first ship arrived, dozens followed, and regular systematic trade became the norm. This was the case in Africa, and it would be the same in the Indian Ocean, which the Portuguese also opened up to direct European trade at the end of the fifteenth century. Nor did the Portuguese enjoy their monopoly for long; even on the Gold Coast, interlopers from the major European naval powers had definitively broken that monopoly by the 1540s. Europe clearly was unique at that time in its ability to mobilize capital and labor over very long periods. This was the result of strong state institutions; a rising merchant class with access to government support; credit mechanisms that were capable of generating large quantities of capital for longtime investments; a reasonable distribution of wealth and savings due to control over natality through late marriages and limited bastardy; and a large free peasantry, recently released from serfdom and accustomed to responding to wage incentives and a free labor market.

While this explains why the next centuries have been labeled the "European Period" in world history, they do not fully explain the relative development of European and African contact. This, as we will see in the next chapter, is highly correlated with the opening up of the Western

Hemisphere to European conquest. But this was not the only factor influencing that contact. Aside from peaceful trading in gold, slaves, ivory, and other local products, the Portuguese were also concerned with conversion. Like the rest of southern and eastern Europe, they were locked into a deadly battle of survival with the Muslims of the Ottoman Empire. Especially where Islam had not yet fully established itself, or did not exist, they saw a possibility of conversion. Already by the 1480s their agents had reached the Kingdom of Ethiopia in eastern Africa, the only independent Christian state in Africa. In 1490 they mounted a major fleet to support a Christian pretender to the Jolof throne in Senegambia, which failed in its effort. In 1491 Christian missionaries were sent to the Kingdom of the Kongo, south of the Congo River, and there had more successes, even enthroning Affonso, a powerful leader, and a Christianized African as head of the state in 1506. But within a generation the missionaries were expelled and the Kongo reverted to traditional religious beliefs. In 1514 they sent missionaries to the Oba of Benin, and this attempt ended in failure. Finally, in their desire to control the Shona goldfields of East Africa, the Portuguese in 1569 mounted a 1,000-man expedition, that included missionaries, to expel the Muslimized Swahili traders and Christianize the local miners. The Portuguese army went up the Zambezi River toward the mines only to see the majority of the Europeans die of malaria and the expedition end in failure.

The only result of all these Portuguese efforts at penetration and conversion was the unintended one of the creation, from Senegambia in the northwest of Africa to Mozambique in the southeastern part, of a mixed Afro-Portuguese free merchant class, which claimed Portuguese identity and adopted Catholicism but rejected the sovereignty of the Portuguese state. Some of these communities not only occupied key settlements along the coast, but often penetrated deep into the interior. They colonized the Benguela highlands in Angola and even created ministates with African followers and slave armies in the interior of Mozambique on their "estates" or prazos. This model in turn was followed to a lesser extent by the creation of local Afro-English and Afro-French merchant groups along the West African coast in the seventeenth and eighteenth centuries. In each case, these were racially mixed elites who intermarried with members of the local African establishments and were deeply involved with the regional African states and societies and who no longer obeyed the commands of the European states that had fostered them.

The great push toward Christianizing Africans through either conquering the Islamic groups or evangelizing and converting the religiously "primitive" peoples ended with these Portuguese attempts. This also meant the end of any thought of actual conquest and colonization in Africa as well. This forced acceptance of African autonomy was due to several factors. First were the difficulties of maintaining troops, missionaries, and bureaucrats in the African environment because of extraordinarily high European deathrates from yellow fever and malaria. There was also the military balance that existed between Europeans and Africans. Though here as everywhere else in the post-1500 world the Europeans controlled the seas, the rapid transmission of European and North African military techniques throughout Africa meant that firearms and even cavalry were used by African states, making it extremely difficult to conquer inland. Finally, the unqualified hostility of these states and/or their peoples to any intervention, or missionary activity, eventually destroyed the few military gains that the Portuguese obtained in either West or East Africa. Respect for religious and political autonomy therefore became the norm in African-European dealings, and the Portuguese and those Europeans who followed them were even forced to deal with the many Muslim groups of the western Sudan region in peace and acceptance.

This does not mean that the coming of the Europeans to the Atlantic and Indian Ocean coasts of Africa had little impact on internal African society and economy. Far from it. But it should be stressed that the coming of the Europeans by sea varied in its impact depending on the nature of the local society and its previous contacts with the non-African world. In the region from Senegambia to the Cameroons, and in East Africa, it was less a revolutionary event than in the Central African regions of the Congo and Angola. This had to do with the prior existence of long-term trading arrangements across the Sahara, which reached as far south as the Bight of Biafra in the west and intimate long-term relationships with African trading communities along the entire Eastern African shoreline. While sea transport was cheaper than land transport, it did not eliminate traditional relationships or the constant movement of goods to North Africa. Even at the height of the gold trade in West Africa, for example, the Europeans only took a minority of the local output by sea, with a majority of the gold still crossing the Sahara. Nor was the political impact of the European arrival in this zone very profound. The slave trade initially was a minor movement of peoples with little influence over warfare or raiding and the Europeans' inability to conquer any territories or send in armies limited their influence over local events, no matter how much trade routes were reoriented. Thus, the great Songhai Empire in the Upper Niger region – the largest empire in West Africa – was weakened by the coming of the Europeans, but it was actually destroyed by a Moroccan invasion from across the desert. In 1591, a revived Moroccan state not only drove the Europeans out of most of its coastal cities and even killed one Portuguese king in doing so, but the Moroccans headed south across the desert and seized Timbuktu from the Songhai. The blow destroyed this Sudan empire. Though smaller secondary states continued in this region, the fall of the Songhai state meant the end of large empires in this area until the nineteenth century.

It was also clear that Swahili and Arabic traders had dominated the East African trade routes long before the arrival of the Portuguese. Though the Portuguese aggressively moved to control Mozambique, they could not drive further north against these Muslim traders or seize the independent state on Madagascar Island, and found that they could not even monopolize the gold trade of the Mozambique hinterland itself. Thus, many traditional trade networks initially remained unaffected by the European contact despite very aggressive European activity.

Moreover, so long as the Atlantic slave trade remained small, which was the case through most of its earlier period, it had a relatively limited impact even on the internal African slave markets. Estimates of all the slave trades to 1600 suggest that the Atlantic slave trade took only a quarter of all slaves leaving Africa and was still considerably smaller than the trans-Saharan slave trade. It was only in the seventeenth century that the Atlantic route forged ahead as the dominant slave trade, accounting for close to two-thirds of all Africans leaving the continent. Even so, until 1700, slaves were not the most valuable product taken by the Europeans from West Africa. Rather the most important export was gold, followed by ivory, hides, pepper, beeswax, and gum. Slaves were still only a small part of the total value of African exports. At the end of the fifteenth century the Atlantic slave trade involved the shipment of no more than 800 to 2,000 slaves per annum, all of whom were being sent to Portugal or its Atlantic island possessions, such as Madeira and São Tomé, that began using slaves to produce sugar starting in 1455 and the 1490s, respectively. Portuguese extraction of slaves was estimated to have risen to some 4,500 slaves per annum in the first decades of the sixteenth century as slave shipments to Spanish America had begun. This movement was still not that different in volume from the slave trade going across the Sahara or out of the Red Sea ports at this time. It was also of a far different dimension than the close to 80,000 Africans per annum shipped to America at the height of the Atlantic slave trade in the decade of the 1780s (see Table A.1, in the Appendix).

This changing volume of the Atlantic trade, as well as the wide regional variations of ecologies, economies, and political organization in Africa from which the slaves traded, most influenced the impact of the trade on the African continent. Though the Europeans could quickly tap into the local movement of slaves who were previously destined for domestic use or for export by land to North Africa and the Middle East, it was only through the establishment of new caravan routes and ports that they could generate more numerous slave purchases and steadier supplies. Even despite their best efforts to satisfy local African markets with the goods they desired, whether of Asian, European, American, or African origin, it was impossible to develop a major supply of slaves if the local groups or the interior states and trading communities did not wish to participate. This explains the varying nature of the origin of the slaves, both in terms of how they were taken and from where they were shipped.

In the period before the eighteenth century, American demand was steady but did not exceed local supplies, so that slave prices were relatively stable. This meant that the Europeans could purchase slaves from the regular flow of local slaves taken in limited raiding or as judicial offenders in any given region, plus the large quantities of slaves that were produced in local warfare. In almost all these later cases, the wars among the Africans were caused by local political, economic, or religious conflict among competing peoples. The by-product of these wars was, of course, the male slaves of the defeated peoples who could be profitably eliminated through forced migration. This episodic origin of war captives explains why some regions would come in and out of the Atlantic trade over time, often without an increase or decrease of European demand for slaves. Thus, places such as Senegambia suddenly had major slave exports in the years from the 1720s to the 1740s during local Islamic religious wars, only to return to a minor movement of slaves for many decades. The same occurred with the Gold Coast in the Gulf of Guinea, which shipped virtually no slaves until the Asante wars of expansion after the 1680s suddenly led to thousands of slaves leaving its local ports.

There were other cases, such as the Kingdom of the Kongo to the south of the Zaire or Congo River, which quickly organized the slave trade from a region that had only limited local slavery, and became a steady exporter of slaves from its hinterlands from the sixteenth to the late nineteenth century. Its peoples developed local raiding into a major source of slaves over long periods of time. There was also the case of the Kingdom of Benin, which was well located to become a major intermediary in the local slave trade from the Bight of Benin (also known as the Slave Coast): it simply decided in 1516 to restrict the export of male slaves from the kingdom, and eventually closed the trade altogether, just as its neighbors such as the Kingdom of Dahomey was, like the Kongo state, becoming a major and long-term trader of slaves.

Most scholars agree that the increasing American demand eventually brought about changes in the voluntary nature of the trade after the mid-eighteenth century. Though the Europeans could not force any region to enter the trade against its wishes, and many remained closed to the trade, the rising prices for slaves – driven by increasing American demand due to increasing European consumption of American slave-produced goods – powerfully influenced local African developments where the slave trade was well established. Large-scale warfare, in which obtaining slaves for the Atlantic trade was a major theme, now became more common. Entire trading networks, especially in such regions as the Congo and Angola, as well as the Bight of Biafra, produced a steady volume of slaves for America and large parts of their local economies became intimately tied to the supply of slaves to the Atlantic economy.

The evolution of the trade along the coasts of West and East Africa varied over time and place. The first region encountered by the Portuguese as they rounded Cape Bojador and arrived in the western Sudan just south of the Sahara, was the area called Senegambia, which took its name from the Senegal and Gambia Rivers, its two most prominent features. The Portuguese concentrated their effort on the zone south of Cabo Verde and tended to send their boats into the Gambia River to trade. They also settled the uninhabited Cabo Verde Islands in the 1460s, a zone that would eventually produce sugar with African slave labor. Very quickly, individual Portuguese traders also settled along the navigable Gambia River and by the end of the seventeenth century there arose a powerful set of Afro-Portuguese communities made up of Portuguese who had intermarried with the local African populations. Except for their island settlements and a few key coastal cities, this in fact would be a common pattern for the Portuguese from Senegambia to East Africa. Given the high mortality experienced by Europeans and their inability to conquer the interior, only mixed Afro-Portuguese merchant communities were capable of survival. For most of the first century here, the Portuguese traded for gold coming from the Bambuk goldfields in the Gambia-Senegal Rivers hinterland, hides from the interior savanna cattle herds, and other local products along with slaves, who came both from the coast and from the Upper Niger interior savannas. On these savanna coasts the Europeans dealt with the Muslim states long tied to the Mediterranean through the Sahara caravan routes. By the time of the arrival of the Portuguese the great empire of Mali had broken down into smaller states within the Gambia region, while the Senegambia successors to the great Jolof state were also quite small agricultural and trading communities of Mande speakers.

The Senegambia was an exclusively Portuguese zone of interest only for the first two centuries. By the late sixteenth century the region was being contacted by the English and French traders on a regular basis. The English settled the James Island in the Gambia River, and the French established themselves on the island of San Luis just off the Senegambia River, from which they concentrated their trading efforts. By then the local Afro-Portuguese trading river communities, though claiming to be Catholic and Portuguese, were totally independent of the mother country and traded freely with all Europeans along with all the local African merchant groups. Interior trading was in the hands of the Jahaanke peoples, who brought their slaves, ivory, and other local products by caravan from the Upper Niger to the river merchants, who then boated them down to the coast. They also brought such products as iron, cotton textiles, and kola nuts for the local coastal markets, and brought back not only imported products from Europe, but also mats, textiles, and sea salt produced on the coast for their interior customers.

In this complex of local, long-distance, and international trade, the slaves were just one element. The slaves taken here were mostly war captives and so the movement of slaves tended to be more random than steady. Though slaves were obtained from the coastal communities, after 1700, most of the slaves being sold to the Europeans came from the interior. They also were most definitely a by-product of the long series of Islamic wars among the states of the Upper Niger region. This included the Moroccan destruction of the Songhi Empire in the 1590s and the resulting local warfare, which lasted until well into the seventeenth century, as well as the mass movements of the 1720s to 1740s and again in the 1780s and 1790s when interior clerical-led jihads of fundamentalists against more lay-oriented leaders led to major civil wars in many of these Islamicized states. Europeans also obtained slaves after the droughts of the 1590s and those which struck the region again from 1639 to 1643. The seventeenth and early eighteenth centuries represented the peak of the Senegambia slave trade. In the eighteenth century alone these two rivers produced something like 337,000 slaves for the Atlantic trade, though even in the nineteenth century the reduced trade from this region still produced over 200,000 Africans for the American plantations.

Further to the south the Europeans finally encountered the rain forest zones in the region called the Upper Guinea or Sierra Leone Coast (from current-day Guine-Bissau to southern Sierra Leone). Here, there were numerous ministates and even stateless local governing communities, and Islam was less well embedded in the local culture. The prime local product here was the kola nuts sold in the interior African markets. But the Europeans took beeswax, camwood, ivory, and gold as well as slaves from this coast. Although the migration of Mane peoples into the region produced lots of slaves in the mid-sixteenth century, the area languished as a slave-exporting zone until the Muslim religious wars of the eighteenth century, when slaves finally became the prime export. In fact, it was this region, more than Senegambia, to which the defeated troops of the jihad wars were sent. In the 1590s the Portuguese had set up a trading post at the north end of this coast at Cacheu and by the late eighteenth century the French were at Gambia Island in the Sierra Leone estuary and the English had settled a trading post on Bunce Island. During the eighteenth century this region sold some 726,000 slaves into the Atlantic slave trade – double the number of slaves that came from Senegambia. These Sierra Leone slaves represented 11 percent of the total leaving Africa in the eighteenth century. Although repatriated Africans taken in the illegal trade were landed by the British on this coast in the nineteenth century, forced migration still remained the norm from this region as a reduced but still important slave trade continued on these coasts until the 1840s.

Just south and due east of this zone were the so-called Grain and Ivory Coasts (including the contemporary states of Liberia and the Côte d'Ivoire), which, unlike the previous coastal zones encountered by the Europeans, had few decent harbors or viable beaches to land on. The Grain Coast got its name from the Malagueta pepper produced in the region, while the Ivory Coast was from early on a major exporter of ivory from the local elephant herds. By the eighteenth century pepper was no longer a major European import and the local elephant herds had been depleted. Thus, international trade was quite small in this region, and relatively few slaves were taken by the Europeans from this coast.

Even here, however, the Fulbe jihad wars for Islamic religious purity in the Fuuta Jaalo kingdoms in the period from the 1720s to the 1740s led to significant slave exports in this otherwise little visited coast, since this region was more intimately integrated into the interior north-south caravan routes. But by the late eighteenth century the slave trade had ended from this region, and in fact this zone would be another net importer of previously exported slaves as Afro-American migrants from the United States began settling the Monrovia region in 1822.

The rain forest continued down southeastward along the coast from what is today central Sierra Leone to the so-called Gold Coast (Ghana), when the open savanna lands broke through the tropical rain forests and again reached the sea in what was called the "Benin Gap." The Gold Coast was initially the most attractive to the Europeans, primarily because of its easy contact to the Akan goldfields centered at Begho on the Volta River. Here, there were good harbors and landing beaches, and because of the gold trade the Europeans quickly built some twenty-five fortified stone forts. Unlike the open "forts" used for regular commerce and the slave trade everywhere on the African coasts, which were really trading posts or "factories," these gold-trading centers were all fortified to protect the gold from other European raiders. In fact, no fort on the African coast existed without the often formal approval of the local African state or community, to which it often paid taxes and from which it obtained its provisions and access to the interior trading routes. The first of these forts to be constructed was that of São Jorge da Mina (Elmina) in the fifteenth century. By the eighteenth century the region was studded with forts from the major and minor powers of northern Europe as well. Several battles were fought among the Europeans from the 1630s until the 1720s for control of these strategic places, with many of these forts changing hands several times. By the late seventeenth century, it was the English and Dutch who predominated, with the French and Portuguese mostly excluded from the Gold Coast trade. Until the 1680s, this was a zone almost exclusively of gold exports, but the decline of gold arrivals to the coast, if not of local gold production, and the wars related to the rise of the local Akwanu and Asante states in the seventeenth century also provided slaves for exports. By the end of this century the value of slaves was approaching the value of all other exports, and they surpassed them in the eighteenth century. So important was this zone in gold and slaves that both the Royal African Company of England and the Dutch West India Company (WIC) had their African headquarters here – the latter at Elmina, which it took from the Portuguese in the late 1630s, and the former ten miles distant at Cape Coast castle. In the eighteenth century, 645,000 slaves were sent off this coast into the trade, which represented 10 percent of West African migrants, though virtually no slaves were sent from this coast after 1800.

The Gold Coast was also one of the first African regions to adapt American crops to African conditions. Although the slave trade was to bring a host of workers, plants, and diseases to America, it also brought many new plants from America to Africa. In this regard, the introduction of American food crops to the African continent would revolutionize food production here as much as did the American potato in Europe and Asia. Early in the period of the slave trade, manioc and maize were introduced into Africa. Manioc, which originated in Brazil, had a revolutionary impact on the forest agriculture, providing a crucial new food crop ideal for forest cultivation and one that could dependably feed and maintain more dense populations. In turn, maize became an important food crop on the savanna. Tobacco, cacao, peanuts, and a host of other American plants were also introduced, many of which would become important African commercial export crops in later centuries.

Next, eastward along the so-called Lower Guinea Coast region were the two Bights (defined as a wide bay formed by a bend or curve in the shoreline) of Benin and Biafra on either side of the Niger Delta. Together, they formed one of the most heavily slave-traded regions in all of Africa. The coast defined by the Bight of Benin was called the Slave Coast by contemporaries (current-day Togo, Benin, and western Nigeria). The three dominant powers in the region were the kingdoms of Benin and Dahomey close to the coast and the Oyo Empire of the Yoruba in the interior due north of the port of Lagos. This zone was well connected to the Saharan caravan routes and had major state formations going back at least to the eleventh century a.d. What is fascinating about local developments is the contrast that the two key states of Dahomey in the west and Benin in the eastern part of the Bight of Benin exhibited in their response to the slave trade. In Dahomey, the state controlled the port of Ouidah and used it to dominate local slave movements. The slave trade was at first a royal monopoly and, even in its nonmonopoly phase, was heavily taxed by the state. In turn, when the Oyo cavalry defeated the Dahomean musketeers in 1730, the Yoruba too became intimately tied to the trade, from which they derived significant wealth, opening up their own sea outlet at Porto Novo and reaching the height of their slave exports in the 1780s. In contrast, the more easterly Kingdom of the Benin prohibited the export of male slaves as early as 1516 and kept that embargo in force until the eighteenth century. Instead it traded for firearms and other European products by exporting ivory, pepper, cotton textiles (usually for African consumption), and beads.

So efficient did the Dahomey and then the Oyo trade systems become that the Bight of Benin became Africa's second largest slave trading zone. In the eighteenth century, for example, the region shipped some 1.2 million slaves, or 18 percent of the total leaving West Africa in this period, and in the nineteenth century it shipped another 421,000 slaves. In fact, it was the most active West African region north of the equator and did not end its shipments of slaves until the 1860s. Though warfare was often a major source of slaves for these two regions, as the collapse of the Oyo Empire in the late eighteenth century showed when Yoruba slaves flooded the market, it was not the primary mechanism for obtaining slaves. Given the long-term and very steady nature of slave exports from this region, it is evident that the trade was obtaining slaves from systematic raiding on the frontier as well as from local religious, judicial, and political sources all along the trade routes from the interior.

The area from the Niger River delta east to the Cameroon coast, which formed the so-called Bight of Biafra region (today, eastern Nigeria and Cameroon), was already a well-developed trading area even before the arrival of the Europeans. The local coastal Igbo and Ibibio (Efik) peoples had coastal urban settlements as large as 2,000 people in the Niger and Cross River deltas that supported major fishing and shipping industries – including canoes manned by as many as eighty rowers. These boat traders operated along the local rivers and estuaries formed by the Niger and Cross River deltas, as well as engaging in coastal trade. Though there was lots of commercial contact with the Europeans because of these long trading traditions, this zone did not become a major participant in the Atlantic slave trade until after the mid-seventeenth century. But as with the groups from Benin to the east, the local peoples, who were mostly organized in clan groups and organizations no more complex than multiple village associations, developed extensive peaceful trading networks for obtaining slaves over large territories in the interior. They also soon established ministates along the coast at their major trading towns of Bonny and New Calabar in the Niger Delta and the three towns that came to be known as Calabar or Old Calabar on the Cross River delta to the east. The interior trade was controlled by the Igbo who were organized in merchant and religious associations. In the eighteenth century, these ports on the Cross and Niger Rivers shipped out almost the same number of slaves for America as did the Benin traders, 1.2 million slaves. But in the nineteenth century, although they added another 353,000 Africans to the Atlantic trade, they ended serious trading by the late 1830s several decades before it ended in the Bight of Benin.

From the Bight of Biafra south there were long stretches of lightly inhabited coast that had little appeal to the Europeans, though just off the coast of Gabon stood the islands of São Tomé and Príncipe just at the equator. These volcanic and fertile lands in the Gulf of Guinea were settled by the Portuguese in the last decade of the fifteenth century and by the 1520s had become a major producer of plantation sugar based on African slave labor. They soon replaced Madeira as Portugal's principal sugar producer before the 1580s, when Brazilian sugar production began to dominate European imports. São Tomé nevertheless remained important after the decline of sugar, not only because it was a major provisioning stop for Portuguese and other European slavers, but also because it was a major center of Portuguese settlers who exercised considerable influence over Portuguese activities in the Congo-Angolan region. Not only did they engage in a major local coastal trade with Africans, but they often housed African slaves for subsequent export to America. In 1510, for example, between 5,000 and 6,000 slaves were being held on the island for American transshipment. It is estimated that these islands absorbed almost 64,000 African slaves in the sixteenth century and another 24,000 in the seventeenth century. With the abolition of the Atlantic slave trade they were among the most notorious of the importers of indentured contract laborers, whose service by the early twentieth century was finally defined as slavery in disguise. Its important coffee and cacao plantations in the late nineteenth century imported an average of 4,000 workers per annum, mostly from Angola, who were to serve five-year contracts, though few were ever repatriated.

For all the volume of slaves shipped from West Africa, Central Africa (Gabon, the Congo, and Angola) was to be the single most important source of African slaves for America from the sixteenth century until the late nineteenth century. This was a region that was well settled by the end of the first millennium and had already a thriving copper-mining industry. By 1400 there was a common culture and market encountered throughout most of the Congo River basin. There also arose a major empire called the Kongo in this same period, which was the largest state in Central Africa on either coast. By the time of the Portuguese arrival in the region in the late fifteenth century there were also emerging two other major states in the region: the Kingdom of Loango on the coast north of the Congo River and the Tio Kingdom inland and upriver from the Kongo and Loango states, which was centered on the Melbo Pool – a body of water well up the Congo River. Finally, after 1500 emerged to the far south the Kingdom of Ndongo, which would be located near the Portuguese constructed port of Luanda.

From the beginning in Central Africa, the Portuguese took a very active role in local politics and made their greatest effort at control in the western part of Africa. Missionaries and technicians were sent to the court of the Kongo kings, and while they temporarily converted the royal family, their most successful effort was with Prince Affonso, who became king in 1506. A very dynamic ruler, he not only expanded his territory, but he also became closely associated with the Portuguese, paying for their support and aid through the sale of ivory, copper, and slaves. By the 1520s Affonso had monopolized the slave trade and prohibited the export of any Kongo peoples. He established Catholicism as the state religion and even had a local bishop appointed by Rome. But much of this effort at conversion eventually failed, though Portuguese association with the state remained strong. In 1658 when the Kongo was invaded by the so-called Jaga peoples, they sent in an army to restore the throne and expel the invaders, which took seven years to accomplish. But they also supported the Ndongo Kingdom when it defeated a Kongo army in 1556, and succeeded in extracting the right to establish the port of Luanda and the fortified town of Massangano in the interior of Angola shortly thereafter. But loyalties shifted quickly in West Central Africa and the Portuguese supported the Imbangla against both the Kongo and Ndongo armies when they established their own state at Kasanje.

But the Africans could utilize these political alliances as well as the Portuguese. When the Dutch arrived in 1641 all three states – Kongo, Ndongo, and Kasanje – joined the Dutch side and the Ndongo even laid siege to Portugal's last outpost at Massangano in 1648. But at this point the arrival of a Portuguese armada from Brazil removed the Dutch and in 1665 the Portuguese defeated the Kongo state in the battle of Ambula. Though expelled by the Kongo state again a few years later, internal civil wars would finally lead to the end of the empire by the early eighteenth century.

Throughout all this effort, the Portuguese established settlers in Luanda and then far to the south in Benguela, and there emerged from these efforts and local traders moving into the interior the largest of the Afro-Portuguese communities in western Africa. Although African merchant trading clans controlled most of the trade from just north of Luanda and in the Zaire watershed, most of the trade from Luanda south was in the hands of these Afro-Portuguese traders, at least along the coast and a moderate way into the interior. Although these mixed background traders were willing to deal with all Europeans, the heavy political and military presence of the Portuguese guaranteed a minimum of loyalty. Thus, most of the French, Dutch, and British slaving activity was north of Luanda with the ports of Ambriz and Loanga being important, while the Portuguese dominated to the south. Although controlling the coast influenced who took which slaves, the interior peoples supplying the slaves could easily sell to whomever they preferred, especially given the length of water navigation on the Congo River, which made it a reasonable destination from most interior regions. Even in the Luanda-Benguela regions, it was the Ovimbundu who controlled the interior caravan routes from the 1790s for all of Central Africa. But it also should be stressed that the Portuguese penetrated deeper here than anywhere else in western Africa and by the late eighteenth century they had even begun to settle in the Benguela highlands. This effort resulted in an extraordinary volume of slave purchases. By the end of the century the Portuguese were shipping out 16,000 Africans per annum from the Angolan ports, a figure that would rise to 18,000 in the first decade of the nineteenth century.

The Loango coast in turn proved to be a major region for both British and French slaving activity from the earliest period. But it was in the eighteenth century that this region to the north of the Congo River became the prime trading zone for these two major traders. At the beginning of the century the French were taking 3,600 slaves per annum and by the 1790s they were averaging 12,800 captives per annum. The English experience was similar, beginning the century with annual movements of 2,600 slaves and rising to 11,600 per annum by the 1780s. Despite all the efforts of the Portuguese to close this crucial area to other Europeans, these two nations alone took over 1 million Africans from the Loango coast from 1700 to 1807, making it the single most important region for African slaves for both nations in the eighteenth century.

The volume of slaves leaving the Congo and Angolan coasts was so steady that it had to have originated with both political as well as military initiatives. Prisoners taken in warfare, villagers seized in low-level raids in nonfortified zones, and persons condemned by their respective communities for economic or religious reasons all went to supply such a steady movement of slaves. In the eighteenth century (to 1810), these two regions sent some 2.5 million slaves into the Atlantic trade, of which 1.3 million were carried away by the Portuguese, and another 1.3 million were taken after 1811. These 3.8 million slaves obtained between 1700 and the 1860s represented 40 percent of the total esti-mated Africans shipped in the Atlantic slave trade from East and West Africa over the entire course of its existence, making the Congo and Angola unquestionably the single most important slave-producing area in Africa from the earliest days until the end of the Atlantic slave trade.

Although the Portuguese would penetrate East Central Africa (Mozambique) as quickly and as pervasively as they did in Angola, the slave trade would be a late development in this area. Given the length-ening of the sailing routes, opening up East Africa to the Atlantic slave trade would require slave prices high enough to justify the extra cost and higher mortality suffered in this trade. Initially, it was gold and geographic location that attracted the Portuguese to these shores. The existence of major gold production in the Shona highlands south of the Zambezi River and west of the coast brought initial Portuguese efforts on taking this gold away from the Islamic Swahili traders, who had dominated its export for several hundred years before the arrival of the Portuguese in force in the early sixteenth century. In 1505 the Portuguese settled in the Muslim town of Sofala and in 1508 they were on the island of Mozambique, which they fortified and which became their central residence on the coast and a major provisioning port for the East Indies fleets. For the next few decades they raided all the Islamic towns on the coast as far north as Mombasa, but finally set-tled into peaceful dealings with the local Islamic trading networks by the 1520s.

At first the Portuguese concentrated on the gold trade, shipping major quantities to India to pay for European imports of Asian spices and other goods. But they never fully controlled the goldfields or the gold exports. They did, however, open up a whole new export in ivory to India, which had been of limited interest to the Islamic traders before their arrival. As had occurred in West Africa, shipwrecks and desertions soon created local Afro-Portuguese communities and by the 1560s all the ports from Mombasa southward had these resident Portuguese, and many had moved inland and intermarried with the local groups. All of these semiautonomous communities entered into trade with Muslim and non-Muslim alike. Finally, the major needs of provisioning of the fleets, which sometimes brought over a thousand Portuguese to Mozambique island at any one time, all promoted an integration of Portugal into the Islamic trading networks that had existed before their arrival.

In the 1560s Jesuit missions were in the goldfields attempting to convert the Mwene Mutapa peoples, but with relatively little success. But in the 1570s the Portuguese penetrated inland, using the port of Quelimane at the mouth of the Zambezi River as their starting point. Several major European-recruited armies of conquest were organized in this decade, but the end result was that the goldfields were too dispersed and the local states too small and too numerous to conquer. Malaria, the death of horses, and the iron weapons of the Africans all halted most of these formal expeditions. But the Portuguese did leave behind two forts at Sena and Tete several hundred miles inland, established firm relations with most of the major regional African states, and became a dominant player, either with their own troops or with their Afro-Portuguese allies, throughout the entire Zambezi River valley and most of the interior.

Although the Portuguese remained strong on the coast, it was the Afro-Portuguese who successfully settled the interior. This was a most dynamic community, and beginning in the seventeenth century these mixed background immigrants began to carve out large estates in the Zambezi River valley that soon resembled ministates, with their African followers and slave armies. These so-called prazero lords (named after their grants of lands or estates called prazos) dominated interior Mozambique until the nineteenth century. They also established an extraordinarily tenacious European foothold on the East African coast that no other competitors could ever match or eliminate.

The Indian Ocean monopoly of the Portuguese was ended in the seventeenth century, with major effects on its East African holdings. The loss of its Persian Gulf fortresses of Hormuz and Muscat in 1622 and 1648, respectively, to English and Islamic assaults broke the power of the Portuguese in the Indian Ocean and saw foreign powers arriving en masse into the Mozambique Channel. Turkish raids along the coast in the late sixteenth century resulted in the Portuguese fortifying Mombasa, but this port was lost to the Omans in 1698 and the Portuguese abandoned their northern ports and markets. The arrival of the Dutch and English in the 1590s and early 1600s brought constant warfare until peace was signed with both by midcentury. Mozambique itself withstood four major sieges by the Omans and the Dutch, the last of which ended in 1608. In fact, Mozambique and all the East African Portuguese cities were the only African possessions of Portugal to resist successfully Dutch conquest in the first half of the seventeenth century. The Portuguese were able to hold the coast south of Cape Delgado against all comers in the seventeenth and eighteenth centuries, and even revived the gold trade with new finds north of the Zambezi River in the later century. From Quelimani in the Zambezi Delta to Lorenço Marques at the far end of Delagoa Bay in the south and in the interior along the Zambezi River valley, it developed a major international trade, importing East Indian cloth and beads as payment for the exported gold and ivory. In recognition of its growing trade and importance, Mozambique was finally separated from the Goan viceroyalty of Portuguese India and made into an independent colony in 1752.

Although slavery was present among all the African and European groups living in East Africa and slave armies were common, the international slave trade from this coast only began in the middle decades of the eighteenth century as slaves were shipped to the French Indian Ocean island of Réunion (Ile de Bourbon). The first port to engage in this trade was the southern one of Inhambane, which was shipping out some 1,500 slaves per year in the 1760s and some 3,000 Africans two decades later, making this the second most valuable export after ivory from this port. Although this international slave trade to Indian Ocean colonies of Europeans began in the middle decades of the eighteenth century, the shipments of slaves to America did not begin on a serious basis until the nineteenth century. There were some French and English attempts in the late seventeenth and early eighteenth centuries to supply their West Indies with Mozambique slaves, but the steady volume of shipments to America only occurred in the nineteenth century. The first reported ships from Mozambique arriving in Rio de Janeiro – which would be Mozambique's major American destination port until the middle of the nineteenth century – reached the city only in March 1797. But only thirteen more arrived in Rio de Janeiro by 1811 and they averaged only 272 slaves per vessel compared with double that number for ships coming from the Congo and Angola. Moreover, the mortality of slaves during the crossing was extremely high, averaging 24 percent, when overall mortality was 9 percent for ships arriving from West Africa. Clearly, these were still experimental voyages of a few enterprising captains who had yet to learn how to deliver slaves efficiently from East Africa, or who still found relatively few slaves to bring to America.

But a combination of severe droughts from 1790 to 1830 and major migrations through most of East Africa of war bands from the Transvaal region to the south of Delagoa Bay severely disrupted the economies and polities of the interior regions of Mozambique and promoted slave seizures. This was coupled with an ever-rising demand for slaves and consequent doubling of local prices on the African market. In response to this demand, the Portuguese government permitted free trade for the Brazilian slavers with all the ports of East Africa after 1811, and as a result 85 of the 430 slave ships arriving in Rio de Janeiro from 1825 to 1829 were from Mozambique. These vessels carried over 48,000 slaves for an average of 569 slaves per ship (compared with an overall average of 410 for ships arriving from Angola) and their slave mortality at sea, while still high, was down to 12 percent or only double the 6 percent mortality then experienced by the West African shippers. This mortality reflected the different times at sea between West and East Africa, with the average East African ship taking sixty days compared with just thirty-three days for those coming from Angola. Also, port specialization was now evident, with Quelimane on the Zambezi Delta being the second biggest port of exit for Brazil with 31 ships, following the island of Mozambique with its 44 slave ships. Also, the southern ports around Delagoa Bay were represented with Lorenço Marques (Maputo) from the southern end sending 7 ships and Inhambane on its northern edge organizing 4 slaving expeditions. By the late 1830s, it was estimated that on average some 10,800 slaves were still being shipped off the coast.

Whereas Mozambique had shipped some 90,000 slaves to the Indian Ocean islands and America before 1811, after that date 386,000 East Africans entered the Atlantic and were forced to migrate to America. This meant that Mozambique was the third largest supplier of slaves in the nineteenth century – ahead of Biafra and just behind Benin – accounting for 14 percent of those shipped in the nineteenth century from anywhere in Africa.

As can be seen from this survey of the evolution of the slave trade on the coasts of Africa, the Atlantic slave trade evolved relatively slowly over a long period of time. In the first three centuries the volume of shipments was relatively low and the trade simply tapped into the traditional internal slave markets of Africa and obtained slaves from the normal local sources. Thus, it was mostly war captives who filled the holds of the American slavers, though there were some Africans condemned to slavery in their local societies for various reasons, as well as small-scale raiding of unprotected peasant groups. In these first two or three centuries of the trade, it was mostly people living within fifty miles of the coast who were taken across the Atlantic. But rising demand in America and consequent rising prices increased the movement of slaves in the eighteenth and nineteenth centuries. The Atlantic slave trade then became a qualitatively and quantitatively different trade than before. Annual movement of slaves across the Atlantic in the second half of the eighteenth century was constantly rising, reaching the 80,000 per annum level shipped by the peak decade of the 1780s. This increasing movement forced some significant changes in the provisioning of slaves. Regions such as the Bights of Benin and Biafra and the Congo-Angola area now developed more long-distance trade for slaves into the interior. Whole trading networks now evolved just to move slaves to the coast on a steadier basis. Equally, the sporadic nature of warfare was no longer a sufficient source for slaves. A steady level of raiding on the various open agricultural frontiers now became the norm in selected areas, and the slow abandoning of unprotected fields now began to occur as a response to the new intensity of the Atlantic trade. Moreover, the source of slaves now moved further inland and more of the West and East African population became involved in the trade.

The increasing intensity of the trade, which would remain a major movement of peoples into the middle decades of the nineteenth century, clearly began to distort traditional patterns of government and trade in certain selected regions of Africa. As we have seen, whole regions, such as Senegambia or the Gold Coast, simply ceased to trade slaves in the nineteenth century as local groups became involved in other trades or refused to engage in this particular commerce. Others, such as the populations in the Portuguese lands of East Africa, were in the throes of massive ecological and political change, which produced many slaves regardless of American or Indian Ocean demand for slaves. But in areas such as the Bight of Biafra or the Congo and Angola, no such local disasters or dynastic struggles or migrating war bands created a large enough pool of slaves to maintain the steady outpouring of Africans that these coasts experienced. Therefore, the trading states had to engage in systematic raiding to supply the steady demand for slaves, and, in so doing, the Atlantic slave trade can be said to have finally influenced in several important ways the evolution of local societies. Quite evidently, viable agricultural lands in the interior of many of these exporting regions were abandoned because of the raiding against defenseless peasants. Equally, the trade became so important that some groups were willing to engage in warfare to satisfy the demand for the imported goods that the slaves produced.

This said, that impact was not uniform across Africa, but varied by locality. It is generally agreed by most scholars that only one or two of the major civil or interstate wars in the late eighteenth and early nineteenth centuries may have been influenced by this demand for slaves, but that the rest can be best explained by the usual problems of succession in highly centralized regimes, migration of peoples for purposes of conquest of new resources, or conflicts for control of territories and economies. Equally, an internal slave trade existed both before and after the end of the Atlantic slave trade, and even as the export of humans was replaced by the export of palm oil in the early decades of the nineteenth century, slaves were often used to produce this product along with free workers. The end of the trade to America did not end slavery in Africa. Nor did its ending destroy the economy of any major African states or their basic source of wealth. Most of the major states of West Africa were able to compensate for the loss of slave sales by turning to palm oil or other exports, often producing more revenue for purchasing ever cheaper industrial imported goods than had been possible in the slave trade era. Moreover, it should be remembered that international trade was only a small part of the African economy, and that the internal market accounted for a much higher percentage of national production and exchange. Even the slave caravans brought ivory and other goods to the coast and returned with local coastal as well as imported products to the interior.

Thus, the Atlantic slave trade, while profoundly influencing many parts of West Africa over some five centuries, was only one part of the complex economic, social, and political history of the continent. It was brought to an end by European intervention, just as it had been created by those same Europeans. But it neither ended African relations with Europe, nor did it end slavery within Africa itself. How the trade interacted with various peoples over time and place and the costs and benefits of the trade for all the participants will be examined in the next chapters.

CHAPTER 4

The European Organization

of the Slave Trade

The Atlantic slave trade was one of the most complex economic enter-prises known to the preindustrial world. It was the largest transoceanic migration in history up to that time; it promoted the transportation of people and goods among three different continents; it involved an annual fleet of several hundred ships; and it absorbed a large amount of European capital invested in international commerce. The trade was closely associated with the development of commercial export agricul-ture in America, and Asian trading with Europe. It involved complex capital and credit arrangements in Europe, Africa, and America and was carried on by a very large number of competing merchants in an unusually free market. Finally, it was the largest movement of workers to the Americas before the mid-nineteenth century.

How did this extraordinary trade develop in Europe? What mecha-nisms were used to get this system into operation and what were the relative roles of the state and of private capital? How was the trade financed and what were the goods used to purchase the slaves? What types of ships and crews were involved in the transport of these slaves and how were they purchased in Africa and how were they sold in Amer-ica? What were the profits generated by the trade and what was their relative importance within the expanding European economy? These are some of the issues I will deal with in this and the following chapter on the African part of the trade.

Given the high entry costs to trading, and the initial lack of detailed knowledge of the various African and American markets, the earliest period of the slave trade was one in which the state played a major role. Though slaves were shipped off the African coast by private European traders from the 1440s onward as part of general exports of gold and ivory, the organization of an intensive slave trade took several hundred years to develop. Africa was a modest source of slaves for southern Europe until the beginning of the sixteenth century, and it was only the opening up of America to European colonization that slave trading finally turned into a major economic activity.

Although the Portuguese were rich enough to allow private contractors to develop some part of the early trade, both they and all the Europeans who followed used heavy state control in the form of taxation, subsidization, or monopoly contracts to get the trade going and control its flow of forced workers to America. In almost every case, the state was needed to subsidize the trade in order to get it organized. The Spaniards even declared it a monopoly from the very beginning to the end of the eighteenth century. Though the Spanish contract holders subcontracted to private or foreign monopoly company firms, the trade was still heavily controlled by the state, and even the Portuguese finally resorted to state monopoly companies in the eighteenth century to get the trade going to colonies that were underdeveloped and lacked the capital to finance the trade.

The relative ability of the American importing colonies to pay for their slaves determined whether a slave trade could develop. In the case of Spain, the silver and gold mined by the Indians would pay for the forced migration of African slaves from the earliest days of the conquest. The trade was a very controlled one, but only for state taxing purposes, as private individuals from all over Europe were given exclusive contracts to carry slaves to the American colonies (the so-called *asiento*) in return for paying the Crown a fixed fee and taxes on each slave delivered. In the case of the Portuguese, their early dominant position in African trade gave them a decided advantage in the slave trade by lowering their costs of entry. In turn, the very rapid development of a sugar plantation economy based initially on American Indian slave labor in Brazil permitted them to generate the capital needed to import African slaves. But all other trades required some use of monopoly companies to provide slaves to those American colonies that did not have the capital or credit to pay for the imported slaves.

From the fifteenth century until the early sixteenth century the Portuguese held a monopoly position in Africa carrying on an exclusive trade in gold, ivory, and slaves. They were also able to establish an effective settlement in Angola and a major trading post at São Jorge da Mina (Elmina). To these continental positions were added several Atlantic African islands, of which the most important were São Tomé and Príncipe off the coast of the Bight of Biafra. By the early seventeenth century, between their own American needs and their supplying the Spanish American colonies, they were probably shipping some 3,000 to 4,000 slaves per annum. But this monopoly situation was challenged as early as the late sixteenth century by the French and then the British. French and then British free traders intermittently visited the African coast from the middle decades of the sixteenth century, but they and the Dutch did not become a major presence with forts and permanent trading links until the seventeenth century. For all of these early northern European traders, it was gold and ivory that were the primary products taken from the African coast, with slaves only a secondary concern. So long as the northern European powers had no major American colonies, their trade in slaves was confined to illegal smuggling to the Iberian colonies. In fact, until 1700, for all traders, gold and ivory were predominant exports over slaves. It is only after that date that slaves become Africa's most valuable export.

It was the Dutch who first seriously challenged the Portuguese monopoly in African trading. As part of their grand rebellion against Spain at the end of the sixteenth century, they eventually challenged Spain's dependent ally, the Portuguese. In 1621 the Dutch West India Company was established with designs on Portugal's American and African possessions. Initially, it concentrated on destroying their opponents and seizing their resources and spent their early efforts attacking Portuguese and Spanish shipping. It was reported by the company that in a fourteen-year period beginning in 1623 it had captured 2,336 slaves from Iberian ships and sold them in America. But it soon moved from piracy and haphazard trading in Africa to creating a systematic presence on the African coast. As early as 1624, it sent fleets to capture both the northeastern Brazilian sugar region of Bahia and the Gold Coast fort of São Jorge da Mina. Though both attempts failed, the Dutch were now committed to obtaining an American colony out of Portuguese America and of making themselves a presence in the slave trade. In 1629 a new fleet seized the Brazilian sugar province of Pernambuco and soon moved to gain direct access to slave supplies in Africa. This African campaign finally achieved its first success in 1637 when the Dutch seized Elmina on the Gold Coast and effectively eliminated the Portuguese from trading in this region. Then in the early 1640s they temporarily seized the coastal forts of the Portuguese in Angola. From the 1630s to the 1650s the Dutch West India monopoly trading company, the WIC, was unquestionably the dominant European slave trader in Africa.

The company had reduced the Portuguese presence everywhere and at the same time still faced no serious competition from other northern European nations in the African trade. In the late 1630s and early 1640s it was delivering some 2,500 slaves per annum to America, and in 1644 it peaked with a purchase of almost 6,900 slaves on the African coast. Half of these slaves came from the Lower Guinea Coast and half from the Loango-Angola region.

Once opened up by the Dutch, the French and the English were not far behind. Long-term trade links were established by the French in the Senegambia region of the African coast from the 1660s, while the English slowly staked out the Sierra Leone or Upper Guinea Coast in the middle decades of the century as their own area. The Dutch for their part concentrated on the Gold Coast. But however much a given European power tried to dominate a region, in the end, everyone traded almost everywhere. In the late seventeenth and eighteenth centuries, for example, numerous European nations, including even the Danes, built forts on the Gold Coast east and west of Elmina. Though all Europeans tried to create a monopoly trade with their slowly developing system of fortified forts or unfortified trading factories, it was only the Portuguese who effectively settled any region of Africa. But even the Portuguese in Angola had to operate in the context of African state politics and were just one element in the total picture – often forced to join forces with various local states to preserve their position. In all other cases the forts and factories were more expressions of claims to exclusive trade against other European powers than statements of monopoly over local African suppliers.

Given the fierce European competition and the generalized African knowledge of this competition, African suppliers had little interest in accepting a trade monopolized by any one European nation. Constant trade created zones of influence, but no coast was the exclusive zone of any nation. Africans traded with whom they wished even in the Congo and Angola regions, and no fort or factory had influence more than a few miles inland. All such European outposts were maintained to keep trade links open to Africans and guarantee continuity of trade rather than creating national or colonial enclaves. Even when monopoly companies were established, the respective nations had difficulty in maintaining their control against challenges not only from other Europeans but even from interlopers from their own nations.

From all this experience, toleration became the norm after the seventeenth-century fratricidal wars among the monopoly companies.

Most slavers traded on the coast with little fear of attack from other European nations in times of international peace, and even cooperated in trading. Moreover, there was room even for smaller trading nations to develop their activities. A Danish West India Company formed in 1625 and a Swedish African Company founded in 1647 all traded on the African coast and set up small establishments. Even the German state of Brandenburg built a fort on the Gold Coast.

But the costs of entry into the trade was so high that only some kind of government support and a corresponding monopoly arrangement seemed capable of opening up a continuous and successful trade. In this case, the Europeans had in view the extraordinary success of the Dutch and English East India models. It was thought that this was the way to develop the trade. Between 1620 and 1700 every slave-trading nation but Spain and Portugal experimented with joint-stock monopoly trading companies. All achieved some initial success, often opening up systematic trade for the first time, but all would eventually fail and be replaced by free traders from their respective nations. Though ultimately replaced, these companies bore the costs of opening the trade and creating the contacts, credit, and shipping practices that would eventually be the norm for all free traders who followed them.

While French interlopers had involved themselves in the Atlantic slave trade from early in the sixteenth century, serious French participation began only with the development of the monopoly trading companies in the second half of the seventeenth century. After many partial and incomplete attempts, the French finally organized a monopoly Compagnie des Indes Occidentales in 1664, which was granted trading rights in America and Africa. But this largely state-financed effort was already granting licenses to private traders by the end of the decade. Nevertheless, French state interest was strong, and a French fleet took many factories from the Dutch in Gorée and the Senegambia region in the 1670s. Then, in 1672, the French government offered a bounty of ten livres per slave transported to the French West Indies. This offer encouraged the establishment in 1673 of a new and separate African monopoly company to control the French trade to the northwestern African coast known as the Compagnie du Sénégal. By 1679 the Senegal Company had twenty-one ships operating in the trade. Although successful in establishing several trading factories on the African coast and even fighting wars with other Europeans, this and subsequent monopoly companies that followed eventually faltered. Even with active state participation and support, trade for the French company was still too risky an adventure, and it could not raise sufficient private capital to maintain its power. By the 1690s most of France's African trade was in the hands of private entrepreneurs, though it was not until the 1720s that free traders finally succeeded in definitively breaking the company's control over trading.

The use of both monopoly companies and later free traders was part of the French government's efforts to promote viable plantation economies in the West Indies, and followed a pattern similar to the English. Colonizing the islands of the Lesser Antilles in the first half of the seventeenth century, the French, with the aid of Dutch technology, capital, credit, slaves, and markets, began to develop a thriving sugar export economy by the second half of the century. With the successful development of Martinique and Guadeloupe, the French sugar empire in the Caribbean received a major impetus and, from then on, never ceased its growth and expansion.

The Dutch West India Company was initially the most successful of these early monopoly companies, the one most involved in delivering slaves to colonies of the other European powers, and the one that shipped the most slaves to America. From its founding in 1621 it operated both as a commercial company and as a military institution with quasi-statelike powers. It seized major territories from the Portuguese, becoming in the process a sugar producer in Brazil and a major slave trader in the Gold Coast and Angola. It even made war on the Spaniards and succeeded in capturing one of the American silver fleets. But by the 1670s it was reduced to a few American possessions and to its Gold Coast forts, with the Portuguese having retaken most of their lost possessions. At this time the company was reorganized and lost most of its trading monopolies, with complete free trade coming to the Dutch African regions in the 1730s. Nevertheless, from the 1620s to the 1730s, it moved some 286,000 slaves from Africa, whereas free traders moved just 256,000 slaves from the 1730s to 1803. In the period of its monopoly, the Dutch West India Company even competed for the Spanish asiento, and overall from the seventeenth century until 1729 some 97,000 of the slaves that it shipped to America were delivered to the Spanish colonies in America.

The last major company established in the seventeenth century was the English Royal African Company, which, like the Dutch company, was based primarily on private capital. It grew out of a series of earlier English monopoly companies and was put together in 1672. It was modeled along the lines of many such joint-stock incorporated companies in England and would enjoy monopoly control over the English slave trade and England's trade with Africa in commodity goods. It also actively transported sugar and other products from the West Indies to England. Like all such African adventures, it was required to invest heavily in fixed costs, such as forts and armaments. The English probably started trading with Africa in the 1550s and tried some slave trading to the Spanish colonies in the 1560s. But without major American tropical colonies of its own, there was relatively little incentive to enter the trade. This of course changed with the expansion into the Lesser Antilles in the early 1600s and the taking of Jamaica in the 1650s. By the 1630s the British had their first fort in Africa, on the Gold Coast, and were regularly trading in slaves. By the 1660s several companies had been established and forts settled, and open warfare with the Dutch on the Gold Coast had become the norm. Thus, even before the final company was established, an active trade had developed. With the Royal African Company in operation, the trade became brisk. From 1672 until 1713 the company transported over 350,000 slaves to the English colonies of the West Indies. Nevertheless, the pressure from the free traders was such that the company gave up its monopoly on slave trading in 1698, though it continued to maintain its forts and charged the free traders a fee for their services.

Thus, by the first decades of the eighteenth century free trade in slaves had come to most nations. In all cases the basic infrastructure had been well established largely by the respective monopoly companies, and free traders could now use these well-established routes with low risks. Although direct trade between Africa and Europe was often still a monopoly trade, by the eighteenth century individual entrepreneurs who organized one or several voyages had become the norm in the trade from Africa to America. Even the closed Spanish colonial market, which allowed only contract providers to participate, was largely supplied by free traders obtaining subcontracts from the original asiento holders. In turn, this system was eventually abandoned in 1789 when the Spaniards decided to turn their West Indian islands into sugar-producing colonies and opened up the slave trade to their American colonies to all nations.

The last experience with monopoly trading companies was the late eighteenth-century Portuguese use of such companies to develop the far northern regions of Brazil. Although the Crown retained a large part of the African commodities and mineral trade to Europe, the slave trade had been a free enterprise trade from the sixteenth century. It had been heavily taxed from the beginning but was open to all Portuguese or Brazilian merchants. But the marquis of Pombal in the second half of the eighteenth century wanted to develop new plantation and slave economies in Brazil's northern Maranhão and Pernambuco colonies and decided that monopoly companies were the only solution. To get the capital needed, he agreed to give the Portuguese merchants who invested monopoly rights in the exports from these Brazilian provinces and even subsidized some of the African trade. The two companies were set up, in 1755 and 1759, respectively, and their object was to promote the development of the respective regions. Both companies were given the exclusive rights to import slaves into these two colonies. Of the two companies, the most important as far as Angola was concerned was the Pernambuco and Paraiba Company. Of the grand total of 49,344 slaves this company shipped to Brazil between 1761 and 1786, 85 percent came from the port of Luanda. For the Grão Pará and Maranhão Company, 68 percent of its 28,083 slaves came from the Upper Guinean ports of Cacheu and Bissau. These two companies accounted for a quarter or more of the slaves leaving the major trade port of Luanda, Angola, in this period, as well as the majority that the Portuguese took from the ports of Cacheu and Bissau. Given the infrastructure already in place in Luanda it is not surprising that the slaves were cheaper and the costs of shipping them to Brazil were less from Angola than from Cacheu-Bissau. With the disappearance of the Maranhão and Pará monopoly companies, the movement of slaves from Africa to the northern ports of Brazil temporarily declined, though eventually free traders picked up the flow again as these regions continued to grow with slave-produced cotton and sugar becoming important.

Although the monopoly companies varied as to organization and function, they all failed. This mostly had to do with their high fixed costs in forts and ships or their obligations to deliver a fixed number of slaves into a given region no matter what the demand or the costs – obligations that were often too expensive to maintain. They usually tied up too much capital for too long a period and found it increasingly difficult to raise new funds. In the free-trade era these companies were universally replaced in all trades by temporary associations of merchants who joined together to finance individual voyages. Thus, merchants in the sending port committed their capital to relatively short periods or spread it over many different slaving voyages. Moreover, they delivered slaves only in the quantities demanded in the New World and to zones that were capable of paying for them with cash or exportable products that could be sold for a profit in Europe.

Although some formal joint-stock companies were established, it was more common to form a trading company as a partnership of from two to five merchants. If it was two partners, both usually worked actively in the enterprise, but if it was more than this number, there was usually an active partner who organized the expedition and a group of more or less passive partners. Interestingly, most of these associations engaged in other trades as well as that of slaves, indicating the diversification of risk of the entire transaction. The contract that the partners signed, or which founded the joint-stock company, was usually for seven years' duration, which was the time needed to completely close the books on a slaving expedition. Kinship and friendships were among the major ties that brought partners together.

But given the high costs of entry into the trade, many of the partnerships or joint-stock companies offered stock or shares in the individual voyages they financed. Thus, while one of these slave-trading companies might undertake several voyages, each voyage attracted a different set of investors. The owner and outfitter of the ship (called an *armateur* in French) sold parts of the expedition or the ship to outside investors. In so doing he thus formed a minicompany that handled just that one expedition. In the premier French slaving port of Nantes in the late eighteenth century, for example, an armateur typically sold slightly over 60 percent of the ship and its cargo to outside investors. Often these investors were other outfitters, and it was common for the principal company or association itself to invest as a temporary shareholder in ships outfitted by other companies. Some 20 percent of such temporary shareholders in Nantes were in fact other *armateurs*, and another 25 percent were local merchants, many of whom were in colonial trade. Some 10 percent of the shares came from investors from all over France and the colonies. To attract investors, many of the outfitters published brochures promising returns of 30 to 50 percent. The remaining shares in an expedition came from the captain and the crew who often were allowed to invest on their own account. In over half of the expeditions mounted from late eighteenth-century Nantes, captains invested and typically held 10 percent of the shares in the expedition. On rarer occasions, the crew was also given rights to invest and subsequently to trade in slaves. Finally, outfitters sometimes paid for part of their cargoes in shares in the expedition rather than in cash. Often these shares were sold to third parties, especially on ships mounted by the largest and most successful companies.

The actual purchase of the ship, collection of the cargo, and the arrangement of final papers and insurance typically took some four to six months to arrange. After the owners, the second most important participant was the captain. Whether he bought shares or not, most captains were given 2 to 5 percent of the sale of all slaves he delivered in the Americas. Successful captains could obtain a respectable fortune in just two to three voyages. They could well earn 20,000 livres per voyage, representing 10 percent of the total value of the outbound cargo taken to purchase slaves. It was the captain who had the most responsibility, being in charge of both sailing the ship and doing all the trading in Africa. Many captains and crew carried out repeat voyages, although there were great risks involved. Among the 186 Dutch captains employed by the Dutch West India Company in the seventeenth and early eighteenth centuries, the average was for 1.4 voyages per captain – but this was highly concentrated since two-thirds of the captains made only one voyage. Moreover, captain, crew, and slave mortality was high, with the latter averaging 11 percent per voyage. Clearly, these mortality rates were related to lack of knowledge of local disease environments and other hazards of the trade, for by the eighteenth century these mortality rates had dropped. Thus, in the case of the 310 free-trader Dutch captains making the slaving voyage in the late eighteenth century, the mortality on the entire trip was just 7 percent and the average was 2 trips per captain, with only 49 percent making just one trip.

A large complement of subofficers and skilled persons was needed aboard the ship, including a ship's doctor, a carpenter, and a cooper or barrel maker. The doctor cared for the slaves and crew but had really few skills with which to combat disease except the basic rudiments of hygiene. The carpenter was the highest paid nonofficer on the ship and the person who designed the holds for the slaves when they were collected. Just below him in status and wages was the cooper, who was in charge of the crucial water casks. The average French and Dutch slaver in the seventeenth and eighteenth centuries took from 30 to 40 sailors for its crew, the majority of whom were poorly paid common seamen. In the eighteenth-century French trade, three months of the crew's wages were paid before the voyage and the rest when they landed. For a variety of reasons, slave ships were unusual in the number of sailors they carried. Between the needs of coastal trading in Africa and the potential for violence and the need for tight security on the African coast and in the Atlantic crossing, all slave traders carried double the number of crew that a normal merchant ship of their tonnage would carry.

Slave ships clearing for Africa were a third to a half the tonnage of regular ships clearing directly for the West Indies from Liverpool in the 1780s, and in those engaged in the similar droitue or direct West Indian trade from Nantes in the same decade. But despite the size advantage of West Indian trade ships, they carried much less crew than the typical slaver. Thus, the crew per ton ratio of some 252 ships that left Liverpool outbound for Africa between 1785 and 1787 was 0.17 crewmen per ton, whereas the 249 ships leaving for the West Indies from this same port carried half that number, or 0.09 crewmen per ton. Nor was this much different from the French slave trade. In Nantes, between 1749 and 1792 on the 870 slave ships outfitted for trade with Africa the average slave ship carried 0.18 sailors per ton, compared with 0.10 crew per ton on the 3,140 cargo ships engaged in overseas trade. From a larger sample of slave ships in the period from 1750 to 1799 in which the tonnage has been converted to a modern uniform standard, these same patterns hold as well, with the average crew per ton ratio for over 4,000 English slavers leaving Europe being 0.19 sailors per ton, and for the close to 1,000 French slavers that left Europe for Africa in the same period the ratio was 0.16. Except for fishermen (which averaged 0.30 crewmen per ton) and privateers and warships (which averaged 0.77 crewmen per ton in Nantes), the slave trade used the largest crew of any trade in the merchant marine. This high usage of sailors was, of course, related to both the demands of sailing, and the need to trade for and guard the captured slavers. Given the length of time on the coast to purchase slaves, and the necessity for the captain and other officers often to trade from small cutters and other boats sent out from the main ship, a large demand for sailors existed even to purchase and oversee the slaves on land. Whatever the pattern of slave purchases on the African coast, however, there was always a need for a large number of sailors to control the slaves once aboard the ship. In the second half of the eighteenth century, French ships on average carried a crew of 36 and the British one of 30 – the difference being that the French ships were a third larger than the English ships – but in fact they both had about the same high ratio of 6 tons for every sailor.

Given the fact that fewer sailors would have been needed to man these ships had no slaves been carried, it is no accident that problems arose with the crew once the slaves had been sold. One of the major findings of the late eighteenth-century English Parliamentary Commissions examining the slave trade was that slaver captains with regularity discharged a large number of their crewmen in the Caribbean and paid them off in devalued colonial sterling. This ill-treatment of sailors, in fact, was one of the most important issues used by the abolitionists to discredit the slave trade. Even as the number of slaves per ton declined in some of the early nineteenth-century trades, the number of sailors still remained quite high and usually did not decline. It is clear captains considered a minimum number of crew absolutely essential for survival and safety when handling slaves.

Nor were these needs unique to the British trade. In all slave trades where the data are available on crews, tons, and slaves, there is the same high correlation between the numbers of slaves carried and the number of sailors manning the ships. Even where tonnage cannot be made comparable, there is the same difference seen between slavers and regular merchant ships. Thus, for some 12 ships engaged in the slave trade to the Spanish Indies in 1637, the average of 7.7 slaves per sailor for these seventeenth-century Spanish American ships was quite similar to a sample of 525 French slavers from the first half of the eighteenth century, which carried 7.5 slaves per crewman. Moreover, as was to be expected, in all the slave trades the number of slaves per crewman kept rising over time, reflecting an increasing efficiency of the slave ships, reaching the 9.5 range for almost 1,500 slavers in the second half of the eighteenth century. But however efficient these ships became, all slave ships on average needed twice the crew size to man their vessels as the West Indian cargo ships of their period.

Clearly, ships of the same tonnage or larger than the slavers did not need one crewman for every 6 tons simply to man the ships. Half that number was sufficient. Equally, crew-per-ton ratios on slavers behave exactly like slave-per-ton ratios, both diminishing sharply as the tonnage of ships increases – further proof of the lack of ship's size, as expressed in tonnage, from being the primary factor influencing the number of sailors needed to man the slave ships.

Unique to the Brazilian trade was the large number of American slaves who made up the crews of the slave ships. As was indicated in the standard registers, the use of Brazilian-purchased slaves to make up crew complements was always justified by the lack of free sailors. This crisis in sailors must have been considerable since 42 percent of the 350 slave ships arriving in Rio de Janeiro from Africa between 1795 and 1811 indicate slaves in their crew. The average number of Brazilian-owned slave sailors in the crew for the 148 vessels that had them on arrival was 14. This meant that the slave crewmen probably made up between one-third to one-half of the crew in these slave ships if the total number of sailors the Portuguese were carrying was approximately the same number of crewmen as the French slavers at the peak of the eighteenth-century trade. This would have meant an average of 35 sailors per vessel. Clearly, these slaves were used to man the ship, while the free sailors of whatever color must have been employed to guard the slaves.

Despite these crew sizes, and the special nature of these slave ships, the biggest outfitting expense was always the cargo, which averaged between 55 and 65 percent of total costs. This made the slavers unique in almost all the major commodity trades. In France, which has the best data on costs, the cargo accounted for two-thirds of the total costs, and the ship and its crew a mere one-third. There was some variation depending on whether or not the ship was newly built, but, in general, most ships were bought used for operation in the trade, and the cargo costs were between 55 and 65 percent of the total outfitting expenses. The relatively cheap costs of the small cargoes being taken to the West Indies by regular cargo ships explains why the average value of the outfitted slaver per ton was six times the average value per ton of the much larger direct trade ships. This comparative difference in cost was not due primarily to the ships themselves, which were quite comparable in price between the West Indian and African slave trades, but to the cargo. In an evaluation of French ships captured by the English in the Seven Years' War, 8 ships in the *droiture* or West Indian commodity trade were worth 144 livres per ton, compared with 137 livres per ton for the 9 slave ships captured during this same period of 1755–66.

It was African demand for sophisticated imported goods for their slaves that made these cargoes so costly. One estimate has put the average value of the cargo at 200,000 livres. But this may be on the low end. The Nantes slave ship *Reine de France*, weighing 150 tons and with a 47-man crew, transported 404 slaves from Guinea to Saint Domingue in 1744. For this trip it purchased some 247,000 livres of trading goods. The African consumer market was unusual in that the Portuguese, the French, and even the English had to import foreign goods to make up their cargoes. Top on the list were East Indian textiles, which were made up of cotton cloths of white, solid blue, and/or printed design. Also from Asia came cowry shells produced in the Maldive archipelago just off the south coast of India and purchased there and at transit ports in Ceylon and India. Important as well were armaments, which were sometimes produced at home, but often purchased abroad, and Swedish-produced bar iron used by African blacksmiths to make local agricultural instruments. Knives, axes, swords, jewelry, gunpowder, and various nationally and colonially produced rums, brandies, and other liquors were also consumed along with Brazilian-grown tobacco. No one nation could produce all these goods and over time purchases shifted from nation to nation. Early on the French tended to buy English arms, the English preferred cheaper Dutch produced arms, and everyone bought their cloths from the Dutch, French, and British traders on their return from Asia.

There is little question that textiles were the primary product used to purchase slaves. In five selected years (1767, 1769, 1771, 1774, and 1776) slave ships from the port of Rouen shipped a total of 3.9 million livres tournois worth of goods to Africa. Of this figure, 1.4 million livres consisted of Indian textiles. Not only were the Indian cloths the single most valuable commodity being shipped, representing 36 percent of the total value of all trade goods, but they also represented 63 percent of the value of all cloths, European and East Indian combined (with the total textile value coming to 56 percent of the 3.9 million figure). The reason for this great demand for East Indian textiles had to do not only with the brilliance and quality of the colors, but also with the durability of these colored cloths and their ability to hold their color through numerous washings and in hot climates, at least according to a French commercial analysis in the eighteenth century. But Africans also purchased large quantities of cloths produced in Europe and North Africa. The Portuguese had discovered in their Gold Coast trade in the sixteenth century that the Africans often took the simple white cloths and linens they imported from Europe and used their own dyes to color them to local taste. But both colored and white cloths from Europe and North Africa were a standard part of African textile imports through the end of the trade, always complementing the Asian imports.

In a major study of African trade in the seventeenth and eighteenth centuries, it has been estimated that textiles made up 50 percent of the total value of imports into Africa in both periods. Next in importance after textiles came alcohol at 12 and 10 percent, respectively; manufactured goods at 12 and 10 percent; guns and gunpowder between 7 and 9 percent; tobacco between 2 and 8 percent; and bar iron between 2 and 5 percent. Even in the nineteenth century when textiles, though still dominant, dropped to a little over a third of the value of all imports, their volume was impressive. It was estimated that in the 1860s, sub-Saharan western Africa imported 57 million yards of cloth, or enough to provide at least 2 yards for every person in the region.

Even when Europeans used African products to purchase slaves, these in turn were bought with European or Asian or even American manufactured goods. All these goods were purchased by traders for hard currencies. Not only did Europeans purchase African produced beads, textiles, special food, or other products wanted by their African customers, but they imported Pacific Ocean products from textiles to such items as cowry shells, which were an important medium of exchange in many African societies. Unlike most of Europe's colonial trades, the African trade required the purchase of a large quantity of nonnationally produced goods – everything from Brazilian tobacco and Silesian textiles to Swedish bar iron and Dutch furniture. Thus, the trade was often the most costly of overseas trades for all European nations since a very large share of the goods used to purchase slaves in Africa had to be purchased outside their own metropolitan economies with hard currencies.

So important was the East Indian textile component of the trade, that it explains the rise of the chief African slave-trading ports in the French and English trades. Whereas La Rochelle and Le Havre had been major slaving ports in the seventeenth century, by the beginning of the eighteenth century Nantes rose to be the primary port, much as Liverpool would be later in the eighteenth century. Like Liverpool, this dominant position was due to the close ties of the two premier ports in Europe's East Indian trade. Unlike Liverpool, however, Nantes also enjoyed several other advantages that encouraged its very early and active involvement in the slave trade. It was already one of France's leading ports in the seventeenth century, and had developed close ties with the Dutch and other northern European capital markets. This promoted its general interest in Asia as well as the New World trade, even before Africa was opened to its merchants. Finally, Nantes enjoyed special tariff arrangements that gave the Nantes merchants further advantage over their competitor ports. Because of all these factors, Nantes established majority control over the French slave trade as soon as that trade was first opened up to free traders in 1716, and while competition grew in the latter part of the century, it remained the primary slave trade port into the nineteenth century. It is estimated that of the 3,709 slaving voyages outfitted by the French during the course of the trade, half came from Nantes with no other port organizing even a third of its slave-trading voyages. In contrast, Liverpool, though England's largest slave-trading port, accounted for only 39 percent of the 7,642 known

British voyages and was closely followed by London and Bristol, which together outfitted 61 percent of these slaving expeditions.

The trip out from Europe to Africa took anywhere from three to four months. Many ships stopped at other European ports for more cargo on the outward leg, or temporarily stopped to provision in the southern European ports or the Canary Islands. Moreover, the length of the trip also depended on which area of Africa was to be the prime trading zone. Reaching Gorée, a major trading zone in the Senegambia region, for example, left another trip as long again to reach Angola.

The region selected for trade by each European national depended on local and international developments. By the eighteenth century, rough spheres of influence had been established, with the English, Dutch, and the Portuguese most dominant as residents on the African coast with their permanent forts or factories. But no African area was totally closed to any European trader, and there was an extensive published contemporary literature and general European knowledge on the possibilities of local trade everywhere in western Africa. The local forts maintained by some European powers were not military centers, but were commercial stations that facilitated local commerce with the Africans and had little inland activity. Many of these forts would allow foreign traders access to their resources. Even the Portuguese, who were the Europeans most likely to concentrate on a limited set of regions in southern Africa, would conduct trade in other quite open and competitive regions. In the eighteenth century, for example, Portuguese and Brazilian shippers took over half a million slaves from the Bight of Benin where Portugal had no permanent settlers or outposts, at the same time as they took 1.3 million slaves from their controlled ports of Angola.

Of all the major European traders, the French were the most catholic in their selections. They established the fewest permanent establishments on the African coast, with those at the Senegal River and Whydah on the Gold Coast being the most important. Otherwise, the French Atlantic port free traders essentially operated out of seasonal or quite temporary locations all along the coast from Senegal to the Congo, and were even extraordinarily active along the East African coast. The French even became serious competitors to the Portuguese in the Mozambique region and carried on a thriving slave trade from East Africa throughout the eighteenth and into the nineteenth century. Unlike the Portuguese, however, the French East African traders did not carry their slaves to America but rather to a series of Indian Ocean islands off the African coast where they developed thriving sugar and slave plantation colonies.

Even in the areas where these forts existed and which therefore served as well-known local markets for slaves, there was no major "bulking" or warehousing of slaves. The costs to the Europeans of maintaining slaves was prohibitive, and would have made final costs quite high. For example, the fort that the French maintained at Fort Saint Joseph in the 1750s had a capacity of only 250 slaves. But there was little agricultural activity around the fort, and it was virtually impossible for them to maintain slaves in storage once the majority of the slave ships had left for America. On the other hand, hinterland traders could easily absorb slaves into their own agricultural or industrial production as they waited for the return of the slave ships. It is estimated that feeding a slave on the coast for a year would have increased his or her price by 50 percent.

In the overwhelming majority of cases it was the Africans who controlled the slaves until the moment of sale to the captain. Only occasionally in the era of free trade did a local European purchase slaves on his own account for resale to the slaver captains. This had been more common in the earlier age of the monopoly companies, but even then had accounted for only a small volume of sales. Given the lack of arrangements for holding slaves on the coast until late in the nineteenth century, there were few cases when a captain could buy a large number of slaves from any one African buyer even where the local state or its officials controlled the trade. In all the accounts of the trade, as will be seen in the next chapter, it was the norm for slaves to be purchased in relatively small lots directly from the African sellers. Finally, though the African purchase origins were the same, some captains in the eighteenth century were able to buy slaves from each other. Especially if a slave ship had been on the coast a very long time and was trading near recently arrived vessels, it was common to pay a premium and make quick trades among the captains so that the long-trading ship could finally leave the coast.

In almost all cases, African slave traders came down to the coast or the riverbanks in a relatively steady and predictable stream to well-known trading places. The cost of moving the slaves in caravans to the coast was relatively cheap – only the costs for food for the slaves and the salaries of the guards, and the costs of purchase for any slaves lost in transit because of death or escape (a loss for which we have no systematic data for any African interior trade route). The slaves also could be used to move goods at no cost, with each male slave carrying up to twenty-five kilograms of goods and women up to fifteen. It has been estimated that the total ivory exported from Gambia in 1741 could easily have been moved free of charge by the slaves who were shipped to the coast for sale in the Atlantic slave trade. This low cost of transport and free "ballast" of goods that could be carried reduced the costs of delivery of slaves from the interior to the coast. It also promoted an ever deeper penetration of the interior for ivory husks as the coastal elephant population became depleted. Also, given alternative local uses of slaves, inland traders arriving by caravan could respond to low European prices by holding these slaves off the market and using them as workers in agriculture or industry for any time period needed until prices rose again. Equally, they could be sold to local consumers at any time on the trip, and, from the few eyewitness accounts, this seems to have been a common experience. Eventually, many of these slaves would then be resold into the Atlantic trade if demand was strong.

The lack of bulking facilities for slaves on the coast meant that all European traders tended to spend months on the coast or traveling upriver gathering their slaves a few at a time. Even the ports of Luanda and Benguela, the only African centers that maintained a large resident white population, still required a stay of several months for ships going to Brazil to complete their complement of slaves. In a study of 84 Brazilian slave ships coming from the port of Rio de Janeiro between 1827 and 1830, the average stay in the Central African ports was 5 months. It was typical in almost all trading areas for the captain to leave the ship in one spot and take small craft to trade inland, leaving another officer in charge of the ship. He usually was accompanied by the ship's doctor, who then examined each slave for disease before allowing the purchase. On average, it would take several months to fill the ship. In most cases, the slaves were held ashore as long as possible to prevent the outbreak of disease on the ship, but even so death rates were relatively high for this "coasting" period. The best records for this mortality experience come from some 58 Dutch free-trader slave ships in the 1730–1803 period. On average, they spent six months trading on the coast and lost close to 5 percent of the slaves they purchased before sailing to America. Typical of the free-trade eighteenth-century experience was the Dutch vessel the *Vergenoegen*, which reached the Loando coast on 5 September 1794. After the usual gift giving to local African officials, trading began, with the captain remaining on shore during the whole period and sending between 2 to 7 slaves across to the ship every day. The purchase of 390 slaves took a relatively rapid four months to accomplish, but serious illness occurred with an outbreak of smallpox. A rather high percentage, some 26 slaves, died on the coast along with the captain, even before the ship finally sailed for America.

But there were some very well-organized trading zones where local African factors or merchants purchased slaves from the arriving inland traders and then arranged their sale to the ship's captain. This allowed the vessel to stay at one place instead of wandering along the coast and rivers. This pattern was typical in Luanda, Benguela, Elmina, and other well-established trading centers with a powerful local merchant center. But even in these fixed-position trading places, the average time on the coast was measured in months because most purchases were still in relatively small lots.

Good data are available on the "coasting" experience from the Dutch, French, and English trades. The seventeenth-century Dutch West India Company ships averaged 100 days on the coast picking up slaves, which was comparable to 34 British vessels in this period who averaged 95 days on the coast. Time trading on the coast seems to have increased in the course of the eighteenth century. Thus, Dutch free traders in the early eighteenth century averaged 200 days trading in Africa, some 230 French traders needed on average 143 days to complete their purchases in the 1726–58 period, and some 587 independent British traders averaged 173 days at midcentury (1751–75). In the 1763–77 period, another group of 224 French slave ships averaged 168 days of trading, with the Loango coast as usual being above the average, at 173 days for the 55 ships which took on slaves on this West Central African coast. The increasing time needed to purchase slaves is partly explained by the reliance on the forts and local company men to do purchases prior to the arrival of the slaver in the earlier period, which helped reduce the time to an average of just over three months. Equally, the fact that several ships were coming from the same European company meant that often ships traded among themselves to move the earliest ship out faster. Thus, an arriving captain might sell some of his first slave purchases to a departing captain so as to more rapidly complete the latter's loading. But the free traders usually worked for companies or associations that sent out few ships and could not rely on the cooperation of fellow captains.

While accumulating their slaves, the Europeans also took on freshwater supplies if they could from the local coast. During the dry season in many areas and in some African coastal regions at all times, water supplies were simply not available. This led some of the traders to stop at the Portuguese African islands of São Tomé or Princípe to obtain the large quantity of water that was needed. Others stopped earlier on the African coast in regions known to have abundant water supplies. They also purchased food supplies for the voyage at this point or before the trading had begun in other parts of the coast.

In provisioning for the voyage, all traders used common African foods and condiments along with dried foods and biscuits brought from Europe. They also brought with them lime juice for combating scurvy. The Europeans all tried to supply standard foods that local Africans could consume, though this varied from region to region. Most used European- or American-produced wheat flour or rice to produce a basic gruel, which would then be seasoned with local condiments and supplemented with fresh fish and meats as well as dried versions of these foods. Regional taste differences also showed up in food supplied for slaves taken from different regions. In the Sahel region, African-produced millet was preferred to rice, whereas slaves from the delta of the Niger and Mayombe preferred yams. In all trades, whatever the base used for making the gruel, almost all the condiments used came from Africa including the palm oil and the peppers, and all trades provided biscuits for both crew and slaves.

Even in the earlier seventeenth- and eighteenth-century trade when much more European dried foods were used, Dutch slave captains purchased fresh vegetables and small livestock on the African coast, along with the ever necessary supply of fresh water. To the earlier Portuguese provisioning acts of the late seventeenth century, which most concerned water rations, the governor and captain general of Luanda in 1770 decreed a more complete law on provisioning for the slave ships. He demanded that all slave ships be thoroughly cleaned and aired out before they took on slaves. He also demanded that shippers buy the more expensive dried fish as well as the cheaper fresh fish, and that any fresh fish purchased for the slave diet be consumed in the first days of the voyage before it rotted. Beans were to be cleaned before storage. Palm oil, vinegar, salt, and other seasonings were to be provided in their daily rations of flour (most probably Brazilian imported wheat flour) along with a small quantity of rum. Also, along with the fish and occasional vegetables, the slaves were to get some dried beef and be given tobacco on a steady basis. In the French trade, a freshly prepared quart of soup composed of rice and beans was provided at the two meals per day. Corn meal, peppers, and salt were also occasionally given with the soup and here as well some rum or brandy was occasionally supplied. The British in the eighteenth century also provided two meals a day with the first made up of African foods, mostly rice and yams, and the second a gruel made of barley, corn, and biscuits, with meat sometimes added. Fish stock and garnishings of palm oil and pepper could be added to either meal.

The British slave ship the *Brothers* in a fifty-day Atlantic crossing in 1789 provided the slaves with a per diem ration of three pounds and ten ounces of yam, two ounces of flour, three and a half ounces of beans, and ten ounces of biscuits, along with salted beef. On three out of five days the slaves also got a plantain and an ear of corn. Finally, a mouthwash of lime juice or vinegar was provided to each slave in the morning to prevent scurvy. A typical French slaver of 280 tons that carried some 600 slaves for a two-month voyage to America needed some 200 kilograms per slave for their food supplies, which consisted of 40 kilograms of biscuits, beans, and rice, along with other rations. This was calculated to mean a consumption of a little over 2,000 calories per day for each slave during the crossing – a figure lower than that provided for contemporary sick sailors aboard French royal naval vessels (2,385 calories).

As important as food was the water. The French estimated that they needed one cask or barrel of water for every person aboard ship and all traders gave drinking water three times per day, even when meals might only occur twice a day. The ship carrying the 600 slaves for a two-month voyage would thus need one water cask per slave (weighing between 65 and 66 kilograms per cask), which meant that some 40 tons of water casks were loaded for the slaves alone. On some coasts, water was not readily available and often had to be obtained in regions far from where the slaves were obtained. Finally, the maintenance of the casks and the guarantee of their quality was an important part of the responsibility of the captain and the carpenters. The governor of Angola in 1770 formally ordered the checking and cleaning of the water casks and copper caldrons of all slavers leaving his region, and demanded that drinking water not only be stocked in the abundance already ordered by royal decree, but that it not be put in the rum casks. For their part, the French traders, before crossing the Atlantic customarily took their final water supplies from the Portuguese African islands of São Tomé and Principé rather than from the African coast on which they traded because of the excellent quality and abundance of the local waters.

Aside from maintaining a steady and clean water supply, almost all slave traders housed and organized daily life of the slaves in the same manner. The decks usually were divided into three separate living quarters, one for males, one for grown boys, and one for women and children.

Sick slaves were usually isolated in their own compartment. Depending on the number taken, and the number ill, these compartments could be expanded or reduced. Slaves were usually shackled together at night to prevent rebellion and movement, but were then brought up to the deck during the day. On deck they were forced to exercise, often accompanied by African musical instruments. In the Dutch trade, for example, all captains purchased African drums so as to force the slaves to dance as a form of exercise. Usually, the Africans stayed the entire day on deck and had their meals there if the weather permitted. At this time the crew went into their quarters and cleaned them out, often using vinegar and other cleansing agents. While all females were given simple cloths to wear, in some trades the males were left naked if the weather permitted. All slaves were washed every day with seawater.

As is obvious from these details, it was the aim of all traders to keep the slaves and their quarters as clean as possible since there was a generalized awareness of the correlation between cleanliness and disease. Beyond this, all slave trades carried a ship's doctor to care for the slaves and crew and their illnesses. Nevertheless, the details given of the medical cabinets of these "doctors" show little of value for fighting the standard diseases that struck both crew and the slaves. Mortality and morbidity were high among the slaves and little beyond maintaining clean food and water supplies provided any effective remedy for these diseases.

Once arriving in America the slaver had to clear local customs and health registrations and then the slaves were immediately sold to local planters. Among the French it was the custom for the captain to sell his slaves directly, using a local agent who took a commission on all sales. The local agent announced the arrival of the ship via posters and by mail and the sale usually began immediately upon docking, or within a week of landing. Slaves were either sold directly from the ship or brought to a special market on land. Usually the slaves were sold one at a time, with occasional sales of several to one buyer. Thus the French *Duc de Laval* that arrived in the West Indies in 1775 sold its 365 slaves to 72 different purchasers from all walks of life, going from royal officials and leading merchants to artisans buying 1 or 2 slaves.

In the eighteenth-century French West Indies, all able-bodied slaves were usually sold within two or three weeks of arrival. In Barbados in the late seventeenth century, sales from Royal African Company ships appeared to be much more rapid. Thus the *James* that arrived in May 1676 sold 351 of its 373 slaves within the first three days of beginning its sales, but did not sell the rest for another two weeks because of the poor health of those not sold immediately. What is evident from this experience is that if the American demand was strong, most of the healthy slaves could be sold in just a few days, with sales going longer to include those recovering from disease. There is even the practice of some free colored women in eighteenth-century Saint Domingue buying the sickest slaves at bargain prices at the end of several weeks in order to nurse them back to health and then sell them to local buyers at healthy slave prices. All sales were deemed final and it was the responsibility of the new American owner or his agent to move the slave to his new place of residence.

The great problem for the ship's captain and the original outfitter and owner of the expedition was the terms of sale. Once agreeing on the price, usually only about 25 percent down payment was made and the rest was to be paid for in eighteen to twenty-four months. Moreover, even when payment was made it was often in colonial goods and not in cash, which was always scarce in all American colonies. Also, collecting on these promissory notes was very difficult and involved endless conflict between the merchants and the purchasers. The agent determined the creditworthiness of the local purchaser and was required to collect the final payments. He was also required to obtain a return cargo for the slave ship if this were possible. More often than not, the ship was sent off with only a limited cargo and finally would return to Europe some fifteen to eighteen months after having left Europe.

Thus, despite the myth of the so-called triangle trade, the leg of the slaving voyage between America and Europe was the least important part of the slaving voyage and slave ships were not a significant element in the transportation of slave-produced American goods to the European market. This myth assumed a tight relationship between the shipping of European goods to Africa for slaves, of slaves to America, and slave-produced American products being shipped to Europe all on the same ship. In fact, most of the West Indies goods were shipped to Europe in boats specifically designed for that purpose and were both larger than the typical slaver and were exclusively engaged in this bilateral trade. Since many among the crew were supernumeraries after the slaves were sold in America, and the ship's cost was a relatively minor part of the original expenditures of outfitting the slaving voyage, it often happened that slavers ended their voyage in the New World and the captain and a few crewmen returned to Europe on their own. Even when they did return to Europe, they waited only a short time to return and made no effort to wait for the availability of American goods. If a cargo was available, then it would be taken, but more often than not such ships returned in ballast. Thus, of the 195 Dutch free-trader slave ships that arrived in America in the eighteenth century, 65 returned to Europe in ballast – carrying just sand and water – and another 52 carried a small or token cargo. Only 69, or just over a third, came with a full cargo of American products for sale in Europe. There is little question that this trade can be considered to have had a triangle-style relationship, but the slave ships, for all intents and purposes, really made a significant impact only on the outbound to Africa and the Africa to American legs of the trip.

Once in Europe, the captain made his report, and the crew was given its back wages in cash – often necessitating the immediate outlay of 100,000 to 200,000 livres in cash. The *armateur* then immediately sold the imported sugar or other goods to local shipping merchants who handled such trade and then proceeded to concentrate on obtaining all the remaining funds due him for the credit sales of the slaves. This sale of the goods brought back on his slave ship brought the outfitter usually no more than one-third of his original outlay. For the rest of his return on slave sales, it usually took three full years to complete, with the merchant constantly needing to sell the constantly arriving colonial goods (by which most of the slaves were paid for) to local importers. The bulk of the credit sales were completed by the end of six years, though outstanding bills sometimes were never paid. It was the last three of the six years when the profit of the trade was made. Apparently, the period in which the debts were paid off was shorter in the British trade, with one study estimating that at the end of the eighteenth century it was completed in about two years.

The size and amount of the profit generated by the slave trade has been an issue of intense debate for some time. There is little question that the thousands of ships that sailed for Africa to engage in the slave trade did so because it was profitable to European merchants to invest in such a commerce. Thus, despite the very long-term nature of these investments, there was always a large number of European and American merchants and others willing to invest their capital in this enterprise. The trade was also profitable to most of the coastal African states exporting slaves. There was always a supply of slaves brought to the coast by African slave trades who found it profitable to do so, and most African nations resisted attempts by the British after 1808 to close their trades. Even when the more valuable palm oil trade became a major export after the 1820s, these same African palm-oil-exporting regions were still willing to trade in slaves.

But the question remains how profitable was the trade to the Europeans and to the Africans who controlled it and what were its larger social and economic costs? The traditional literature saw the trade as a European monopoly from which the Africans received little compensation and in which slaves were bought for worthless goods at illusory prices and shipped at modest cost across the Atlantic. Profits were therefore assumed to be extraordinary by the standards of the time, and it was then suggested that they were so large that this slave trade profit combined with the profit generated out of slave-produced goods traded from America generated the capital to finance the Industrial Revolution.

But just how profitable was it for the Europeans? The polemics have been intense about the overall economic benefits of the slave trade to the Europeans themselves. These debates began with Eric Williams and have continued on into the most current journal articles. The discussion can be divided into three general questions: was the slave trade profitable at the firm level and were these profits excessive; what impact did the slave trade have on the economic growth of Europe; and, finally, what impact did the slave trade and slave labor have on American economic growth?

From the work of the European economic historians, it is now evident that slave trade profits were not extraordinary by European standards. The average 6 to 10 percent rate obtained was considered a very good profit rate at the time, but not out of the range of other contemporary investments. But if profits were not "astronomic," was the trade an open one, or a restricted one that created concentrated oligopolistic profits that could then possibly serve as a fundamental source for capital investments in the European economy? It has been suggested that high initial costs of entrance, plus the long time period needed to fully recover profits (up to five years or more on a typical slaving voyage), meant that only highly capitalized firms could enter the trade. Most merchants spread their costs around by offering stock in slaving voyages and otherwise trying to insure themselves against catastrophic loss on one or more lost voyages. But the costs of entrance, the experience of contacts, and the international nature of the complex negotiations suggest that there were limits on the number of merchants who could enter the trade. While this specialization seems to have taken place (and there are cases of quite major houses operating in both England and France), it is also impressive just how many independent merchants participated in the trade and how many ships were outfitted for the trade in any given year. At the height of the trade in the 1780s, for example, some 260 or so ships, almost all with different owners, were needed to move the 79,000 slaves per annum who were sent to America.

There have been numerous studies on profitability of the trade at the level of the individual firm. Earlier English research by Anstey and others estimated a gross profit of 10 percent per voyage. In a recent analysis of the eighteenth century French trade, Gullerme Daubin, using modern economic accounting found the internal rate of return to be 6 percent. This, he estimated was also the average for most overseas commercial trades, and in fact the French slave traders were much less specialized than the British, with most of the biggest slave traders also actively engaged in other more normal trading ventures. In turn he asked if there were better rates of return to local capitalists in land rents, private credit arrangements or public bonds, and found that both the slave trade and all overseas trades produced higher average returns of between 2 and 5 percent. Surprisingly the slave trade and general commercial voyage investments were less risky and more liquid (that is capital could be extracted) and needed less time to garner returns than all other forms of possible investment in the eighteenth century. But given the high risks of all overseas voyages risk itself was controlled by buying shares in multiple voyages. This need to control for high market wide risk meant that there were barriers to entrance into the trade. To be profitable an investor had to have committed a large volume of capital. Information barriers also existed because of the need to have good contacts and knowledge about the quality and experience of individual voyage organizers. The result was that most of the investors were in fact wealthy merchants and were local to the port where the ship voyages began.

It has also been argued that the credit mechanisms used to finance the trade were among the most sophisticated employed in long-distance trading. Though this is correct, it turns out that most of the credit mechanisms implemented by the traders and their suppliers and customers were in place before the trade fully developed. Thus, while the slave trade was unusual in its very high use of credit, of which the British made the most use, such credit sales were not unique to this trade nor did their use alone foster the evolution of English or continental credit institutions considered so crucial to the evolution of modern economic society. It is interesting to note, however, that English credit facilities would be intimately involved in the slave trade even long after British direct participation ended in 1807.

This debate on the relative rates of merchant participation and control and of the sophisticated use of instruments of credit has generated a lively analytical literature. In this debate, however, no current scholars have been able to show that the gains from the trade were directly invested in the earliest industrial enterprises of Great Britain. All the studies of the sources of industrial capital in England suggest local origins from agriculture and/or European commerce. Nevertheless, the thesis first developed by the historian and former prime minister of Trinidad and Tobago, Eric Williams, which had suggested such a linkage between slave trade profits, profits from slave-produced sugar, and the capital used to promote the Industrial Revolution in England, has come in for some support. Thus, French scholars have suggested the important role played by Africa as a market for European manufactures, especially of the more basic sort. It has been suggested that the French armaments industry was completely dependent on the African trade (which was paid for by slave exports) during times of European peace. Several other industries on the continent and in England can also be shown to have been highly dependent on the African market. Since much of early industrial activity involved production of cruder and popularly consumed products, it can be argued that the African market played a vital part in sustaining the growth of some of Europe's newest infant industries. Thus, while the more extreme position that Williams suggested has not been supported, scholars have suggested various linkages between European industrial production and the African market.

Another area that has yet to be explored is that of the use of the capital generated from the slave trade within America itself. In many trades, American owners and investors participated along with Europeans in the Atlantic slave trade. The West Indians, the North Americans – Virginians and, above all, the New Englanders – and the Brazilians clearly were an important group of owners within the trade. In terms of volume and capital generated, there is little question that few American regions compare with those of Bahia and Rio de Janeiro. The number of ships provisioned for the African trade in these areas suggests a major involvement of local capital. The capital dedicated to the Brazilian slave trade came from many sources. Merchants in Angola outfitted and paid for numerous voyages, and capital was invested from Portugal itself. But a large share of the financing came from merchants in the port cities of Rio de Janeiro and Salvador de Bahia. Given the unusual importance of Brazilian produced goods in African importations – above all, tobacco, alcohol, and arms and ammunition – and the complex wind and current conditions of the South Atlantic that made any potential triangular trade extremely difficult, Brazilian resident merchants had a higher participation ratio in the slave trade than any other American merchant class. For example, of some 42 slave ships which were involved in legal issues before the *Junta do Comércio* (commercial court) in Rio de Janeiro, 10 were owned by Portuguese African-based merchants, one by an English merchant and the rest pertained to Rio merchants. Moreover, even European or African owned vessels probably had shares sold to Brazilian capitalists. And the slave trade merchants of Rio de Janeiro had extensive contact with Luanda merchants who operated as either co-owners of their slave expeditions or as their agents. Although Brazilian-produced goods were to be found in every outbound slave ship going to Africa, only an estimated 14 percent of early-nineteenth-century slavers carried only Brazilian produced goods for purchase of slaves. The most valuable part of the trade, even in Brazil, was Asian-produced textiles, which had to be imported from Goa, either via Lisbon or delivered directly to Luanda from India. Thus, the Brazilian trade, like all others, involved a complex amalgam of metropolitan, African, Indian, and American capital. But equally it is clear from studies of merchant records that Rio de Janeiro merchants either as organizers of voyages, owners of the slavers, or even as insurers of the ships and their cargos had a major capital investment in the Atlantic slave trade, and were probably the single largest American investors in the slave trade. What happened to this Brazilian capital tied to the slave trade after 1850 is difficult to assess. Thus, the end of the slave trade to Brazil in 1850 involved a major reallocation of local capital. It has been suggested that all this capital went into consumption of imported goods or financial speculation, but that is doubtful. It is most likely that most of the capital went into coffee, the internal slave trade, the construction of new steam mills for sugar and the beginnings of infrastructural investments in railroads and tramways, all of which experienced major growth in the next three decades. A similar process of alternative deployment of slave trade capital may have occurred in other American importing zones after the abolition of the trade.

Whatever the revisions that can be expected in our knowledge of the economics of the trade, there is little question that the basic outlines are well established. The older popular literature that stressed the cheapness of slaves, the passivity of the Africans, and the extraordinary profitability of the trade has been thoroughly challenged by the available documentation. It is evident from all the studies of provisioning costs in the trade and of the organization of the African market that slaves purchased in Africa were not a low-cost item. The goods exported to Africa to pay for the slaves were costly manufactured products or high-priced imports from other countries or even other continents, and were the single most expensive factor in the outfitting of the voyage, being more valuable than the ship, the wages for the crew, and food supplies combined. An officer in the Royal Navy presented a typical cost estimate to Parliament in the late 1780s, which noted that the cargo taken on board a typical slaver leaving Liverpool was close to double the combined costs of the ship, its insurance, and the wages of the crew for twenty months. Even when all the final commissions to the captain, other officers, and agents from the final slave sales, the interest on loans, and the port fees were included, the costs of the outbound cargo used to purchase the slaves still represented the single largest expense incurred by the owners and over half of total costs for the entire enterprise. Two-thirds of the outfitting costs of the French slavers in the eighteenth century were also made up of the goods used to purchase the slaves.

Along with the myths about the cheap cost of slaves, the popular literature stressed the dependent position of the African merchants in the trade. It was thought that prices demanded for slaves were low and invariant, that the trading was all dominated by the Europeans, and that the Africans were passive observers to the whole process. These issues will be examined in more detail in the following chapter, but at this point it is worth noting that all studies show that the mix of goods that went to make up the price in each zone tended to vary over time and reflected changing conditions of demand and supply. Thus, African merchants adjusted their demands for goods in response to market conditions. Africans were also astute and persistent in preventing the Europeans from creating monopoly conditions. The European forts in West Africa and even the Portuguese coastal and interior towns in Southwest Africa were ineffective in excluding competing buyers from entering the local market. The forts exercised dominion for only a few miles inland and were more designed to fend off competitors than to threaten suppliers. As for the unique Portuguese settlements, these were unable to prevent the French and English from obtaining Congo and Angolan slaves on a massive scale. Yet these were supposedly domains totally monopolized by the Portuguese.

Finally, even if the "triangle trade" idea is essentially incorrect, the Atlantic slave trade was one of the more complex of international trades that existed in the modern period. It intimately tied cowry and textile exports from Asia to African imports and involved massive movements of people across large land masses and great oceans. It tied up European capital, ships, and crews for long periods of time and involved very complex credit arrangements for the sale of American crops in European markets. Thus, while an actual "triangle trade" may not have existed as a significant development for ships in the trade, the economic ties between Asia, Europe, Africa, and America clearly involved a web of relationships that spanned the globe. At the heart of this system was a Europe committed to consuming American plantation crops at an ever expanding rate, crops that ranged from luxuries to basic necessities within the European population. Until European immigrants replaced them in the late nineteenth century, it was African slaves who enabled this consumption revolution to occur. Without that labor most of America would never have developed at the pace it did.

CHAPTER 5

The African Organization

of the Slave Trade

Did a market for slaves exist in Africa, and were slaves purchased in an economically rational way? These seemingly innocuous questions have created enormous debate as some writers have even denied the existence of such a market, assuming that all slaves were taken by piratical seizure of European traders. Thus, the first question to ask is, Did a market exist? The answer from all known sources is that all African slaves were purchased from local African owners and the exchange of goods for slaves represented a real market by anyone's definition. Although early in each European trade there are cases of ignorant slave captains seizing local Africans who appeared before them on the coast, these practices stopped quickly. European buyers were totally dependent on African sellers for the delivery of slaves. European traders never seriously penetrated beyond the coast before the late nineteenth century because of the military power of the African states and the threat of disease. The coastline itself was often lightly populated and had few slaves. Slaves in numbers sufficient to fill the holds of the slave ships only arrived to the coast via African merchants willing to bring them from the interior. The complexity of this exchange was such that it explains why slaves were purchased in such small numbers on the coast and why Europeans took months to gather a full complement of them for shipment to America. Given this balance of resources and power relations, the Europeans quickly discovered that anything but peaceful trade was impossible. Those who did not adapt were rapidly removed from the trade, sometimes by force.

Aside from a commitment to peaceful trade, Europeans had to deal with the special demands of established states if they wished to purchase slaves. Almost all traders paid local taxes for their purchases and otherwise dealt with the African traders as autonomous and powerful foreigners who controlled their own goods and markets. Everywhere, Europeans quickly adapted to local trading practices. It was estimated that in the Kingdom of Whydah on the Slave Coast in the late seventeenth and early eighteenth centuries, European slave traders had to pay the equivalent of 37 to 38 slaves (this cost valued at £375) per ship in order to trade for slaves in the kingdom. These costs included a royal tax on the right to trade, payments for royal officials handling the movement of slaves to the ships, the costs for African government interpreters – one for each of the foreign lodges then trading on the coast who knew English, French, Dutch, and/or Portuguese – and even a privileged first sale of a small number of royal slaves before all others could be purchased. Then came a final export tax. Such taxes and payments for the right to trade existed on virtually all coasts. The European observers on the African coast record all these taxes without comment, taking them as the normal cost of dealing with powerful foreign states, and only complaining of what they thought of as corrupt or arbitrary practices favoring one group over another.

In an unusual arrangement, the same Whydah government guaranteed a standard price for all slaves sold to one ship – a practice clearly favoring the European traders – but even here it varied that price from ship to ship depending on supply and demand factors, and would even work out different standard prices for ships of the same nation trading at the same time. Though European traders constantly petitioned the Whydah king for a fixed price for all ships, the government refused all such demands. More common in most trades was for prices to vary for each slave sold, and there were constant complaints by traders that prices of slaves tended to rise toward the end of their trading, as Africans knew that they were anxious to complete their sales and leave. The Europeans were even required by the Kingdom of Whydah to use a given set of African brokers who arranged all trade and received a sales commission fee beyond the taxes and port fees, a practice rather common not just on the Slave Coast of the Bight of Benin.

Aside from these costs, since Europeans had to remain on the coast for several months, they had to purchase all their water and supplies from local merchants in whatever currency or goods demanded. There even developed a very active credit market, with Europeans giving goods to local officials or merchants to purchase slaves for them in the interior, as well as Europeans obtaining slaves on credit with the promise of goods. This led to conflict and judicial proceedings, with the African governments often holding resident European merchants captive, or expelling them from the coast for failure to pay debts. The existence of these powerful and independent local states was in fact a guarantee for the Europeans of a steady trade relationship. This explains why Whydah and Dahomey (which conquered Whydah in the 1720s) provided some of the largest numbers of slaves for the Atlantic trade.

Nor was all of this trading in slaves something unknown to the Africans. Both an internal and international slave trade existed in Africa before the arrival of the Europeans, and Europeans found it convenient to adjust to well-established local African markets and trading arrangements already in place. In many cases, the Europeans only deepened preexisting markets and trade networks. Africans were also quick to respond to European needs beyond the slaves themselves. Coastal Africans developed specialized production to feed and clothe the slaves arriving at the ports and to supply provisions for the European trading posts and their arriving ships. New trade routes were opened up as European demand increased beyond local coastal supplies, and with it more long-distance trading became the norm everywhere. It was said that white and black Muslim traders from the Saharan region finally began trading at Whydah at the beginning of the eighteenth century, as the complex Saharan routes were now linked to the European Atlantic ones in the so-called Benin gap – the open savanna lands in the Lower Guinea Coast.

Coastal trading states got their slaves from the interior, purchasing them with both their local products such as salt, dried fish, kola nuts, and cotton textiles, as well as European goods. Unusual trade routes opened by Europeans were often developed as well by the Africans. The Dutch initiated direct oceanic trade on a systematic basis with small coastal yachts between the Gold Coast and the Slave Coast in the seventeenth century in order to purchase African products demanded on the Elmina markets for gold. Africans in oceangoing canoes soon followed and created a major new cabotage trade for regular African commercial goods between these two coasts for the first time. This in fact explains the origins of the settlement at Little Popo on the Slave Coast, which was a portage stopping point for Gold Coast canoes transferring from the ocean to the inland lagoon shipping channels. At the same time new American foodstuffs that were imported by Europeans for their own needs were quickly adopted by African producers. These imports included such fundamental crops as maize and sweet potatoes, along with manioc (casava), coffee, and cacao. Already by the 1680s the Slave

Coast communities were supplying maize to the European slave ships. The Europeans also introduced pigs and such unfamiliar Asian products as citrus fruits. Many of these crops slowly replaced or supplemented traditional African foodstuffs, often permitting denser and healthier populations. Although some of these products were integrated into traditional food production arrangements, others became the basis for new local industries. There was even the case of imported European woolen cloths being unraveled for their thread and rewoven by Slave Coast weavers to produce new-style cloth for consumption on the Gold Coast. This is aside from the well-known importation of Swedish bar iron, which was used by African blacksmiths to produce agricultural instruments for clearing bush and planting crops. Nowhere on the coast were the Africans incapable of benefiting from European trade or the introduction of new products and using them to their own ends and needs.

A thriving market economy with specialization of tasks and production and a well-defined merchant class, in existence before the arrival of the Europeans in most areas of Africa, goes a long way toward explaining the rapidity and efficiency of the African response to European trade. Gold and slaves had been exported from Africa for centuries. From the Saharan caravan traders of the western Sudan to the stone cities and gold fairs organized by Swahili Islamic traders in East Africa, Africans were well accustomed to market economies and international trade well before the arrival of the Portuguese on the West African coast. This does not mean that these were necessarily full capitalist markets, since local monopolies, kinship, and religious constraints, along with state intervention, often created unequal access and restricted markets here as they still did in most of Europe in the fifteenth century. But in general, prices defined in whatever currencies, units of account, or mixes of trade goods fluctuated in response to supply and demand across the entire continent. Nor were traders reluctant to expand their markets or adopt new technologies.

Thus, Africans had little difficulty in dealing with Europeans and trading with them from the beginning. An extensive slave market already existed before the arrival of the Europeans, and though domestic slavery in Africa would be substantially different from commercial slavery in America, the whole process of seizing war captives, enslaving criminals and debtors, taxing dependent groups for slaves, and even raiding defenseless peasants constituted well-known market activities. Slaves were purchased by local groups and individuals throughout Africa and were also shipped north and east to satisfy Middle Eastern and Mediterranean markets. Thus, Europeans were able to tap into already developed supply markets. Moreover, long-term contact with the Islamic states in North Africa and the Near East, and even longdistance trade between Asia and East Africa prior to the arrival of the Europeans, meant that Africans could negotiate from a reasonable knowledge of international markets what items of European or even Asian production most appealed to them.

If African markets existed and slaves were marketed throughout Africa prior to the European arrival, and if Africans were definitely not passive economic actors, what about the price they received for their slaves? What did a slave cost on the African coast and did this price change over time? These remain fundamental questions in dealing with the economics of the slave trade. To determine the price for which slaves were sold in Africa to Europeans is a very complex calculation. For the Europeans the price was the European cost of goods that they needed to purchase and offer in exchange for obtaining a slave. This European cost of goods was called the "prime" price. On the African coast, these goods were often doubled in value when sold to the Africans, and these prices were called the "trade" price. Almost all the European accounts when estimating their own costs used the "prime" price. But even using the trade price for what the Africans had to pay is a complex calculation. The actual mix of goods used in any purchase was expressed in both European currencies as well as in African monetary accounts, which included such monies as cowry shells, copper wires, or even palm cloth, or was defined in such units as a trade "ounce," which originally meant the value of an ounce of gold, "bundles," and other arbitrary units. These African currencies or units of account were not uniform across Africa. Cowry shells, for example, were a primary money used in the Gulf of Guinea, but not on the Congo-Angola coast. The "ounce" was very common in the Gold Coast and associated areas, but not used elsewhere, while a "bundle" of goods was common in the trade to the Loango and Angolan coast. Silver coins minted in Spanish America were used in the Upper Guinean ports and on both the Gold and Bight of Biafran coasts in the eighteenth century and they were carried by all Brazilian slave ships going to East Africa to purchase slaves in the nineteenth century. Gold dust was used to purchase slaves in many regions, but especially in the Bight of Benin. Thus, Europeans were often required to spend their own currencies directly in their commerce with the Africans.

Finally, to determine an average price on a ship filled with 450 slaves is also complex, since there was not a uniform price paid for all slaves in a given port at a given time. Prices varied quite widely based on the age, sex, and health of each slave. Women were on average 20 percent cheaper than men, and children were even cheaper still. Moreover, "prime-age" males were 20 percent more expensive than older males, and so on. Thus average prices varied depending on the slaves purchased, though in general between half and two-thirds of any group of slaves carried off the coast were made up of prime-age men. Slave prices also varied depending on local trading competition and supply conditions and even varied over the time of trading for an individual voyage. This variation in "average" price per slave is well reflected in the records of Dutch free traders in the eighteenth century. Thus, the slave ship *Nieuwe Hoop* that traded at Senegambia three times between 1767 and 1771 averaged a different price each time, going from 262 guilders per slave on one voyage to 325 guilders per slave on another. The *Philadelphia*, which made five successive voyages to this same coast between 1753 and 1760, also paid a different average price per slave on each expedition, going from a low of 230 guilders to a high of 337 guilders per slave. This pattern of variation was common throughout Africa and no two Dutch ships ever averaged the same price. Moreover, the actual prices paid for each slave varied quite considerably from this mean, since each purchase was made with a variety of goods of markedly differing costs for the Europeans. Thus, one English observer calculated that though the average price per slave on a given group of slaves was £3 15s., those purchased with cowry shells cost £4 each, those with beads and iron bars cost only £2 15s, and those sold for pieces of Indian cotton goods were valued as high as £6.

Nor were the goods sold by the Europeans over the several centuries of the trade of the same quality, quantity, or price. Nor were the products that the Africans wanted for their slaves the same over time and place. While beads and brass bracelets did well in the seventeenth century, the number needed to purchase slaves increased to such an extent that they were worthless in such exchanges in the eighteenth century, as African sellers no longer expressed interest. Moreover, while gold was mostly exported from Africa, there was even the case of the Portuguese obtaining large numbers of slaves on the Slave Coast in the early eighteenth century by buying them with Brazilian gold. Portuguese traders also used Spanish American minted silver coins, the famous pieces of eight (a peso worth eight reales), in trade on the Upper Guinea Coast in the seventeenth century, which were used by local African buyers as currency and for making jewelry. The last thirty years of the eighteenth century also saw the need of the English to purchase the slaves sold by the Asante with gold, since they refused to accept British goods for these purchases, at a time when the Dutch had no trouble trading their European goods for slaves in the same markets. Nor were European goods or East Indian textiles or Indian Ocean cowries the only products used by the Europeans to purchase slaves. There were also large quantities of American goods imported including Brazilian tobacco and North American rum. Often, African goods were also employed. Cotton textiles of African make, salt, dried fish, kola nuts, various woven cloths, and other local coastal products were also used to purchase slaves in the interior markets, along with European goods. On the Senegambia and Upper Guinean savanna coast north of the forest areas, there were even imports of horses brought by Portuguese vessels from Arab sources in North Africa that were used to purchase slaves, gold, and ivory. In the Cross River zone of the Bight of Biafra it was necessary to buy local copper rods to be used to purchase slaves and in the Loango Bay north of the Zaire River and on the river itself it was customary to purchase locally produced palm cloth of the Vili group of Loango Coast to pay for slaves in the early centuries of the trade from the Congo and Angolan regions.

Finally, some regions eventually found little interest among the goods offered by the Europeans. It has been suggested that the limited level of participation of the ports of Senegambia in the Atlantic slave trade in the eighteenth and nineteenth centuries had little to do with declining supplies of slaves and mostly to do with the increasing disinterest in the European goods offered in trade and the ability of Senegambian groups to supply most of their needs through North African trade. Even in their earliest contacts with the Portuguese, local traders demanded North African cloths. This was an ideal region for European traders: it was the closest to Europe, had the shortest sailing times to America, and was the zone that produced the highest ratio of prime male slaves of any in Africa. But limited demand for European or East Asian goods, and high slave prices and limited offerings because of competitive North African markets, guaranteed that this would be a minor European zone of slave trading.

Despite all of these variations there were some long-term trends evident in the selling of African slaves to the Europeans. Almost everywhere slave prices remained low or even declined from the early period

to the end of the seventeenth century, suggesting that the growing supply exceeded any increased demand in most cases. Though American
demand for slaves was on the increase, especially after the middle of the
sixteenth century, the steady level of African wars due to state expansion and the European exploitation of new areas of the coast more than
satisfied American needs. Slave prices on the Slave Coast, for example,
which only developed as a prime source for slaves in the early seventeenth century, saw average prices decline for most of the century until
the 1690s, when they began a long but steady period of growth. Thus, an
average price for a slave (in this case considered the totality of the slaves
bought for any single ship and including about two-thirds males and
80 percent adults) in terms of "prime" prices went from £3 per slave in
the early 1680s to £10 in the mid-1730s. In a detailed survey of English
prices, this trend of rising prices is clearly evident everywhere the British
traded. A plateau seems to have been reached in the 1690s to the 1750s
period. Although there was wide annual and decade fluctuations, prices
for slaves remained relatively steady at levels achieved late in the seventeenth century. But a longterm secular rise in constant prices began
at midcentury with only modest pauses until the nineteenth century.
By the early 1760s, constant prices were double those in 1700 and then
took off at an even more rapid pace, being four times those of 1700 by
the late 1790s and five times higher in constant British pounds by the
early 1800s.

This rising trend in prices represented the dual impact of growing
American demand outpacing increased supply, and the overabundance
of European goods in African markets forcing down prices of imports.
Thus the number of bars of iron needed to purchase a slave increased
far more than average prices expressed in European currencies. Also,
the constant and unremitting competition of the Europeans kept prices
rising, as they could never monopolize any trade zone for long. The
constant theme of all African states trading with the Europeans was
to maintain open competition, always favoring newer arrivals for fear
of becoming dependent on traditional traders. Though the Portuguese
were excluded from the Gulf of Guinea by the Dutch in the early
seventeenth century, for example, the local states, which had often
been hostile to them in their monopoly days, welcomed their return and
allowed them to trade despite strong northern European opposition. At
the same time, the Kongo Kingdom south of the Congo River often
shipped its slaves north of the river to be exported from the Loango
coast in order to escape Portuguese monopoly control in its own area

of trading. There are cases not only of local kings forcing traders to remain neutral while their mother countries were at war, but also of their engaging in international diplomacy. Thus the king of Allada on the Slave Coast in the late sixteenth century sent an official emissary to the French court to encourage France's entrance into the local slave trade to counterbalance English and Dutch influence. At the same time, the Kongo king Afonso II sent an embassy to Rome demanding an autonomous bishopric be established in his kingdom separate from the one at the Portuguese island of São Tomé.

In short, the Africans were neither passive actors nor peoples innocent of the market economy, and were able to deal with the Europeans on the basis of equality. They were already well integrated into a market economy and responded to market incentives as well as any peoples of western Europe. They also fought against European attempts to place monopoly constraints on their trade and, in turn, were able to limit the more excessive demands placed by the Europeans on their local trading arrangements. Though their consumption demands may have been different from the Europeans', these demands were determined by different economies, ecologies, and social organizations. Even some of their seemingly more quaint customs, at least to contemporary Europeans, made good economic sense to modern-day economists.

Nowhere is this more evident than in the use of Indian Ocean shells as money, above all in equatorial Africa. To modern readers this may seem a primitive instrument of exchange that marks the backwardness of the Africans of the time. But, in fact, cowry shells had a history of use as a money in Asia long before their implantation in Africa. They were used in China until the thirteenth century and were a common currency in Bengal and other parts of India until the nineteenth century. Cowries were used throughout the Pacific islands and even appeared in Hudson's Bay among the Indians of North America.

The choice of cowries as money was a more than reasonable one. They were produced in relatively fixed amounts from one unique source, they were durable and could be stored indefinitely, and they were easily identifiable and impossible to falsify. Nor were these shells the only form of money in use, but were commonly used alongside gold, silver, and copper. In both India and Africa they were used as the cheapest form of payment and would eventually be replaced by copper coins or paper money.

Cowries were a floating currency with no fixed exchange rate and would vary in worth by time and place, influenced by their intrinsic value (the cost of producing and transporting them) and the demand and supply for them. The only unique feature of cowries is that the Europeans who used them on the African coast as money refused to accept them as payment for anything they themselves produced – at least during the era of the slave and palm oil trades when Africa was independent. In the late nineteenth and early twentieth centuries, however, cowries were accepted as money for taxes that the Europeans collected in some of their new African colonies and they continued to be used up until the 1920s in some areas.

Moreover, European traders were not the only ones not to use cowries as money. For in fact, the region within Africa in which cowries were used was a limited one. It included essentially the region of the Bight of Benin and the Niger River basin. This cowry zone ranged from the western part of the contemporary state of the Ivory Coast to the western edge of present-day Cameroon and included Ghana, Togo, Benin, large parts of Nigeria, and southern Mali. But it was not used as money in the area northwest of the Bight of Benin (from Liberia to Senegal), or to the south (from the Bight of Biafra – at least in the earlier period – south to Angola). Thus, while it included one of the most important of slave-exporting zones, it did not encompass all or even most of western Africa.

The cowries were first introduced across the Sahara by Muslim traders before the opening up of the coastal trade by the Portuguese in the fifteenth century. They came from the Maldive Islands, a series of atolls, just off the south coast of India. Though the animal that produced the shells could be found throughout the Pacific region, including East Africa and Zanzibar, it was the variety called moneta that was most heavily concentrated in these Pacific islands. These produced the smallest and most distinctive shell. These snaillike animals were taken live from the sea, allowed to die on shore, and their shells were then cleaned and gathered together and shipped to both Ceylon and India. Like all things Asian imported into Europe, these shells were first a Portuguese monopoly trade, then a Dutch one, and finally dominated by the English. Though the islands remained independent of all foreign domination and were under their own sultan, the key regions that traded with them were Ceylon and India, and it was European domination of these regions that guaranteed their respective monopolies.

After being cleaned and sorted, the small shells were packaged in coconut-leaf baskets containing a standard 12,000 shells and this socalled *kotta* was then shipped by local or Indian traders to Ceylon and

India. These shells were usually exchanged for rice and other foods not produced on the atolls. Europeans purchased these shells with gold and silver coins, but found that they made ideal ballast – as opposed to sand or other noncommercial materials – for ships sailing to Europe. Thus, they were almost a costless item to transport.

These shells were brought by the Portuguese in the 1510s to the western African coast, where they were already in use as money. The Portuguese, in contrast to other Europeans, traded directly with the Pacific island producers and could transport their shells from the Pacific to Africa or Lisbon. But the Dutch who replaced them in the early 1600s had difficulty with the producers and bought their shells from local shippers in Ceylon or India, as did the British who followed them. The Dutch and English then shipped their shells directly to Europe. There the shells were cleaned and sorted once again and put into casks, for in the African trade using them as ballast would have made it difficult to access them quickly as trade goods. Amsterdam and London became the big markets for cowries, and to these markets came all the Europeans who traded with Africa, from the Swedes to the Portuguese. By the peak of the Atlantic slave trade in the eighteenth century, the Dutch and English alone were importing some 40 million shells per annum in a normal year, and it is estimated that the two imported 10 billion shells in the 1700–90 period.

In Africa, the shells were either bagged or pierced and put on strings. The basic unit was a string of 40 shells called a *toque* (or tokky), which like all the units was a Portuguese word or a corruption thereof. Five toques made up a *galinha* of 200 shells and 20 *galinhas* made up a cabess (or *cabeça*) of 4,000 shells – though a "small" cabess was also used of only 10 *galinhas* of 2,000 shells. By the eighteenth century, the English translations for these terms were "string" for toque, "bunch" for galinha, and "head" for cabess – though meaning the small cabess of 2,000 shells (here considered to be made up of fifty strings). Ten "heads" made up one "bag" of 20,000 shells (weighing around fifty pounds) which is what one man could carry on his head. The prime means of moving cowries within Africa was by "headloading" – meaning on the heads of human porters.

The value of the cowries varied by time and place, with a "head" of 2,000 shells averaging around one pound sterling in the early eighteenth century in Whydah. In the course of the eighteenth and nineteenth centuries there was a steady inflation of values because of the massive importation of shells and the relatively slower growth of the local and regional economies. Thus the price of a slave in cowries varied considerably, going from 10,000 to 30,000 shells in the 1680s, to 40,000 to 50,000 of them in the 1710s, to 80,000 cowries by the 1760s, and double that number a decade later. Most transactions included other goods along with cowries as the price for a slave.

Within their trading zones cowries were used as money, though everywhere in Africa and even in Europe they were used in jewelry. They often circulated with other currencies from gold dust produced in Africa to American silver coins minted in Potosí. Everywhere they were the small change and used for the simplest transactions. Moreover, given their weight, they often did not travel great distances in exchange transactions. Often they were used as money of account and items were paid for in other currencies or goods, such as salt, kola nuts, livestock, or slaves.

If the shell currency used by the Africans made economic sense, their import demands also reflected a sophisticated buying public which experienced major local changes in consumption and fashion over time. Thus, on the Slave Coast, guns and gunpowder were a minor item of trade for slaves in the seventeenth century, but became a major item in the eighteenth century as local states revolutionized their armies and manner of undertaking warfare. Indian cottons were in great demand in the seventeenth century, to be replaced by German-produced linens from Silesia in the early decades of the 1700s as the prime textile import. Brass bracelets went out of fashion by the 1690s, to be replaced by brass basins, which were cut up by local artisans to make their own jewelry. While liquor in general and American rums in particular were never important on this coast, French brandy became a significant import for a while in the eighteenth century. With Brazilian gold suddenly abundant after 1700, the best prime slaves were purchased by Portuguese traders only for gold. Although Bahian tobacco had been known in the trade from the earliest days, it only became a mass consumption item on this coast in the mid-eighteenth century.

What occurred on the Slave Coast occurred everywhere in Africa. The reports of the Europeans are filled with constant news of changing market demands and the need to respond to them. There is a neverending effort by the Europeans to introduce new wares, some of which became high-demand items and others that failed to attract any customers. All of this reinforces the idea of a relatively complex and ever changing African market driven by basic economic and social factors common to all market economies of the period. Since no European nation ever totally dominated any slave market, competition was the rule. Africans fought all attempts at monopolizing their markets, and no nation could offer goods that were not in demand. Lack of quality goods led to a decline in trading. Though some writers have suggested that Africans were seduced by shoddy goods and enthralled into permanent dependence on the trading of slaves, the history of European imports everywhere shows unique local markets with constant changes in demand reflecting changing tastes, as well as changing abundance of goods. Moreover, the entrance as well as the exit of various regions from the overseas slave market showed that volition existed on the part of the Africans in terms of participation, at least for the sellers of slaves. In short, the Europeans alone neither created this market, nor did they dictate the goods used in the trade.

If determining the supply of foreign imported goods to this market was difficult, equally complex was estimating the supply of African slaves. Their origin and the manner in which they were obtained are among the more difficult areas to detail. It is evident from most sources that coastal peoples were able to supply sufficient slaves from groups close to the sea for the first century or so of the trade. By the eighteenth century, slaves were being drawn from interior groups far from the coast. But who these groups were and how far from the coast were they situated is an issue difficult to resolve. Much of this difficulty is due to the ignorance of the European traders of the interior developments within Africa. They had only the vaguest notions of the names of interior groups or of their placement and relative importance. In fact, in order to determine the African origin of the slaves, African historians have had to rely mostly not on the European traders who visited the coast, but on lists of slaves produced by American officials and planters, which were taken from the origin names the slaves themselves provided. They have even had to resort to the lists of slaves captured on the high seas by the British navy in the post-1808 era of embargo. Otherwise, no ship's manifest lists the ethnic origin of the slaves it carried to America, just their port of purchase.

Most commentators have suggested that the slaves taken to America in the first two centuries of the trade came from the coastal areas probably no further than a few days' march from the sea. Densely populated regions along the Senegambian, Guinean, and Congo coasts were a major and constant source of slaves over very long periods of time. But it is assumed that slaves were coming from much further inland by the second half of the eighteenth century as the trade expanded and intensified.

Some diminishing of coastal slave trading must have occurred as local groups either were incorporated into more powerful states and obtained protection from raiding and enslavement or migrated out of range of the slave hunters, thus forcing local traders ever deeper into the interior. But even in the late eighteenth and early nineteenth centuries the majority of the slaves in most zones still came from relatively close to the coast, despite often cited European notions that peoples were arriving from hundreds of miles from the interior. Thus, for example, the major exporting ports of the Bight of Biafran coast – Bonny and New Calabar (in the Niger River delta) and Calabar (in the Cross River delta) – took the majority of their slaves from the Igbo and Ibibio language groups who were densely settled between the Niger and the Cross Rivers quite close to these ports. This was the pattern from the earliest days until the trade came to a close in the 1830s and 1840s. Though Hausa, Nupe, and Kakanda peoples far to the north passed through these ports, they were definitely a minority. What occurred in this major exporting zone was probably typical of what occurred in most regions. Traditional areas, if they were still exporting, were still the major source for slaves, and these were mostly located close to the coast. The one exception to this rule seems to be the movement of slaves to the Loango and Angolan ports. Although these coastal states continued to supply local slaves, as early as the eighteenth century, interior slaves began to arrive in significant numbers to these coasts along major caravan routes that stretched several hundred miles into the interior.

Of course, long-distance movement was inevitable, especially in the case of war captives. In no known instance did warfare not lead to the sale of slaves. Some captives might be killed, especially the elite, but most were enslaved. While the Dahomean kings, for example, liked to display the heads of their enemies, it was only the kings and nobles that gained this status. The women of the defeated enemies became domestic slaves within Dahomey and the commoners were enslaved, both for local purposes and for shipment into the international slave trade. Among the Asante in the eighteenth century the state even supplied gunpowder to subordinate officials making war in the expectation that they would be repaid with captured slaves. Thus, war-captive slaves were a common commodity throughout Africa, and inevitably war captives even from deep in the interior would arrive on the coast. Moreover, given the universality of domestic slavery, it was not uncommon for captured or kidnaped slaves to serve as slaves in a local situation until such time as transport could be arranged for shipment to the coast. They could also serve as porters for moving other goods from the interior to the coast just as they themselves were being sent there to be sold.

The percentage of total slaves leaving Africa as war captives is difficult to estimate. All studies agree that there were numerous ways to enslave peoples. Aside from captives taken in war, there was largescale raiding for slaves along with more random individual kidnaping of individuals almost everywhere, especially on the poorly defined frontiers of the larger states. Common to most societies was the judicial enslavement for civil and religious crimes and indebtedness. Larger states often required dependent regions to provide tribute in slaves, which could then be shipped overseas. One estimate suggested that the Asante in the 1820s taxed their people in gold and in slaves when gold was not available, and thus produced some 2,000 tribute slaves for the central government annually. There were even suggestions that the Aro merchant communities of southeastern Nigeria used their oracle and religious institutions to enslave peoples, though this use of religion was rare and may not have been the case even among the Aro.

The magnitude to be ascribed to each of these factors has caused ongoing debate among scholars and led to little consensus because of the paucity of records, written or oral. There is little question that warfare was extremely important in generating captives. Though most scholars stress local motives for military conflict, and show how wars often disrupted markets and trade, there was no question that enslavement "facilitated" war and made it more economically viable. The possibility of selling captives in wars, no matter what their origin, made warfare even more attractive than just the possibility of gaining more lands, vassals, or markets. Even well-defined religious wars, the most famous being the conflicts among Muslims in the eighteenth and nineteenth centuries in West Africa, produced slaves for the American markets. There is also no question that some wars were related directly to control of international trade and thus to the impact of the Atlantic slave trade. The long conflicts between the Allada, the Whydah, the Dahomeans, and the Oyo kingdoms on the Slave Coast were clearly related to control over the slave trade and European commerce as well as about local markets and production. Sometimes the effects of these conflicts were counterproductive. This is well illustrated by the rise of this same Kingdom of Dahomey. It destroyed the peaceful trading states of Allada and Whydah to seize control over the trade, and in so doing badly disrupted normal slave trading for some time in the Bight of Benin. Full-scale war could only last a short time, without seriously disrupting traditional trade routes and bringing slave markets to a complete halt. This often happened on the coast when one or more states went all out to destroy their neighbors, and this resulted in what contemporary European accounts reported as "closing the paths" or traditional routes to the coast and, thus, stopping all commerce.

Aside from religious or trade wars, the absolutist nature of many of these states and the large number of royal pretenders due to polygynous royal marriages meant dynastic conflict was a constant in all major states and this often led to civil wars. Even in those kingdoms that had councils of elders that selected monarchs, such as in the Kongo Kingdom south of the Congo River, dynastic struggles were a constant occurrence. The Mali Empire in the Upper Niger region was fairly unique in its use of a powerful royal household to select the monarch and this is often cited as one of the reasons for its unusual centurieslong longevity. Given the relatively poor communications within Africa, the lack of a professional royal bureaucracy in most regions, the failure of some authoritarian rulers to respect traditional local rights, and the fact that most states only had part-time armies because of agricultural constraints meant that increasing state size also led to increasing rebellion at the periphery. In short, Africa was in many respects at the same level as medieval Europe in terms of its state organization and administrative coherence. All this led to a fair amount of civil warfare at all times even in the best-managed states. Some of this warfare, if it represented rebellions of outlying local groups against a relatively secure central power, could lead to a major increase in slave trading without a disruption of traditional networks and markets.

But in the cases of full-scale disintegration of central states, the effect on slave trading could be more negative than positive. In such times of state disintegration, migrating groups forming new states would often go through a phase of banditry. Although such banditry would produce slaves by constant raiding, it ultimately made the trade routes unsafe for travel and destroyed traditional market networks. This was the case with Little Popo on the Slave Coast that was set up by defeated people coming east from Accra. For some time after its foundation, the people of this port city were more a group of bandits than a formal state. Some of this banditry paid off in slave sales, but Little Popo did not become a significant trader with the Europeans until it moved out of the banditry stage and became an essentially peaceful and law-abiding trading society.

Different types of warfare provided varying numbers of slaves for the Atlantic slave trade, but sometimes at a cost to the effective functioning of the slave trade. But Africa was not constantly at war in all places and at all times. A small but steady volume of slaves from essentially peaceful regions was necessary to maintain the trade. Clearly, raiding/trading expeditions mounted by the coastal traders or interior traders was one possibility. Small armed groups of merchants both traded and captured farmers in quick raids. This is what an English observer saw when he visited Old Calabar in 1787. He joined such a raiding/trading fleet made up of some twelve canoes with armed rowers. Going up the Cross River, he noted that:

> in the day time we called at the villages we passed, and purchased our slaves fairly; but in the night we made several excursions on the banks of the river. The canoes were usually left with an armed force: the rest, when landed broke into villages and rushing into the huts of the inhabitants, seized men, women and children promiscuously. (Donnan, *Documents*, 2: 572)

Obviously, this type of activity was more successful in the densely populated but small village systems common among the Ibio in this region. Such raiding would also have been common on the frontiers of larger states where well-integrated multicommunity states did not exist, as well as in more amorphous states where central authority was only lightly exercised at the local level. But in well-integrated states with professional soldiers, constant raiding by outsiders would have been difficult.

It would also be surprising for this type of raiding to go on for too long without a reaction from the local people, either in terms of banding together to protect themselves, or in migrating away from poorly defended places. That these Old Calabar canoe raiders were still using this method on the Cross River after a century of heavy slave trading in this zone seems highly unusual. To both trade and raid in the same area could only occur in places where raiding had not previously occurred on any major scale.

Individual acts of kidnapping in all regions are reported, and these less well-organized and smaller acts of capture were difficult to control even in the most powerful states. In many communities, in fact, kidnapping was considered a crime punishable by enslavement and was considered as serious as murder and adultery. It is also obvious that kidnapping could easily pass over to more structured raiding and that in times of crisis this activity was common.

Given the lack of formal jails, all crimes were either punished by physical acts or enslavement. Officials, royal pretenders, and rebel leaders were often executed. The Europeans reported with some regularity, for example, how the Dahomean king executed his local governors for malfeasance in office or because they represented a threat to his autocratic rule. In 1754 three successive viceroys of the Dahomean king in the port of Whydah were executed, along with two other lesser officials – all during times of internal peace. Murderers, and others considered to have committed vile acts against the community or the local religion, would be killed. But all the more common crimes such as theft, adultery, kidnapping, blasphemy, and witchcraft were usually punished with enslavement. Also, there appears to be enslavement for indebtedness. Though almost all states held that such judicially created slaves were to be used only as local domestic slaves, these judicial proceedings were abused in places, and such slaves were often sold to traders who removed these slaves from their home communities.

The relative importance of each of these means of enslavement must have varied by time and place. In a few well-defined cases, such as the complex trading and regional market network set up by the Aro peoples in what is today southeastern Nigeria between the Niger and Cross Rivers, it was evident that judicial activity with some low-level raiding was the prime source for slaves. In this, the most densely populated zone of West Africa, the Aro created a very complex market through the establishment of small colonies of peaceful traders among large groups of non-Aro peoples. They developed this network from the early seventeenth century to move slaves into the Atlantic slave trade, peacefully linking themselves with other trading networks to the north, east, and west and using other intermediaries to the south to move their slaves to the Biafran coastal ports. Though they employed mercenaries from time to time, the Aro traders worked in an essentially peaceful environment from the seventeenth to the nineteenth century. Here, there were no states, just small landholding communities, and there was little formalized warfare over state construction, dynastic conflicts, or control of trade. This trading network easily moved from slaves to palm oil in the nineteenth century and was still a vibrant and powerful force until British colonial occupation at the end of the nineteenth century. Moreover, it was a reliable organization that delivered a steady volume of several thousands of slaves per annum over decades to the ports of the two Calabars and Bonny on the coast.

This same type of steady trading in local markets has also been reported from the Gold Coast where both the Fante and the Asante got most of their slaves from interior groups at well-defined markets within their own territories. These warrior states also taxed, imprisoned, and fought wars in which slaves were a major booty, but at the same time they peacefully traded for slaves with their neighbors.

As this survey demonstrates, there was no one dominant source of enslavement even in a given region, though force was ultimately the basic instrument used everywhere to obtain slaves. The fact that almost all African states recognized domestic slavery meant that enslavement was an accepted institution within the continent and that the cost of transportation and security of slaves was much less than otherwise would have been the case. The slave coffers coming to market were respected by local peoples, so long as their own members were not affected, and slaves were found in almost all internal markets as well as coastal ones.

Equally, it is evident that since force was required and trading involved many communities and states, the costs of entrance into the slave-trading business were relatively high. Merchants had to organize porters, buy goods for trade, and have extensive personal, kin, or religious contacts over a wide area so as to guarantee peaceful passage, and they clearly needed soldiers or armed followers to protect their purchases from others or prevent their slaves from escaping. In turn, those who raided for slaves had to outfit well-armed and mobile groups, which also needed to be able to resort to peaceful markets as well. All this meant that only relatively wealthy individuals, or well-defined associations of small merchants (found everywhere from Nigeria to Loango), could engage in the slave trade. These merchants had to be skilled in determining local market conditions and to be able to trade with the Europeans, along with using and obtaining credit from all their contacts, including the Europeans, all of which required long-term training and extensive knowledge. Though managed state trading existed in some places, and kings and royal officials traded on their own everywhere, the market for slaves was dominated by merchants, who are reported to have been major actors everywhere, even in such royally dominated trading kingdoms as that of Dahomey. But all studies of the economics of the trade suggest that these merchants never had a monopoly of the market. Europeans were free to trade anywhere on the coast and often refused to trade in areas where prices were too high. In turn, the Africans refused to be confined to any one trading nation and actively fostered competition among buyers. The result was that slave prices varied according to supply and demand and tended to be uniform across all the coastal regions of West Africa.

Moreover, it should be recalled that the African slave trade was ultimately a trade made up of relatively few slaves sold in small groups everywhere. Even with the best organization, and the availability of secure and steady sources for slaves, the purchasing of slaves took time and was done in relatively small lots. Thus, fifty-seven Dutch slavers between 1730 and 1803 spent, on average, 200 days (or over six months) on the African coast purchasing slaves and, on average, bought less than 2 slaves per day. Even in the best of conditions, purchases were usually of small groups of slaves. Thus, for example, the best "loading rate" was 8 slaves per day achieved by the ship Pins Willem V, which in 1759 went to Loango Bay and loaded 478 slaves in 60 days, whereas the worst rate was that of the *Zanggodin*, which went to the Guinea Coast in 1773 and took 377 days to load 127 slaves. The longest stay on the coast for any of these Dutch free-trader ships was the *Geertruyda & Chistina*, which also went to the Guinean Coast and took 508 days to load just 276 slaves. Though earlier Dutch West India Company ships trading from 1687 to 1734 at the fixed fort locations at Elmina took on average just 100 days to load their slaves, they still purchased less than 5 slaves per day.

What occurred for Dutch free traders as well as earlier Dutch monopoly company ships, whether trading on the Gold or Slave Coasts in Guinea or the Loango coast north of the Congo River, was common to all trading ports for all Europeans. Thus, the Portuguese ship *Nossa Senhora da Agua de Lupe e Bom Jesus dos Navegantes* took over three months to purchase 410 slaves in Luanda in 1762–63. Even though most of the slaves purchased were from Portuguese middlemen traders who had time to accumulate slaves on the coast, it took 74 individual transactions averaging just over 5 slaves per transaction to accumulate this number of slaves. The largest purchase was of some 43 slaves, but the modal transaction was just 1 slave per day. Thus, even in the best of conditions, the movement of slaves to the coastal ports was still done in relatively small lots, which makes it even more difficult to determine their origin in terms of warfare, raiding, kidnapping, or judicial enslavement. In fact, the small-lot slave trading would also suggest multiple sources for the slaves in terms of the type of captures accumulated.

Even when European merchants were resident on the coast, their purchases were in small groups. Thus the English merchant Richard Miles, who was governor at the English Cape Coast Castle in the late 1770s and purchased slaves on his own account for later sale to arriving ships, needed 1,308 separate purchases to obtain 2,218 slaves between

1772 and 1780. These slaves were purchased up and down the coast from Accra in the west down to the Cape Coast Castle in the east and were often kept by him for several weeks before the arrival of visiting ships. His ability to "bulk" the slaves – to accumulate them and hold them in pens – enabled him to sell them in large groups to the Europeans at higher than the going prices. His average cost per slave was sixteen pounds sterling worth of goods and he sold them to the arriving ships at twenty pounds sterling worth of trade goods. Most captains were willing to pay this commission in order to load their ships more rapidly and thus cut down on all the costs associated with remaining for long periods on the coast, from local anchorage charges to increasing disease and death. Although he could sometimes make significant purchases of slaves from big local traders, the majority of sales were from unknown merchants for a few slaves. It would also appear that he advanced goods on credit to local African merchants for purchasing slaves in the interior.

This type of what is called "bulking" the slaves in rather large groups for a onetime sale was typical of the early monopoly trading companies. This resulted in much faster turnaround times. This is why the Dutch West India Company ships in the late seventeenth and early eighteenth centuries were able to purchase all their slaves in just over three months, or in half the time that it required a free trader to load his slaves later in the eighteenth century. But such a system required major capital outlays in fixed properties such as forts, and full-time resident merchants, common on the Gold and Slave Coasts and in Angola but rare elsewhere. This was ultimately too expensive a proposition, and in the end free traders dominated in most regions and they abandoned these fixed-cost arrangements for cheaper though longer-term temporary boat trading. It was only under the pressure of the British blockading navy in the mid-nineteenth century that Cuban and Brazilian merchants returned to this practice on the African coast. Needing to load slaves quickly to escape detection by the patrolling British warships, the post-1830 traders set up permanent barracks on the coast for buying slaves over a long period of time so as to load them in a few days when the slave ship arrived from America. But this was an exceptional experience.

If the trade was a normal market arrangement, and particular African merchants obviously profited in the exchange, what were the costs of this trade to the African societies and economies in general? In short, what were the macroeconomic consequences of the slave trade to Africa? This question really raises two fundamental issues: did the goods purchased with slaves add to or detract from African economic development, actual and potential; and, second, what was the demographic impact of the loss of such a large population, both in local and continental terms?

The question of the European imports and African economic growth turns on the issues of the type of goods imported – consumer or capital goods – and their relative impact on local African industrial activity. This is not a simple or easy question to answer. To give just one example, iron bars were a major import throughout Africa and were used by local blacksmiths to produce tools, weapons, and utensils of all kinds. But the importation of this high-quality northern European iron had a negative impact on the African iron mining and smelting industry, since the imported product was cheaper and possibly better than the African made one. It is also argued by some scholars that the East Indian cotton goods were a determent to the local textile industry in many parts of West Africa. These were often used as wraps and not processed in any way by local seamstresses. They were also thought to replace coarser locally made cotton and palm-leaf cloths. But in all regions of Africa, local artisanal textile production continued into the post-slave-trade era, which suggests that local cloth was probably quite competitive with European imports at the lower end of the scale, at least until the British were able to introduce their coarser cloths in the late nineteenth century on a massive scale.

The consumer goods introduced by the Europeans obviously led to increased consumption but had a varying impact on the local production of competing goods. Liquor, for example, was already produced in Africa before and during the trade. Palm wine and various grain beers were consumed by the Africans, who also now consumed American cane-produced rum or European brandies. European traders did not introduce this form of consumption, nor did these imported goods eliminate local production, which continued on through the period of the slave trade. Even tobacco imports had some positive effects. Brazilian and American-produced tobacco was a new item introduced into the African market, creating a demand that led to some local tobacco production within Africa itself.

Sumptuary items such as beads and jewelry were clearly imported by upper-status individuals and tended to mark elite distinction from the masses. Some of these sumptuary items were incorporated into traditional dress and furthered artisanal activity, and some of it replaced traditional jewelry and bead production within Africa itself and led to the decline of local industries. The importation of large quantities of cowry

shells was in fact a positive feature since it promoted the monetariza-
tion of the West African economy, which in turn deepened traditional
markets and encouraged regional specialization and market integration
of previously subsistence agriculturalists in many parts of Africa. All of
this market activity greatly stimulated local production, either in terms
of expanding traditional industries from fishing and hunting to farming
and mining, or creating new local industries that long survived the end
of the Atlantic slave trade.

The slave caravans also opened up new complex trading links and new
local markets, thus integrating the Mediterranean with the Guinean
Coast markets far to the south, or linking together most of Central Africa
from ocean to ocean. These roads and paths were opened to domestic
trade as well as slave trading, which in turn further monetarized the
continental economy and increased the level of exchange, trading, and
production. Finally, many slaves were purchased with African goods or
were fed with African-produced supplies, thus fostering a major agricultural growth, which was spearheaded by the European introduction of
American crops, above all, maize and cassava (manioc). But even with
all these new goods entering the local markets, their impact was small.
Even at the height of the importation of European goods in the late eighteenth century, European imports only reached £2.1 million sterling of
goods per annum, which probably represented less than 5 percent of the
total West African income for the 25 million or so resident population.

Although prior to 1700 Africa could export large quantities of ivory
and gold, which found ready markets overseas, and would produce palm
oil for export from the 1820s to the 1860s far outdistancing the value of
slave exports, from 1700 to about 1820 the primary export was human
beings. While the loss of these people was probably not as great in
relation to resident population as the loss of emigrants to the resident
populations of such classic emigration countries as Ireland or Portugal
in the eighteenth and nineteenth centuries, there was a fundamental
difference. To produce those slaves, violence was used and it did have
a cost in terms of economic growth. Though there are conflicting ways
in determining African population growth or decline, there is enough
evidence to show local population decline on the western coast as a
result of wars and banditry and the abandonment of viable agricultural
lands because of the fear of slave raiding. It was especially this negative
economic factor and its accompanying diversion of resources to military
activity that most negatively affected the West African economy.

After numerous attempts at estimating the African populations –
none of which was officially counted in the slave trade era – historians
and demographers have come to a rough consensus that the population
exposed to the Atlantic slave trade numbered some 25 million in 1700.
This was about half of the total population of sub-Saharan Africa. At
most, this population was growing at around 0.5 percent per annum.
This growth estimate is based on the calculation of a very high crude
death rate of 35–45 per thousand, and a high crude birthrate of some
40–45 per thousand population, leaving an approximate positive growth
of 5 per thousand in most years. Though all African women married and
experienced fertility early, long lactation periods and various cultural
practices kept the spacing between children to some three years and
resulted in lower numbers of children being born than otherwise might
have occurred in this natural reproductive environment. This crude
birthrate is greater than the crude birthrates among slaves in the West
Indies, but lower than the 55 per thousand births reached among North
American continental slaves. Death rates were quite high due to serious
ecological problems within Africa that in many regions led to drought
and famine, but also to a very severe disease environment. Even though
Africans had a less violent response to many of the diseases that were
fatal to Europeans, malaria and other tropical diseases were killers and
kept mortality rates high.

If one accepts a 0.5 percent rate of growth for a population of
25 million, this would give a hypothetical increase of some 125,000
new persons every year. If at the height of the slave trade some 80,000
persons were being forced to enter the trade, they represented almost
two-thirds of the potential growth and would have reduced that growth
rate from 0.5 percent to a barely positive rate of less than 0.2 percent. Even those who challenge this model accept that the ratio of
out migrations was probably no higher than 2–3 per thousand in this
period. This is obtained by estimating an average of 60,000 persons
being shipped across the Atlantic from the mid-eighteenth century to
the mid-nineteenth century. If one accepts an even lower growth rate
of 0.3 percent per annum, which could be reasonably accepted as a possible lower-bound estimate, then the 75,000 surplus population barely
exceeded the out-migration of slaves, especially if the eastern slave trade
migrations are included.

A more radical estimate of the impact of the slave trade on African
populations recently has been proposed by using a controversial ap-
proach of backward projections from known contemporary regional

populations. It is argued that the population of western Africa actually declined by 2 million between 1700 and 1850. The estimate is that the western African population declined from a projected 25 million to 23 million in this 150-year period. Had the population grown at a conservative 0.3 percent per annum in the same period, it would have reached 39.3 million in 1850. Thus, the Atlantic slave trade could have cost a total loss of 16.3 million Africans in 1850 – the 2 million less in 1850 than were estimated to have been resident in 1700, and the 14.3 million potential persons who would have been added had the population grown at 0.3 percent per annum from 1700.

Whatever these various estimates of loss, it cannot be denied that the transatlantic slave trade did have an impact, at the very least, in slowing African population growth considerably, if not in bringing on an actual decline. Unquestionably, the estimated 4.3 million slave and free persons of African descent who were resident in America in the 1790s would have made a significant contribution to the growth of the African population had they remained in Africa.

If total West African population changes cannot be fully assessed, there is little question that detailed studies of local regions have suggested quite important population declines. The 1 million or so living in Senegambia in 1700 suffered their most severe population losses in the early eighteenth century but seem to have recovered positive growth in the post-1750 era. In contrast, the 2.5 million or so in the Upper Guinea Coast did well before 1750 and only experienced declining population in the second half of the eighteenth century. The 2 million plus of the Gold Coast, because of the late beginnings of the slave trade, apparently suffered the least, with perhaps no decline in the resident population. The over 4 million in the Bight of Benin, of which the Slave Coast was the most important part, suffered the most severe decline of any region in western Africa. From the 1690s to 1850 its resident population was in constant decline from probably close to 4 million persons to about half that number in the worst estimation model. Moreover, documentary evidence seems to support this conclusion. It was reported from the Slave Coast, for example, that elephant herds were repopulating the coast in the early nineteenth century after their virtual extinction from this region in the early eighteenth century, which argues for a decline in local human hunting populations. The Biafran coast and its 4 to 5 million people did well until the last decades of the eighteenth century and then probably experienced a decline in population until 1850. To the south, the close to 4 million people in the Loango coast region experienced a steady decline from 1700 and do not seem to have reached positive growth rates until well after 1859. In contrast, the negative impact in Angola was far less with its over 5 million population growing until 1750 and then recovering in the midnineteenth century well before that of neighboring Luanda. Finally, the very late start of the Mozambique trade meant that its 3 million or so peoples did not experience negative growth rates until the middle decades of the nineteenth century and then recovered relatively quickly.

What does this pattern of growth mean? Clearly, it is comparable with, if less intense than, the experience by such major out-migration countries as England, Ireland, Italy, and Portugal in the eighteenth and nineteenth centuries. But it would appear that the Atlantic emigration of Europeans, which finally passed the volume of the slave trade in the 1840s, had a much higher amount of out-migration within a higher rate of population growth, thus bringing its impact closer to the African pattern. These countries were either underdeveloped or developed with little relationship in and of itself to the intensity of out-migration and population loss. Population loss alone does not necessarily lead to economic decline even if the resident population suffers a long-term pattern of negative demographic growth. But unlike the European migrants, close to half of whom returned to Europe, there was very little return migration of Africans, nor was there any repatriation of immigrant savings to the Old World, which was so important to the economies of Ireland, Italy, and Portugal. Thus, the loss of these young workers was total for Africa, with no inflow of savings possible. This loss, coupled with the violence expended to enslave these workers, makes the negative impact of population change obvious and important in the African case. Moreover, the Atlantic slave trade was not the only out-migration of slaves from Africa in this period. It is estimated that roughly 18 million Africans were exported from Africa from 1500 to 1900, but only 11 million of them were shipped into the Atlantic economy. These other slaves were shipped into the Indian Ocean or across the Sahara to slave markets in the East, and they also became permanent losses to their countries of origin.

One lasting impact of the slave trade within Africa was the growth of the internal slave trade. Although slavery within Africa preceded and accompanied the Atlantic slave trade, it would now become even more important after the Western trade in slaves ended. It has been estimated that at the height of the slave trade, there were as many slaves held domestically within Africa as there were in America – probably on the order of 3 to 5 million. As these international slave trades declined, local slave prices declined and slavery within Africa actually increased, so that by 1850 there were more slaves in Africa than there were in America – probably now numbering close to 10 million. Slaves were now used by Africans to produce new exports such as palm oil and rubber for world markets. They also became a basic component in local agricultural production and an important element in the transport network of porters and canoeists. Though free farmers and producers remained a major component in both the local and export markets, slavery now played a much more important role within the African economy until the very end of the nineteenth century. Thus, the end of the Atlantic slave trade did not bring an end to enslavement within Africa.

CHAPTER 6

THE MIDDLE PASSAGE

Having been purchased on the African coast, the slaves destined for America would cross the Atlantic in a journey that became known as the "Middle Passage." The manner in which these slaves were carried and the mortality they suffered have been one of the most notorious issues in the study of the Atlantic slave trade. A popular literature has painted this part of the slave experience as uniquely evil and inherently more inhuman than any other of the horrors of the slave life. This has a great deal to do with the early abolitionists who found that this part of the African enslavement process was the most easily attacked. The merchants of the trade could be opposed with impunity, whereas the American slave-owning class could not be attacked as easily. A group of eighteenth- and early nineteenth-century British propagandists developed their portrayal of the trade out of the belief that the entire transportation experience was an unmitigated disaster. But even one of the most important of these early writers, Thomas Fowell Buxton, argued that only some 18 percent of the mortality suffered in the trade occurred aboard ship, and that almost 71 percent occurred in the transportation of the slave to the coast, and the rest was due to the adjustment to New World conditions after landing. To put the so-called Middle Passage in context, it should be recalled that the water crossing on average took a month from Africa to Brazil and two months from the West African coast to the Caribbean and North America. But most slaves spent at a minimum six months to a year from capture until they boarded the European ships, with time waiting on the coast to board the ship alone being on average three months.

Nevertheless, for European and American writers, the Middle Passage has tended to capture the popular imagination and absorb the moral outrage directed at the whole slave experience. As to why this occurred may be explained not only by the initial interest of the abolitionist, but by the fact that it is the part of the slave trade system that provides the best recording of information dealing with the numbers of slaves involved and their mortality in transit. The European practice of detailed record keeping and of government regulation of the transatlantic traffic in slaves provided abundant information on this leg of the trip, compared with the little known internal movement of slaves within Africa. Finally, there is the undoubted importance of the European involvement in the Middle Passage.

Thus, shipboard mortality became the focus of many of the debates in western Europe regarding the slave trade, and there was concern with both the mortality of slaves during the transatlantic passage and the deaths of the crew. While the shipboard mortality of slaves was used to demonstrate the harshness of the trade, it was the high mortality among the crew that was used by the British abolitionist, Thomas Clarkson, in his arguments to end the slave trade. To those who supported the slave trade as a "nursery for seamen," Clarkson argued that, to the contrary, the rates of mortality of the crew on slave ships were considerably higher than for crews on other routes, including the commodity trade with Africa.

Although these earlier abolitionist writers were familiar with the trade and did not make the argument that slaves were almost costless to the Europeans, this became a major theme of later writers. It was assumed in this popular literature that the low cost of the slaves made it profitable to pack in as many as the ship could hold without sinking and then accept high rates of mortality during the Atlantic crossing. If any slaves delivered alive were pure profit, then even the loss of several hundred would have made economic sense. But if the slaves were not a costless or cheap item to purchase, then the corresponding argument about "tight packing" also makes little sense.

In previous chapters, it has been shown that the purchase of slaves on the African coast was not a costless transaction, nor were the African middlemen passive bystanders. The African market was well connected to the world market and Africans demanded Asian, European, and American goods for their slaves. The more European demand developed for slaves, the higher was the African charge of trade goods that went to make up the slave price. If these goods were expensive items for the Europeans to purchase – and, as noted, two-thirds of the cost of a slaving expedition was made up by the cost of goods used to purchase slaves – then any loss of slaves en route would directly affect the ultimate profitability of the voyage. In fact, high slave mortality on the crossing resulted in financial loss on the trip. It has been estimated for the eighteenth-century French slave trade – which has the best information on costs – that each transatlantic slave death on a ship carrying 300 slaves would reduce profits by 0.67 percentage points. Thus, a mortality rate of 15 percent could reduce trading profits by as much as 30 percent.

Clearly, losing slaves in the Middle Passage meant losing profit on the trade. Does this mean that the Europeans provided slaves with unusual accommodations and/or amenities for the voyage? Far from it, since slaves were carried in the most dense configurations of any group transported by Europeans across oceans in the sixteenth to the nineteenth century. But it does mean that the manner of carrying slaves, however "tightly packed" they were in the ships, did not create any increased mortality. Slaves had less room than did contemporary troops or convicts being transported. In almost all the trades, the average-size ship was small by contemporary standards – usually half the size of a normal cargo ship of the period. The Liverpool slavers clearing for Africa in the late 1790s averaged 201 tons per vessel, with two-thirds of the vessels being between 177 and 241 tons. These slavers carried 1.6 slaves per register ship's ton, with 5 to 7 square feet of deck area given to each slave. Most of the ships were outfitted with partial decks and platforms in the space below the main deck and above the second or 'tween deck. All of these ships had been specially modified for service in the slave trade. A typical ship of 200 register British tons (which in fact was close to the alternative Burden ton figures) would have a keel length of 68 feet, a beam of 24 feet, and a hold about 12 feet deep.

In terms of internal arrangements, this space aboard slave ships was left open and would be divided into different decks depending on the number, age, and sex of slaves to be carried and the registered tonnage of a vessel. For the ships of 250 tons and above, it was usual to construct between 2.5 to 3.5 decks, and for the smaller ships 2 to 3 decks were the norm. Clearly, all but the very smallest ships were converted with partial deck platforms and other spaces for transporting slaves. Drawings of internal arrangements for slave spaces are extant for the *Brooks*, an English slave ship operating in this period and pictured in all the subsequent studies of the trade, and also for *La Vigilante*, a French ship from earlier in the century. For the *Brooks*, 4 decks were used with partial platform decks above the second deck and above the main deck. The Brooks weighed 300 tons, and the drawings show about 609 slaves.

This arrangement gives a deck area estimated at over 3,000 square feet, which provided an average of just under 7 square feet per slave. *La Vigilante* is shown at 240 tons with 347 slaves and probably marks the lowest bound estimate with a deck area that results in 5.6 square feet per slave. For some British slave ships measured by Parliament in 1788, the average space allotted was between 6 and 7 square feet. These results agree very closely with data for many other English and French ships in the late eighteenth century at the height of the trade, and before the various English acts regulating space were enacted – the one of 1799 calling for 8 square feet per slave aboard ship.

Given these temporary deck arrangements and the basic internal space available, it is evident that increasing tonnage did not greatly increase space available for slaves. Also, the smaller the ship, the larger the deck space available for the slaves. Taking two extreme examples from the eighteenth-century trade to illustrate this point, we can see how it functions. What is the difference in space available for each slave in a vessel of 400 tons taking on 600 slaves (or 1.5 slaves per ton, which was close to the average) and a 100-ton vessel carrying 300 Africans for a very high ratio of 3 slaves per ton? The latter ratio of slaves per ton would seemingly indicate very crowded conditions. But in fact the 400-ton vessel contained only two-and-a-half times more deck area (not four times the deck area) than the 100-ton vessel. Thus, the smaller ship was able to carry 3 slaves per ton compared to just 1.5 slaves per ton with little significant difference between actual space available. The impression is that the larger ship provides much more space per slave with reduced crowding. By the ratio of deck areas, however, only 21 percent more space is available on the larger ship. This is not very significant as the smaller ship provides 5 square feet of deck area as compared with the larger ship's 6 square feet.

In fact, for a large sample of eighteenth-century English slave trade vessels, smaller ships usually stuck close to the average of 1.6 slaves per ton and thus consistently had much more deck space available for slaves. Thus, with all ships averaging close to 1.6 slaves per ton, those ships weighing 101 to 150 tons offered an area of 5.8 square feet per slave, for those from 151 to 250 tons the area was 5.5 square feet per slave, and the over 250 tons provided an average of 5.1 square feet per slave. But whether giving 5 or 6 square feet per slave, or carrying 1.6 slaves per ton or above, in no large collection of slave voyages currently available is there a correlation between the manner of carrying slaves (either using a tonnage or space indicator) and the mortality they suffered. So, while slaves were very obviously packed tightly together, their mortality was not significantly affected by the pattern of housing them for the transatlantic voyage.

But slaves were not the only ones carried in limited quarters on sailing ships, and the question remains as to how high their mortality was in comparison to that suffered by convicts, troops, and free immigrants. Thus, while the manner of carrying slaves did not influence changes in their mortality rates, those rates may have been higher in general than for other large groups of people engaged in transoceanic travel. Studies of other types of voyages and their comparisons with the slave trade indicate that, while mortality rates for ships carrying convicts, contract laborers, military troops, and free immigrants may have been as high as for slaves in the eighteenth century and earlier, these rates dropped far faster and to lower levels than was ever achieved by slave ships. As did the slave ships, these voyages experienced declines in their mortality rates over time, and in a number of cases, the magnitude of the decline exceeded that of the slave ships. In all such transportation trades of the Europeans, the number of persons per ton on the slave ships was always higher than the persons per ton experienced on other migrant voyages. This means that while the numbers carried per ton might help explain why slave ships had higher or less declining mortality than did other transport vessels, within the general range of slaves per ton carried there was no additional effect, despite the arguments made in the "packing" debate.

Even at the sometimes achieved low 6 percent mortality rate shown in the Angolan trade in the first decade of the nineteenth century, these mortality rates for slaves would appear high for other comparable migrant population movements by sea in the nineteenth century. Of these movements, the best studied so far is the convict labor transportation to Australia. These convict ships, despite their much lower ratios of persons carried to tonnage (averaging less than 0.5 persons per ton), experienced mortality rates not dissimilar to the slave trade. Thus, in the period from 1787 to 1800, some 10.4 percent of the total of 7,547 convicts on 41 ships (whose crossing averaged 191 days) perished on the high seas. This rate, however, quickly dropped to 4.1 percent for the 8,778 convicts who left in some 55 ships in the period from 1810 to 1815 (with average sailings of 168 days). Thereafter, though the volume of convict migration kept increasing, reaching its maximum level in the late 1820s and the 1830s (averaging some 4,785 per annum), the rate of mortality was consistently below 1 percent of those who left Europe. It should be recalled when comparing these rates, that these were longer voyages, and may have had much higher numbers of elderly persons subject to higher risks of mortality. But what is most impressive about these data is that the death rates fell so rapidly in this trade and then remained consistently low for the rest of the century. They were in fact somewhat lower than the regular emigrant movements from Europe to America in the same period.

Although the more useful comparison for the slave trade would be with the eighteenth- and nineteenth-century data from the European peasant migrations to America, surprisingly much less systematic data are currently available than for the slave or convict migrations. What little that does exist, however, would seem to suggest that the eighteenth-century immigrant mortality rates were similar to the slave mortality rates in the same period. That these rates may not be quite comparable should be stressed here, since it is possible that among the emigrants there were larger ratios of very young children and older persons, which would mean that the emigrant population had a higher proportion of its members at risk than among the slaves. Nevertheless, though these mortality rates were similar in the eighteenth century, immigrant mortality dropped as dramatically as convict mortality in the early decades of the nineteenth century, reaching the consistently low figure of 2 percent mortality and under in the midcentury crossings. Thus, the 132,246 emigrants who shipped from Liverpool to New York in 1854 experienced a death rate of 1.2 percent. A year earlier, American records show that the mortality of 96,950 immigrants in 312 vessels arriving in New York in the four-month period from 1 September to 1 December was 2.0 percent, while the 395,325 immigrants who arrived in all American ports in the year 1853 reported a rate of under 1 percent.

Until the late 1850s, sailing ships predominated in the carrying trade of immigrants, and their rates of mortality in the sea voyage were consistently higher than steam vessels. Of the 950,916 steerage passengers who arrived aboard steamers between 1864 and 1869 in the port of New York, the mean mortality was only 0.18 percent, and this was for an average of 425 steerage passengers per voyage. At the same time, the sailing vessels on average carried only 219 steerage passengers, yet their mortality was 0.9 percent for the sea voyage. This average mortality, just as in the slave trade, had a high degree of variance. But even in the epidemic year of 1866, steamers experienced a mortality rate of only 0.5 percent while sailing ships went to a high of 1.1 percent. What these figures would seem to suggest is that time at sea was as important an

indicator of immigrant mortality as it was in the earlier slave mortality.
Also, it can be assumed, at least until the early 1860s, that the average
immigrant mortality on the trip to America in the nineteenth century
remained at the 1 to 2 percent level, since sailing vessels continued to
predominate. Thus as late as 1856, only 3 percent of the immigrants
arriving by steerage to America came by steamer; and in the port of
New York, sailing vessels still predominated in the immigrant trade
until 1864, a year in which they accounted for 57 percent of the landed
immigrants. The big killers in the mid-nineteenth century immigrant
trade were somewhat different from those in the slave trade, being, in
order of importance, "ship's fever" or typhus, cholera, and smallpox.
Unlike the slave trade, there also appeared to be a sharp difference in
the mortality experience of the European ships engaged in the trade,
with the English immigrant ships consistently having the highest disease
and mortality rates in the trade.

But what was the mortality rate of the slaves shipped across the
Atlantic? Did it change over time? Was it "high" or "low" and what were
the factors that most influenced its incidence? These are the questions
which I will try to answer in the following part of this chapter. In dealing
with the mortality rate, most writers have defined it as the number of
slaves who died on ship in the Middle Passage either recorded directly in
the contemporary records or calculated as the difference between slaves
who boarded and slaves who landed divided by the number of slaves
loaded on the African coast. The most significant pattern for understanding mortality in the Middle Passage is the very wide distribution
of mortality rates by voyage. This is found even when holding other
features constant, such as sailing times, ship sizes, African embarkation
areas, and the age and sexual composition of slaves carried. There was
a broad range of outcomes, with very many quite different experiences,
even for the same captains or the same nationality of shippers. Very high
mortality rates tend to be associated with unexpectedly long voyages,
or to unusual outbreaks of disease, but, in general, it is the very broad
range of outcomes rather than any bunching at specific mortality rates
that has been the main characteristic of the transatlantic slave trade for
most of its existence.

From the earliest recorded voyages in the late sixteenth and early
seventeenth centuries when the death rates averaged 20 percent, slave
shipbound mortality declined to less than one-half this level in the
late eighteenth century. While the decline was relatively steady over
time, there was an especially large decline in the last quarter of the

eighteenth century. As sharp as was the decline in the mean of slave mortality rates, the median of slave ship mortality declined even more rapidly, with the entire distribution of mortality rates shifting down. There was a great increase in the share of voyages coming in at relatively low mortalities. Correspondingly, the percentage of ships with mortality rates above a selected threshold level fell, meaning that over time there were relatively fewer ships with very high mortality rates (see Figure 6.1), and more and more ships were coming in at close to the mean mortality.

The progressive decline of average, modal, and median death rates from the sixteenth through the nineteenth century is seen in all European trades (see Table 6.1). In the last thirty years of the slave trade, the period of the so-called illegal trade, mortality rates may have risen somewhat, but they did not reach pre-1800 levels. Although all European carriers saw the ships arriving with fewer slave deaths, it was probably the British who experienced the most rapid decline in mortality rates in the eighteenth century, even if they did not have the lowest rates on any particular route. Nevertheless, it was still the Portuguese who achieved the lowest known rates in the trade, with ships arriving in Rio de Janeiro in the 1825–30 period experiencing a 6 percent mortality rate in the Middle Passage. This being the case, recent attempts by some Anglo-Saxon scholars to see the Portuguese as particularly "dirty" or unusual in their handling of slaves is quite strange. It is evident that all the trades with the comparable timing and volume of migrations experienced similar rates of African slave mortality. The English may have generated higher returns from lowered costs than most other traders, but there is no other indication to distinguish them in terms of the manner by which they carried their slaves, housed them, fed them, or otherwise treated them from any of the other trades. Slave rebellions aboard ship occurred in all trades, and the British were not immune. They, in short, were no more humanitarian traders than were the Dutch, French, or Portuguese.

Although there were no fundamental differences in mortality rates among European flag carriers over time, there were persisting differences in mortality from various African ports of departure (see Table 6.2). These differences in the mortality rate remained even as overall rates declined. A rough measure of this pattern can be seen by examining the seven general African exporting regions for five time periods.

The results show that three regions are either always above or always below the average mortality rate for that time period, and two differ

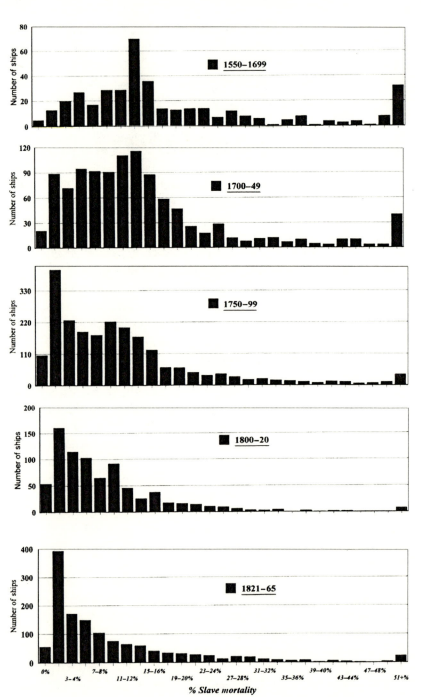

Figure 6.1. Slave mortality in the Middle Passage, 1550–1865.

Table 6.1. *Average Slave Mortality in the Middle Passage by Flag Carrier, 1590–1867*

Period	Portuguese		Spanish		French		English		Dutch		Total		
	Mortality	Ships	Mortality	Ships	Mortality	Ships	Mortality	Ships	Mortality	Ships	Mean	SD	Ships
1590–1699		n.a	29.8%	67	n.a	n.a	21.3%	195	14.3%	139	20.3%	16.1	401
1700–1749		n.a		n.a		n.a	15.4%	176	15.8%	427	15.6%	14.2	1,091
1750–1807		262		n.a	15.6%	488	11.1%	955	13.9%	613	12.0%	12.2	2,571
1808–1829	8.8%	1,211	14.4%	50	12.5%	698					8.8%	11.2	1,350
1830–1867	11.3%	239	9.5%	98	13.3%	21					11.5%	12.7	553
TOTAL	8.7%	1,712	17.0%	215	13.8%	1,210	13.1%	1,329	14.6%	1,180	12.4%	13.1	5,966

Notes: The Dutch and English trades were illegal after 1808; in all other cases, n.a. means data not available. SD = standard deviation.

Source: David Eltis, Stephan D. Behtendt, David Richardson, and Herbert S. Klein, *The Transatlantic Slave Trade, 1562–1867: A Database CD-Rom* (Cambridge, 1998).

Table 6.2. *Average Slave Mortality by African Region of Departure, 1590–1867*

Period	Senegambia		Sierra Leone-Windward		Gold Coast		Benin		Biafra		West Central Africa		South-east Africa	
	Mortality	Ships	Mortality	Ships	Mortality	Ships	Mortality	Ships	Mortality	Ships	Mortality	Ships	Mortality	Ships
1590–1699	13.6%	33	11.0%	12	21.6%	69	17.5%	83	29.5%	30	22.9%	103		
1700–1749	10.6%	94	12.0%	17	15.5%	243	17.1%	301	43.2%	24	12.1%	169	29.5%	1
1750–1807	15.4%	109	9.3%	190	12.4%	660	13.5%	186	14.9%	283	10.0%	705	25.1%	13
1808–1829	4.7%	9	4.9%	38	4.2%	68	7.5%	88	19.4%	81	6.6%	855	17.1%	185
1830–1867	8.8%	5	6.6%	39	7.5%	1	6.5%	106	12.0%	84	11.0%	227	20.6%	54
TOTAL	12.8%	250	8.6%	296	13.2%	1,041	13.7%	764	17.4%	502	9.5%	2,059	18.3%	253

Source: David Eltis, Stephan D. Behrendt, David Richardson, and Herbert S. Klein, *The Transatlantic Slave Trade, 1562–1867: A Database CD-Rom* (Cambridge, 1998).

in direction in only one period. All regions had mortality rate declines over time and generally had their lowest rates in the nineteenth century. While the lowest rate recorded involved those slaves coming from the Congo and Angola (the so-called West Central Africa region), and this is for the region with the shortest average sailing times to America, in general, the times at sea cannot alone explain the magnitude of differences in mortality rates by African port. It has been argued that port mortality differences are due to factors local to Africa. Thus, some ports were more affected by malaria and yellow fever than others, with this seemingly the case in the Gambia River region (Senegambia) and along the Biafran coast. Other regions from time to time were affected by ecological or political crises that affected food production and distribution, and in turn weakened the migrating population and created more intense disease environments. These regional differences expressed themselves not only in differing mortality, but there was also a difference in the age and sex of the departing migrants by port of exit as well as time. How this relates to specific African conditions is not totally understood, but it has been suggested that increasing "exports" of children and women from given areas reflect a serious crisis in local societies, be it ecological or political. This in turn would also reflect itself in differing mortality results. Finally, it has been suggested that local African food crises would affect the mortality rates and the spacing of mortality in the voyage, with most of the deaths coming in the early stages of the voyage and therefore still reflecting conditions in the ports of origin.

Given that the level of mortality at sea was mostly defined by the shipboard experience, the differences in the transatlantic mortality rates based on African port of departure more likely reflected the conditions in Africa than the characteristics of the ships and the voyages from these regions. Local disease environments, long-term ecological changes, and short-term shifts in weather and growing conditions were obviously important influences. Equally, changes in catchment areas within Africa, and shifts that occurred because of local political and economic changes, influenced the age and sex composition of the slaves sent as well as their overall physical condition. Given differing mortality rates for children and adults, for example, the higher ratio of children sent, the higher the overall mortality would be. Finally, African diseases or famine would also have an impact on adult mortality in the trade because of overall poorer health conditions resulting from these events.

In regard to length of voyage, there was some increase in mortality with numbers of days at sea, particularly for those unexpectedly long voyages on which water and provisions ran short and accelerated the spread of disease. For the great number of voyages, however, there was little variation that could be directly explained by the differences in the number of days at sea. Moreover the sailing times remained relatively stable for most of the eighteenth century and only started to decline in the mid- to late nineteenth century. But in both periods, there was little difference that the length of a voyage from a given port made in the mortality rates.

From studies of numerous immigrant and troop migrations in the nineteenth century, the important role played by administrative reforms and the various empirical approaches in the absence of correct medical knowledge were seen to be the major factors in lowering the rates of mortality over time. In the case of the slave trade, state regulation, though it appeared as early as the seventeenth century, probably played a more limited role. Rather, it was largely privately initiated changes in technology and organization that most likely explain the general trends in mortality over time. It would seem that early experiences of very high mortality led traders to reform two basic elements in their trading practices. The first was to move slowly toward a modal ship's size that was best designed both to trade along the coast and rivers of Africa and to transport the slaves most swiftly and efficiently to America. This size ship would be unique to the slave trade and would be the norm for almost all national slave trades in the eighteenth and through most of the nineteenth century. Governments were not indifferent to this problem of carrying capacity and mortality. The Portuguese pushed for a space limit on slaves carried as early as 1684, and the English would seriously enforce such changes beyond what had been already achieved privately in 1799. But the traders themselves anticipated most of this legislation in creating a special fleet to deal with the trade. They were even the first of the merchant fleets to adopt copper sheathing, a major factor in increasing speed and ship longevity in tropical waters and previously limited to warships. Along with changes in carrying slaves, there developed common arrangements for provisioning the slaves en route. Although there was some pressure from state regulation as early as the seventeenth century, the more efficient provisioning of food and water for the slaves for expected voyage length came about through trial and error and a slow evolution of common standards on all routes and among all traders. Both of these elements were vital to the effective delivery of healthy slaves to America, and this information was passed from trader to trader and across national boundaries.

The general trend in ships' sizes was to move from a wide range of ships with the majority being of very low tonnage often carrying high ratios of slaves to a middle-range-tonnage vessel carrying fewer slaves per ton. Moreover, this trend was common to all slave trades regardless of the local national tonnage measurements used. This meant that there was a progressive increase of slaves carried per ship as average tonnage increased and a more steady ratio of slaves per ton was achieved. This was a common and progressive trend among all traders. The best data for this come from the English and French slave trades of the late seventeenth and early eighteenth centuries. While the English and French tonnage figures are not the same measure, they are comparable, especially for broader-tonnage categories. The early French ships exhibit a strikingly similar pattern of distribution as that shown by the Royal African Company ships trading for slaves from England in the 1691–1713 period. Of the 113 slavers that sailed from Nantes in this earlier period, only 55 percent were in the mean tonnage range of 100 to 299 tons. Of the 184 comparable English ships, only 57 percent were in this category. The only major difference between the two was the fact that the smaller vessels of under 100 tons were more heavily represented among the French traders than among the contemporaneous English traders.

Clearly, such a dispersion of ships' tonnage proved a detriment to efficient trading, for both the English and French trades of the eighteenth century showed a remarkably similar movement toward the concentration of ships in the mean tonnage range of 100 to 299 tons. Thus, the French ships in the mid-eighteenth century increased their share of these ships to 68 percent, a figure that jumped to 82 percent in the post-1763 period. This later figure is, in fact, almost identical to the British tonnage distribution of 130 slavers that traded to Jamaica in the 1782–1808 period, which registered 80 percent in this mean tonnage category.

That an optimum type of ship was emerging in the trade of the eighteenth century is especially evident when we compare slave tonnage to that of the tonnage of other trades. Just as average slave tonnage in the Liverpool trade of the eighteenth century was quite low compared, for example, with the average tonnage of the West Indian merchantmen, so too, the same pattern was evident among the Nantes slave ships with their equivalent West Indian merchant ships. Thus, in the period from

1749 through 1783, some 2,266 West Indiamen sailed for America from Nantes and averaged 261 tons. The 575 slave ships that left Nantes in this period, and whose tonnage is preserved, averaged only 157 tons, a full hundred tons less. Nor was the average tonnage of these *négriers*, as the French slave trade vessels were called, appreciably above the average tonnage engaged in the coastal (or cabotage) trade, whose 1,046 ships during this same period averaged 127 tons. Thus, like the English, the Nantes merchant fleet clearly differentiated between the smaller *négrier* and the larger *droiture* or West Indiamen vessel. Despite somewhat different manners of estimating tonnage, all trades were carrying 1.5 to 2.5 slaves per ton and averaging at the height of their trades between 350 and 450 slaves per voyage, meaning that the average ships were in the 150–250 tonnage range at the height of the trade.

That this same approximate tonnage was the basic range among all European traders up to the last two decades of the trade in the late nineteenth century, indicates that this size of ship seemed best to fit the successful carrying potential of the trade and the ability to navigate the rivers and ports of Africa. As was noted earlier, the fact that these slave-trade vessels were much smaller ships than Europeans used in either the West Indian or East Indian trades, goes a long way to explaining why the belief in a triangular trade (European goods to Africa, slaves for America, and sugar for Europe all on the same voyage) is largely a myth. The majority of American crops reached European markets in much larger and specially constructed West Indian vessels designed primarily for this shuttle trade; the majority of slavers returned with small cargoes or none at all; and in the largest slave trade of them all – that of Brazil – no slavers either departed from or returned to Europe.

Not only was tonnage smaller than for normal trading ships, but slave ships of whatever sail arrangement or construction also had design elements unique to the slave trade. Their temporary decks used to house the slaves were all divided by bulkheads that were made of open grates, and the deck hatches were also covered by such open latticed grates. On several of the ships for which designs exist, particularly the L'Aurore built in Nantes in 1784 (Figures 6.2–6.4), there were even opened ventilation ports (with hatches to be closed in inclement weather) on the sides of the ships between the gun ports and above the platforms built over the lower deck, creating air flow across the platforms. With all these openings in operation, outside air was forced into the slave rooms through these "side lights" or ventilation ports, circulated through the bulkheads, and escaped through the deck hatches, creating an unusual

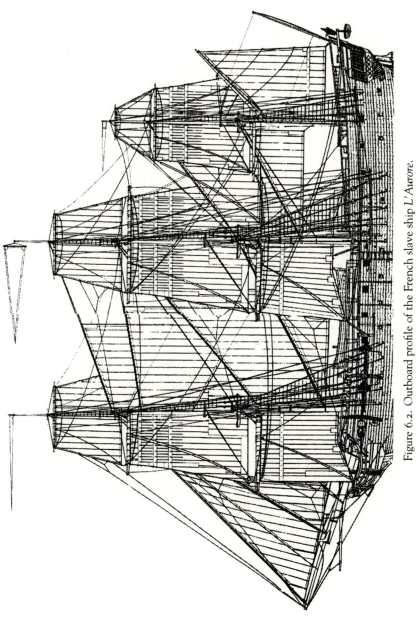

Figure 6.2. Outboard profile of the French slave ship *L'Aurore*.

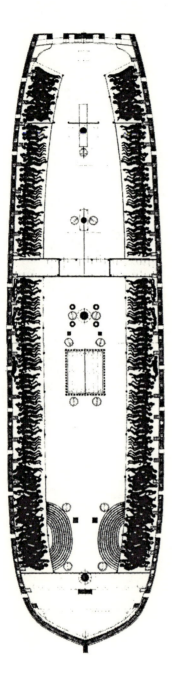

Figure 6.3. Sleeping arrangement for slaves on the lower deck and the platform.

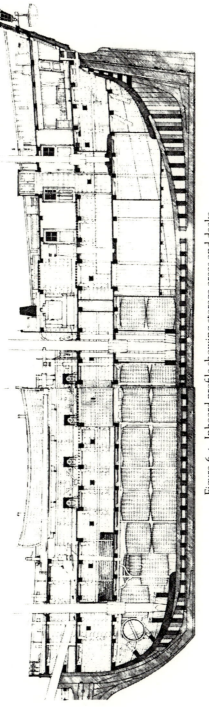

Figure 6.4. Inboard profile showing storage areas and decks.

and reasonably efficient air circulation arrangement. These design features were unique to slavers and were specifically designed for bringing
air into the sleeping quarters of the slaves. Late eighteenth-century
British vessel measurements recorded for 9 slaving vessels (including
the famous Brooks), show that they all divided their internal space in a
common pattern with the men's rooms on average three times the size
of the boys', and twice the size of the women's and infants' quarters,
with the boys' quarters separating the men's and women's rooms. In
this space – estimated to have averaged 3,500 square feet – the divisions were common to all the ships in terms of constructing the half
and full temporary decks used by the slaves for their sleeping and living
arrangements.

As in most things involved in the Atlantic slave trade, the Portuguese were the first to try to deal with standardization in the manner
of carrying and provisioning for the slaves transported. From scattered
references in the pre-1700 period it seems that provisioning and carrying arrangements were haphazard at best. Thus, as early as 1684 the
Portuguese were the first to regulate both slaves-per-ton ratios and the
quantities of food and water which were to be taken aboard ship. By
the law of 1684, the Crown determined that each vessel was to have
its legal capacity to carry slaves recorded in its registration papers. This
capacity figure, involving different measures for different areas of the
vessel, worked out to between 2.5 and 3.5 slaves per ton, depending
on the construction of the ship – with tonnage being determined by
contemporary Portuguese standards. What is interesting is that by the
early eighteenth century most Portuguese slavers arrived in Brazil with
less slaves than legally permitted and this number of underregistration
voyages and ships increased over time.

In the early eighteenth-century Luanda trade to Brazil only the
smaller vessels reached full capacity (which, it should be stressed, was
generous in the extreme to the shipowners), and the majority of ships
came in with below the numbers allowed for by law. The larger the
capacity, the less likely were the ships to carry their full complement
of slaves, and this pattern was consistent throughout the eighteenth
century. At the same time, the average number of slaves carried per trip
was constantly on the increase over the course of this century rising
from the 340 range to the 440 range by 1800. This suggests that it was
probably increasing ship's capacity in terms of the use of larger vessels,
rather than changes in crowding slaves, that determined the rise in the

number of slaves carried per vessel – especially as mortality declined at the same time as the average numbers carried rose. In fact, slaves-per-ton ratios probably declined somewhat during the century, since the smaller vessels that were being abandoned by the end of the century were those most likely to have the very highest ratios of slaves to tons.

This phenomenon of increasing tonnage, declining slaves-per-ton ratios, and higher numbers carried per voyage would be repeated in all trades in which tonnage figures were provided. In both the French and English eighteenth-century trades, the ratio of slaves per ton constantly declined as tonnage increased. This increasing tonnage (however differently defined for each European nation) among all traders over the course of the eighteenth century meant ever higher numbers of slaves carried per ship. By the 1780s, the English were averaging some 390 slaves per vessel delivered in the West Indies, the French in the 1770s were bringing in some 340 slaves per vessel, and the Portuguese were also landing on average 340 slaves per ship arriving into Rio de Janeiro from Luanda in this period.

But while the other traders, especially the Portuguese, steadily increased their ability to carry slaves in the following decades, the carrying capacity of the English vessels steadily declined. Whereas the average number of slaves carried to Rio de Janeiro kept rising into the upper 400s decade by decade into the nineteenth century, especially as an increasing share of the trade was coming from East Africa, the opposite was the case with the West Indies and British traders to Cuba. This was not due to any change in tonnage, which was probably increasing moderately for all traders, but to the British Parliament's decision finally to regulate the trade.

In acts of 1788 and 1799, Parliament reduced the number of slaves per ton ratio as a way of relieving what was viewed as the overcrowded conditions, which in turn were assumed to have caused excessive mortality to both slaves and crew in the Middle Passage. Dolben's Act of 1788 reduced capacity by defining slaves-per-ton ratios, while the 1799 act diminished the legal limits even further by using space measurements below decks rather than crude tonnage as the criteria for the numbers to be carried. The net impact of these two acts was to reduce the slaves-per-ton ratio from 2.6 in the prereform period to 1.0 slave per ton in the last decade of the trade. By the first decade of the nineteenth century, British African slavers were averaging just 289 slaves per voyage.

The one trade that was different in terms of tonnage was the trade from Africa to British North America. Here, the average-size ship used was quite small by the standards of the day. Thus, Virginia-bound African slavers in the 1727–69 period were averaging only some 200 slaves per voyage on ships of some 100 tons – already a low figure by contemporary British standards. But the slaves-per-ton ratio was close to that of all other British trades. This North American trade also showed the standard European pattern of decline in slaves-per-ton ratios as the tonnage of the shipping increased. The reason for this common pattern is, as we have argued earlier, structural.

Along with the changes in the tonnage of the ships and their manner of carrying slaves over the course of the first three centuries of the trade, there were also obvious changes in provisioning and the care of slaves during the voyage. The studies of all post-1700 trades show that slavers generally carried provisions and water for double their expected voyage times. They all used fairly standard foods as I have shown in the preceding chapters and they all adopted similar methods of hygiene.

While these firmly grounded statistics on mortality certainly destroy many of the older themes on "astronomic" mortality and "tightpacking," there does remain the question of whether a 7.5 percent mortality for a thirty- to fifty-day voyage for a healthy young adult is high or low. While intuitively it seems that a 5 to 10 percent mortality on the Middle Passage was a low rate, in fact, it was just the opposite. If such a mortality had occurred among a young adult population in England in the eighteenth century, it would be considered an epidemic rate. Thus, the estimated crude death rate for mid- to late eighteenthcentury England was 29 per thousand in times of relative peace and internal prosperity. This was translated into a monthly death rate of 2.4 percent per month of the resident population. If Africans who crossed from Luanda to Rio de Janeiro in the late eighteenth century, a onemonth voyage, suffered a shipboard mortality of 8.8 percent in the crossing, this would represent an annual crude death rate of 106 per thousand – three and a half times the normal rate. This ratio, in fact, understates the difference between the two populations, since this shipboard slave group is a population of healthy adults, not a population such as was resident in an English village, with lots of young children and aged persons who were highly susceptible to death. If such a village experienced a crude death rate of these proportions, it was going into severe decline and it was undoubtedly treated as experiencing a severe mortality crisis situation. Thus, while European slave traders succeeded in reducing the slave mortality rate in the Middle Passage to seemingly low percentages, these rates still represented extraordinarily high death rate figures for such a specially selected healthy young adult population. Equally, while troop, immigrant, and convict mortality rates in the eighteenth century approached the slave death numbers, in the nineteenth century they consistently fell to below 1 percent for transatlantic voyages. For slaves, however, these rates never fell below 5 percent for any large group of vessels surveyed. There thus seems to have been a minimum rate due to the special conditions of slave transport, which the European shippers could never reduce.

Death in the crossing was due to a variety of causes: some had African origins and others were either related to actual living conditions aboard ship or were a combination of the two. The biggest killers were gastrointestinal disorders and fevers, the former accounting for just under half the known deaths by the late eighteenth century, followed by fevers, which accounted for just under a fifth of the deaths. Bouts of dysentery were common and the "bloody flux" as it was called could break out in epidemic proportions and was the most common of the gastrointestinal diseases. Dysentery was also probably the most common disease experienced on all voyages, even when it was not a killer. The exposure of the slaves to dysentery increased both the rates of contamination of supplies and the incidence of death. Nevertheless, even these gastrointestinal deaths could be related to preshipboard experiences. A detailed study of slave deaths aboard British ships for the 1790s shows that gastrointestinal deaths increased steadily from the time of loading in Africa until the third to fifth week at sea and then declined steadily and were not systematically related to either crowding or time at sea. In a survey of 42 voyages undertaken by freetrading Dutch ships in the early eighteenth century, dysentery (caused by both bacteria and amoebas) was the single most common cause of death among the 20,653 slaves carried (of whom 3,563 died). It accounted for 34 percent of all deaths and occurred on all but one of the voyages.

Next in importance to gastrointestinal deaths were various fevers among which yellow fever and malaria were important. It is most likely that many of the poorly diagnosed fevers were brought on board by the slaves from their residence on the African coast, though shipboard conditions clearly influenced their development. Although in previous periods diet-related diseases and smallpox were killers, by the late eighteenth century there were few cases of scurvy, and smallpox was slowly declining as such a ferocious killer since the Europeans had by now learned to control both of these diseases. In the early eighteenth century survey of the 42 Dutch slaving ventures, for example, smallpox occurred on 19 voyages and killed 15 percent of all slaves. Scurvy, virtually eliminated by the late eighteenth century, killed another 15 percent and also occurred on 19 of the 42 voyages. Thus, for example, the Dutch slave ship *Bandenburg* lost 38 of the 409 slaves it was carrying to Surinam to smallpox in 1730, and smallpox was still reported on other Dutch slavers as late as the 1790s. But by this decade general inoculation by the British and other slave traders guaranteed that few slaves were lost to this disease in the Middle Passage. Even earlier, as all the provisioning information shows, all Europeans were using lime juice and other nutrients to prevent scurvy, which by and large had disappeared from the trade by the middle of the eighteenth century, except in those rare and unusually long voyages where provisions had run out.

That some mortality was inevitable for all participants in the slave trade is shown by the very high mortality suffered by the white crewmen who worked the slave ships. In all trades, seamen who worked slave ships suffered higher mortality than those who worked in nonslave vessels, even for trading in Africa. The best data for this mortality experience come from the French and English trades. Though the English traders in the early eighteenth century seemed to have achieved higher rates of slaves per crew, suggesting greater efficiency – a difference that disappeared by the end of the century – they suffered much higher death rates than the French crewmen. In some 1,535 slave voyages, French crew mortality in the Middle Passage was 15 percent per month. In contrast, 158 Liverpool slave trade crews in the 1770s experienced a Middle Passage mortality of 28 percent per month of voyage, while mortality on the African coast was 45 percent per month. Nevertheless, like slave mortality, crew mortality slowly declined in the course of the eighteenth and early nineteenth centuries. Moreover, the mortality experience of the crew became more sharply differentiated. In some 313 Liverpool slave trade ships from 1801 to 1807, ship's surgeons and their helpers suffered the highest mortality, which was almost double the mortality suffered by the ship's officers, and even 20 percent higher than the unskilled and skilled sailors. Clearly, those closest to the slaves suffered the most. In the outbound leg to Africa and the return voyage from the West Indies, the mortality of the sailors dropped to those normal for any naval trade of the period.

The very high rates of African mortality reached on occasional voyages were often due to outbreaks of measles or other highly communicable diseases that were not related to time at sea or the conditions of food

Table 6.3. *Sequential Slave Mortality Experienced by Nantes Slave-Trade Captains Making Four or More Voyages in the Eighteenth Century*

Captain	Sequence of Voyages					
	First	Second	Third	Fourth	Fifth	Sixth
F. de Beau man	17.8	14.2	3.7	9.3		
O. Denls	35.7	13.7	2.6	7.5		
E. Devigne	19.6	8.5	7.0	1.0	42.8	4.9
R. J. Durocher	5.0	3.3	4.8	3.3		
J. B. F. Gaugy	54.0	3.3	4.1	2.1	5.8	
J. Guyot	3.5	13.3	9.2	10.7	unk	22.9
P. LeRay	4.6	39.5	8.8	0.0	1.0	15.5
L. Monnier	2.6	4.5	4.1	6.4		
J. Perron	3.1	8.0	8.4	28.2	5.7	
J. Proust	4.3	13.1	22.9	0.2	4.3	
L. Quatreville	4.5	2.8	2.8	5.3		
A. Vandendriesche	3.7	6.2	5.8	16.4	6.6	

Notes: This is not an exhaustive list of all captains who made more than three voyages, but is only the list for which complete slave mortality in the Middle Passage could be calculated.
Source: Dieudonni Rinchon, *Les armements négriers au xviiie siècle* (Brussels, 1956).

and water supply, hygiene, and sanitation practices. This randomness of epidemic diseases along with periodic breakdowns in water quality and sanitation due to inclement weather or failure of winds prevented even experienced and efficient captains from eliminating very high mortality rates on any given voyage.

This sense of randomness of high slave mortality is further reinforced when the experiences of individual slave captains are analyzed. Although company officials complained that high mortality was due to crew negligence alone, this does seem to be the case. Thus, Sir Dalby Thomas, an irate Royal African Company factor at the Cape Castle fort, wrote to London in 1705 that "when yor. ships have great Mortality unless occasioned by ye Small Pox, you may be assured its thro Carelessness of yor. Captns., Mates, Surgeons & Cooks usage who ought to answer to yor. Honors for it." Although this may explain higher than normal slave mortality on a single voyage of an inexperienced crew, it was clearly not the norm for those making multiple voyages. Thus, in examining the mortality history of twelve French captains who made four or more successful slaving voyages (Table 6.3), the generally random quality of high mortality is clearly evident. The most typical pattern was for relatively low rates of slave mortality experienced on several voyages, followed by one unusually high incidence of death. This pattern would seem to suggest that, within limits, the individual performances of multiple-voyage captains had little impact on slave mortality. Those successful traders who were employed on more than one voyage seem to have experienced either the general mortality rates of the trade, or even rates lower than that on most voyages, with exceptionally high mortality rates occurring infrequently. This would suggest that experience and skill could not in themselves prevent catastrophic mortality rates. Equally, it strongly supports the foregoing contentions that these rates were the most likely results of epidemic diseases and/or an unusually lengthy voyage and its concomitant problems of food supply.

The Middle Passage mortality was only one part of the mortality experienced by slaves after leaving their African homes. Currently, almost as much controversy surrounds the estimates for these other mortality experiences as the debates about the mortality suffered at sea. An area in which the numbers game is once again becoming a question is the estimates of the mortality slaves suffered from their initial capture to the time they were sold to the Europeans. Although no serious documentation has been provided by anyone so far for the mortality that occurred in the slave caravans to the coast and during the entire time between capture and final sale, some recent scholars have accepted quite extraordinary figures. For reasons not very evident, they have even tried to distinguish mortality suffered by slaves taken by one group of Africans or another. Recently, one scholar even argued that slaves taken by Loango traders from interior groups suffered less mortality than those taken in the Congo region over the same distances by Portuguese based pombero and local Kongo traders. These speculations were based on no evidence whatsoever.

Most of the estimates of the preshipboard mortality that have been suggested recently have been based on nothing more than the unproven estimates of Buxton, which I cited at the beginning of this chapter. This has led to speculations on the impact of the Atlantic slave trade that have seriously exaggerated the number of deaths suffered by Africans, and consequently the number of the resident Africans, and finally the total numbers involved in the slave trade to America. While popular writers on the slave trade have come to accept the approximate 11 to 12 million figure of those who were shipped across the Atlantic in the Middle Passage, they have rejected this as a total figure. Instead, they have generated truly enormous numbers on the basis of an assumed mortality in preshipment land transport that was five times or more that experienced by the African slaves in the Middle Passage. While some adjustment for mortality in the capture and travel to the African coast – over time and by different region – is necessary, much research must be done to come to some type of reasonable estimate. Given our knowledge to date, I am sure that the adjustment will still be no greater, if not considerably less, than the mortality suffered in the Middle Passage.

Since little information exists, much caution must be exercised in discussing this mortality. But given the few eyewitness accounts that we have, it would appear that slaves moved with great security along well-traveled routes and were often used as porters as well. It can be assumed that they would have been housed and fed as all other such porters were on long routes and that there would be no especially high rates of mortality they might suffer. The existence of local markets for slaves and developed trade routes meant in fact that most of the original interior captors probably were not those who finally brought the slaves to the coast. Thus slaves were passed from group to group in well-organized markets, and often sold for local use along the way, before eventually being resold for the Atlantic trade. This ability to hold captured slaves in interior communities until sales to Europeans were possible, and the fact that slaves for the Atlantic coast often commingled with slaves in interior communities or along the roads as porters all created a secure and relatively easy transport system prepared to feed and house travelers, both free and slave, as a normal undertaking. As such, captured slaves moved among many legitimate sellers, among peoples who accepted this enslavement as legal, which meant that there was no need for any excessive haste once beyond the sphere of influence of the local community, nor was any other unusual activity called for that might have increased the mortality of the captives.

Thus, in one of the few eyewitness accounts of the capture and transportation of a slave, that by the Igbo Olaudah Equiano who was taken in 1750, it is evident that this young boy went through several sellers before he reached the coast. Moreover, he spent as much as a month at a time living a relatively normal life, even working as an apprentice for a goldsmith. Half the time he was with people who spoke languages similar to his own, and he even learned to speak several of these as well as participate in the local economy. As he concluded of his experience in this phase of the movement to the coast:

> Thus I continued to travel, sometimes by land, sometimes by water, through different countries and various nations, till at the end of six or seven months after I have been kidnaped, I arrived at the sea coast. It would be tedious and uninteresting to relate all the

incidents which befell me during this journey, and which I have not yet forgotten; of the various people among whom I lived – I shall therefore only observe, that in all the places where I was, the soil was exceedingly rich; the pumpkins, eadas, plantains, yams & &, were in great abundance, and of incredible size. There were also vast quantities of different gums, though not used for any purpose, and everywhere a great deal of tobacco. The cotton even grew quite wild and there was plenty of red-wood. I saw no mechanics whatever in all the way, except such as I have mentioned. The chief employment in all these countries was agriculture, and both the males and females, as with us, were brought up to it, and trained in the arts of war. (Interesting Narrative, p. 53)

That he suffered psychological shock and felt tremendous despair Equiano makes abundantly clear. But as this quotation makes equally evident, this long and complex trip to the coast did not destroy his unusual ability to observe, nor does he hesitate in speaking of some good people whom he encountered along the way. In none of his treatment was there any serious threat to his health or his life. That some mortality may have occurred in these caravans and movements to the coast is obvious, especially for peoples forced into new disease areas – say, from a savanna region in the interior to a rain forest on the coast. But what that mortality might be is difficult to estimate, though it probably is on the order of the mortality suffered by the slaves after they were purchased by the Europeans and before they were shipped across the Atlantic.

This second type of mortality, of which we do have some reliable records, is that suffered by the Africans after being sold to the Europeans and before they left the coast. This has been called the mortality associated with "coasting" along the African shore. Either held on shore, shipped in longboats, or carried aboard ships, which then remained stationary or cruised along the coast for many weeks, the newly purchased Africans suffered some mortality. As this period could often be longer than the actual crossing for the first of the slaves purchased for an individual voyage, this mortality could be fairly serious. Thus, for some 55 Dutch West India Company slave ships in the 1675–1738 period, this mortality reached 3.2 percent of the total of slaves purchased, compared with the same slaves suffering a 14.3 percent mortality in the Atlantic crossing. For a 57-voyage sample of the Dutch free slave traders, the coasting time was 200 days and the mortality was 4.8 percent of the slaves purchased, with a mortality of 11.4 percent in the Atlantic crossing.

Thus between 18 to 30 percent of the total mortality suffered by the Africans after being purchased by the Europeans occurred even before they left the African coast.

Nor was this the end of possible deaths associated with the Middle Passage. Another period for which we do have data is for the short time after the slaves landed in America and before they were finally delivered to their American buyers. Given the high rates of morbidity suffered in the crossing, many sick slaves were landed in America and not all of them recovered once they reached land. In many trades, slave ships were initially quarantined, which led to some deaths in the arriving harbor itself and more deaths occurred on landing. Thus, some 314 Dutch West India Company ships arriving in America between 1700 and 1739 experienced an overall mortality upon landing of 0.6 percent. Of some 111,129 Africans shipped across the Atlantic, 18,787 died on the Middle Passage and another 693 died after reaching America, some 168 in port while still on the ship and 525 on landing but before final sale. A similar pattern was found for ships arriving to the port of Rio de Janeiro between 1795 and 1811. Here, of some 170,642 Africans who left aboard slavers on route to Brazil, 15,587 died at sea and 606 died on shore after the ship had arrived, which gives a comparable ratio of 0.4 percent of those shipped. The only major finding differing from this is reported by Jamaican officials who claimed that from 1655 to 1787 some 676,276 Africans had arrived in local ports and 31,181 of them had died in the harbor before landing, which gives a much higher ratio of 4.6 percent. This number, if correct, may mean that there were more strict quarantine arrangements in Jamaican ports that delayed final embarkation and this delay in landing raised mortality rates.

Finally, there was the supposed adjustment mortality suffered by the Africans in the first few months after their arrival in America. Crudely given the term "seasoning" in the contemporary literature, this is another area, like that of the internal African mortality, for which there is little concrete data. Though scholars often repeat that a severe mortality occurred and the eighteenth-century Jamaican Edward Long postulated a 25 percent mortality figure for Africans within eighteen months of their landing in Jamaica, there are in fact no serious records by which this type of mortality can be evaluated. What most modern demographic historians suggest, however, is that such a 25 percent fig-ure seems to be well beyond what anyone might expect in such an immigrant population, however much adjustment to new foods and new disease environments this might entail. Why such an "adjustment" would occur in temperate climates, or even in tropical ones, for arriving African immigrants coming from the same latitudes and from the same disease environment is difficult to understand. That some increase in diseases might have occurred is possible, but not the rates of mortality suggested by Long for eighteenth-century Jamaica. Though there has been some speculation with these supposed death rates and those with the internal trade within Africa to readjust the total volume of forced African migrants to double and triple the current estimates of 11 to 12 million persons initially enslaved, to date, there is no documentary basis upon which to make these claims and much evidence to suggest that these high mortality estimates are impossible to sustain.

As is evident from this examination of the mortality question, the more precise the numbers have become, the more complex the questions raised. If "tight packing" is a myth, there remains the question of the inability of the slave traders to reduce slave mortality to that of the level of immigrants. Equally, if mortality in the Middle Passage is under 10 percent by the late eighteenth and early nineteenth centuries, this seemingly "low" rate produces a crude death rate for a healthy economically active population that is truly astronomic in its level. Finally, the best efforts possible to measure all aspects of the mortality experience of the Africans, as they moved from their African villages and arrived to their new American plantations, still leaves many legs of the trip unexplored and unknown.

That the Middle Passage was a difficult part of the experience of slavery of Africans in America is to be acknowledged. But it was not the totally disorganized, arbitrary, and bloody experience pictured in the popular literature. Over time, the Europeans moved progressively to rationalize the system of transport and to move the slaves with as little loss as possible. They learned from the experience in all the trades and adopted common patterns of housing and feeding slaves and of treating their diseases. From the earliest Portuguese laws of the late seventeenth century to those of the English Parliament at the end of the eighteenth century, they also tried to legislate a manner of carrying slaves that would force the worst offenders to accept this rational position. All this helped to reduce the mortality rates to lower levels, though never to those finally achieved by immigrants and convicts.

Despite all these efforts, death occurred constantly aboard ship, not only from disease and accident, but from rebellion, suicide, and natural disasters. With able-bodied peoples forcibly removed from their native land forever and sea travel in the age of sail a hazardous venture, and even more so in times of war, it was inevitable that mortality would result. Some idea of the importance of what this meant is found in a recently created sample of 24,259 slave-trading voyages from the sixteenth to the nineteenth century whose fates were known. Of this sample, approximately 17 percent of the trips resulted in slaves not being delivered to America for one reason or another. Within this group were 148 ships that were lost at sea and all of whose African slaves on board perished. Slaves rebelled – sometimes successfully – on a total of 313 voyages, and Africans on the coast cut off the slave ships or their small boats on another 70 voyages. Though not all lives were lost, there were 443 vessels shipwrecked, and pirates or privateers seized another 832 vessels. Finally, some 1,871 slave ships were captured and condemned for illegal slaving in the nineteenth century.

While violence and death were a significant factor in the Middle Passage experience, the overwhelming majority of the slaves did reach America. Moreover, despite this atmosphere of violence, the experience may not have been as psychologically damaging as some have claimed. This one- to two-month crossing certainly did not erase the African culture or languages that the immigrants brought with them, as has been supposed. Sometimes, it even reinforced preexistent relations or created new ones. In recent years, numerous documents have been found in the colonial American archives describing friendships made by Africans aboard ship that lasted over decades. Europeans were not humanitarians but pragmatists with the knowledge that slaves delivered to America in as healthy a state as possible guaranteed good profits. It was this attitude that most determined the nature of the Middle Passage.

CHAPTER 7

Social and Cultural Impact of the Slave
Trade on America

Who were the Africans who were forced to migrate to America and what was their impact on the formation of American society? Who determined their demographic profile and what influence did the age and sex of these migrants have on the growth of the respective Afro-American populations? What cultural baggage did they bring with them and how did it affect the societies they helped to establish in the New World? These are some of the questions that need to be answered if the impact of the arriving Africans on American society is to be fully understood.

Given that the Europeans wanted a laboring population to work in their most advanced industries and were willing to pay well for these workers, it was evident that the aged and the infirm were not selected. Not only would they not have survived the transportation experience, but they would have proved useless for the major manual laboring tasks demanded by the American planters and slave owners. Thus, only the healthiest persons were sent into the Atlantic slave trade. These tended to be mostly males – just under two-thirds of the total migration stream whose age and sex is known – and three-quarters were adults.

But these overall age and sex ratios tended to mask sharp changes over time, with both the ratio of males and of children rising through the centuries. In the earlier period – that is, the seventeenth century (from which reasonable age and sex profiles finally exist for the embarked populations) – we know that 60 percent of the slaves were male and some 12 percent children (defined as those boys and girls under fifteen years of age). In the eighteenth century (to 1809), this rose to an overall rate of 65 percent males and 23 percent children and by the nineteenth-century trade the figure was up to 72 percent males and a very high 46 percent children. As we shall see, these changing ratios were due to changing supply conditions all along the African coast.

But there were also sharp temporary variations in the age and sex of the arriving slaves caused by external factors, such as European and American legal decisions. Thus, the Dolben's Act passed by the British Parliament in 1788 and more extensive legislation enacted in the 1790s dictated an increase in the space provided for each slave aboard ship and caused a consequent rise in transportation costs, which led to the reduction of children carried in the last decade of the British slave trade. The cost of transporting children was as high as for adults and the returns were much less remunerative. There was also a rush to import women in the few years before the official closing of each of the major trades to Cuba and Brazil as the American planters sought to provide for as much reproduction potential for their resident slave population as possible.

Though the literature is filled with contemporary and later accounts of the kind of slaves the planters and slave traders demanded, in fact, it was the African suppliers who determined the age and sex of the slaves who were shipped. Though the contemporary literature suggests that planters and ship's captains only wanted adult males, at a rate of two men to every woman, this in fact is not what they got. Though there was a price differential between males and females in the crucial working-age years in America, this price differential was insufficient to explain the low ratio of females in the slave trade. Women performed almost all the same manual tasks as men on the plantations of America and, in fact, made up the majority of most field gangs in sugar, coffee, and cotton. The widespread use of women in unskilled and semiskilled rural and urban manual labor belies any declared preference for male slaves. Not only did women form half of all the planting, weeding, and harvesting gangs on all the plantations of America, they were well represented in all the basic productive sectors of these export industries. The American slave populations were the least sexually constrained laboring population in Western society up to the modern period. Women labored in all sectors of the economy and were the backbone of the field gangs in every plantation society in America. Nor did they experience different rates of mortality than the men in the Atlantic crossing, which might have explained European reluctance to ship them. The answer appears to be that Africans simply presented far fewer women for sale in the coastal slave markets than they did men.

Although more males did arrive from Africa than females, not all of these males were adults. Adult men were, overall, less than half of the Africans arriving in America and their numbers declined from a high of 51 percent in the seventeenth and eighteenth centuries to 42 percent in the nineteenth century. The male ratio was compensated for by the tripling of the representation of boys, who accounted for 8 percent of the total in the seventeenth century and 25 percent in the nineteenth century. But the ratio of girls also tripled, though it started at 4 percent, which was half the rate of boys in this first period. In many ways this compensated for the overall decline of adult women, who were a high of 37 percent in the seventeenth century and dropped to just 17 percent in the nineteenth century.

Equally, the slave populations on the plantations of America had among the highest ratios of economically active population of any working class known to history. Workers probably represented close to 70 percent of the entire slave population, which means that the aged and children were heavily employed in the labor system. Even among contemporary peasant populations, which had unusually high rates of labor participation, the ratio of the economically active populations only reached about 55 percent of the resident population, while free populations in the north and south of the United States in the nineteenth century were estimated to have no more than a third of the total population actively involved in labor. Though there was less interest in shipping children on the part of the traders because of lower profit margins on their sale, planters had little problem in employing these children once they arrived in America.

Thus, whatever preferences the planters expressed in their letters and diaries, they did not get even a majority of adult prime-age males, and were in fact required to purchase half their slaves outside this category. As in the case of age and sex, the same occurred with preferences as relating to African origins. Whatever the contemporary record might report about planters wanting slaves from the Gold Coast and not from Loango, they in fact took what they could get. This meant accepting not only women and children in ever increasing numbers, but also slaves from whatever region provided them. As observed earlier, the trade moved up and down the coast in response to the African supply of slaves. Senegambia and the Windward Coast, which supposedly had the good workers who were supposedly so highly prized by American planters, went out of trade far earlier than other regions and were not even very important at the height of the trade in the late eighteenth and early nineteenth centuries.

Equally indicative that planter demands had little influence on migration streams is that fact that there was not a uniform pattern of emigration of such supposedly desired adult male migrants from all regions of Africa at all times. In all the trades there were sharp regional differences in the age and sex of the migrating slaves. Thus, for example, the Bight of Biafran ports of the eastern Gulf of Guinea had the highest ratio of adult males in the nineteenth century (46 percent of the migrants leaving this region after 1811) whereas the Loango and Angola ports just to the south of them produced the fewest adult males – or just 32 percent of the migrants in this same period. In turn, the Bight of Benin had only one-third of its migrants listed as children, whereas in Angola some 61 percent of the forced migrants were boys and girls under the age of fifteen years. Nor were these rates constant over time. In the eighteenth century, over half of the migrants from the Biafran ports were listed as adult males, whereas children were under 10 percent of the migrants. Again, in just the period of the 1790s, the British took two males for every female off the Senegambia and Sierra Leone coasts, but got close to a balanced sex ratio from these Biafran ports, which now produced a fairly high ratio of children (14 percent).

At the same time American ports had no uniform pattern of arrival of adult males coming from different regions of Africa, since each ship coming west had different ratios of adults and children, and males and females, depending on its port of origin. Thus, planters were faced with a choice of slaves in terms of age and sex, as well as origins, which they were forced to accept if they wished to use slave labor. In short, they accepted what was offered and used these slaves in every conceivable manual labor with little bias as to sexual or even age divisions of labor. It was only when they had skilled occupations to offer that they favored men over women, and this helps explain why women formed the majority of manual laborers in the field gangs of all plantation regimes.

However, because of the fact that African and American regions participated at different times in the Atlantic slave trade, certain broad patterns of variation of regional origins can be discerned in some of the biggest slave trades. Thus, the early participation of the Spanish mainland colonies and Brazil in the trade explains their relatively higher intake of the 604,000 slaves coming from Senegambia, since the major period of Senegambian participation in the trade was in the sixteenth and seventeenth centuries (see Tables 7.1–7.3) In turn, the crucial importance of the West-Central African region to the Brazilian importing ports can be explained by special South Atlantic trade routes and the long-term participation of the Congo-Angolan region in the

Table 7.1. *Estimated African Slave Arrivals in American Colonies by African Region of Origin*

African Origin Region	Brazil	Mainland Spanish Americas	Cuba & Puerto Rico	British Caribbean	French Caribbean	Dutch Americas	Danish West Indies	Mainland North America	Total	(number)
Senegambia	18.1%	24.3%	3.5%	20.6%	16.1%	0.9%	1.0%	15.2%	100.0%	604,423
Sierra Leone	2.7%	0.6%	28.5%	35.7%	13.3%	2.6%	1.1%	13.9%	100.0%	322,612
Windward Coast	2.2%	1.0%	4.7%	51.6%	7.5%	24.8%	0.5%	7.7%	100.0%	284,217
Gold Coast	6.3%	1.4%	3.6%	58.5%	10.6%	9.6%	4.7%	5.5%	100.0%	1,028,177
Bight of Benin	52.3%	1.5%	6.5%	16.0%	16.8%	5.1%	1.0%	0.6%	100.0%	1,677,570
Bight of Biafra	9.6%	1.6%	15.4%	55.8%	9.1%	1.6%	1.3%	5.1%	100.0%	1,276,856
West Central Africa	69.1%	5.1%	5.0%	6.7%	8.7%	3.1%	0.3%	1.9%	100.0%	4,917,434
South-east Africa	65.4%	4.0%	17.1%	4.8%	6.3%	0.1%	0.0%	1.8%	100.0%	426,936

Source: Emory Voyage data set estimates, accessed on September 14, 2009.

Table 7.2. *Estimates of Importance of African Slaves Shipped from Major Region of Embarkation, 1501–1866, by Region*

	Senegambia	Sierra Leone	Windward Coast	Gold Coast	Bight of Benin	Bight of Biafra	West Central Africa	Southeast Africa	Total
1501–1550	7.6%	0.0%	0.0%	0.0%	0.0%	0.1%	0.1%	0.0%	0.5%
1551–1600	11.9%	0.4%	0.7%	0.0%	0.0%	0.4%	2.0%	0.0%	1.7%
1601–1650	7.2%	0.4%	0.0%	0.2%	0.5%	2.3%	9.9%	0.1%	5.3%
1651–1700	10.8%	1.4%	0.4%	8.8%	13.0%	9.4%	10.0%	5.8%	9.6%
1701–1750	18.9%	6.0%	13.8%	38.1%	36.8%	15.6%	15.6%	2.8%	20.5%
1751–1800	29.1%	46.0%	72.1%	45.8%	27.5%	41.1%	25.9%	10.2%	31.4%
1801–1850	14.4%	44.7%	12.9%	7.1%	20.5%	31.1%	33.7%	75.5%	29.1%
1851–1866	0.0%	1.2%	0.0%	0.0%	1.7%	0.0%	2.8%	5.6%	1.8%
TOTALS	100.0%	100.0%	100.0%	100.0%	100.0%	100.0%	100.0%	100.0%	100.0%
(number)	755,513	388,771	336,868	1,209,321	1,999,060	1,594,560	5,694,574	542,668	12,521,336

Source: Emory Voyage data set estimates, accessed on September 14, 2009.

Table 7.3. *Estimates of Importance of African Slaves Shipped from Major Region of Embarkation, 1501–1866, by Period*

	Senegambia	Sierra Leone	Windward Coast	Gold Coast	Bight of Benin	Bight of Biafra	West Central Africa	Southeast Africa	Total	n (000)
1501–1550	89.2%	0.0%	0.0%	0.0%	0.0%	3.2%	7.6%	0.0%	100.0%	64,126
1551–1600	42.2%	0.7%	1.2%	0.0%	0.0%	3.0%	53.0%	0.0%	100.0%	213,380
1601–1650	8.1%	0.2%	0.0%	0.4%	1.4%	5.5%	84.4%	0.1%	100.0%	667,893
1651–1700	6.8%	0.5%	0.1%	8.8%	21.5%	12.4%	47.3%	2.6%	100.0%	1,207,738
1701–1750	5.6%	0.9%	1.8%	18.0%	28.7%	9.7%	34.7%	0.6%	100.0%	2,560,634
1751–1800	5.6%	4.5%	6.2%	14.1%	14.0%	16.7%	37.5%	1.4%	100.0%	3,933,985
1801–1850	3.0%	4.8%	1.2%	2.4%	11.3%	13.6%	52.6%	11.2%	100.0%	3,647,971
1851–1866	0.0%	2.1%	0.0%	0.0%	15.0%	0.0%	69.5%	13.4%	100.0%	225,609
TOTAL	6.0%	3.1%	2.7%	9.7%	16.0%	12.7%	45.5%	4.3%	100.0%	12,521,336

168

slave trade. In fact, this was the premier sending region, accounting for 5,695,000 African slaves (see Table 7.2) embarked, and was the highest producer of slaves from 1550 onward, replacing Senegambia, which had dominated up to that time (see Table 7.3) Because of their greater participation in the regional trade, the Gold Coast was a significant source of slaves only for the British and other West Indian colonies. While all American zones obtained roughly similar amounts of slaves from the ports of the Bight of Benin, the late participation of the Biafran region in the trade meant that slaves from this region were well represented in the West Indies and North America, but were relatively insignificant in Brazil and Mainland Spanish America.

While African supply factors greatly influenced the regional origins of the slaves, American conditions also were influential in which American regions took slaves from which African regions. An American region, even with the credit universally supplied by traders, could not enter the trade without a crop marketable in Europe. Equally, the movement of slaves across the Atlantic was seasonal in nature, owing both to the prevailing currents and winds that influenced the crossing and the seasonality of American demand considerations in terms of harvesting and planting. Though the sailings from East Africa around the Cape of Good Hope were more dependent on local weather conditions, the West African routes seemed to respond to planter harvesting needs in America.

If seasonality in the movement of slaves was influenced by American demand factors, the nationality, sex, and age of the slaves entering the transatlantic trade were primarily determined by African conditions. The sexual imbalance in the departing Africans was especially determined by African supply conditions. African women, both free and slave, were in high demand within Africa, and it was this counter demand that explains why fewer women entered the Atlantic slave trade. In some African societies women were highly valued because they were the means of acquiring status, kinship, and family. One of the distinguishing features of several West African societies was their emphasis on matrilineal and matrilocal kinship systems. Since even female slaves could be significant links in the kinship networks, their importance in the social system was enhanced. Also, slave women were cheaper to acquire than free local women in polygynous societies and were therefore highly prized in societies that practiced this marriage arrangement. Even more important was the widespread West African practice of using women as the primary working group in agriculture. For all of these reasons, women had a higher price in local internal African markets than did men. Moreover, this was a vast market that absorbed a large number of slaves. Though exact numbers are difficult to obtain, the consensus of most African scholars is that slaves made up roughly a tenth of the resident population in Africa. This would mean that at the end of the eighteenth century slaves within Africa numbered any-where from 2.2 to 2.5 million persons, a figure not too distant from the 2.9 million African and creole slaves then resident in America.

Finally, to this demand for women in the internal slave market must be added the demands of the other overseas slave trades into the Red Sea and eastern Mediterranean. These trades also paid higher prices for women than men. Though these markets were smaller than the overseas transatlantic trade, they were still substantial. It is estimated that some 1.6 million slaves were shipped across the Sahara and through the ports of the Horn of Africa in the period from 1500 to 1699, which is just half a million less than the number of Africans sent into the Atlantic slave trade in that period, and that another 900,000 slaves were shipped into the eastern Mediterranean trade from the savanna region and the Horn of Africa after 1700. To these migrant Africans, most of whom were women and children, can be added another 2 million who were shipped off the East African coast in the eighteenth and nineteenth centuries, though this trade, a major part of which did not go to the New World, was more sexually balanced, since many of the workers were used in agricultural production in the Pacific island colonies of the Europeans.

If the factors affecting the offer of women to the Atlantic slave trade were most influenced by African supply considerations, the offer of children to this market was influenced both by European concerns as well as African supply constraints. There was, to begin with, the relative reluctance of shippers to move children across the Atlantic. Although children suffered no higher mortality rates in crossing than any other group of slaves, their low sale prices and their costs of transportation being equal to adults discouraged slave captains from purchasing them, even if their initial costs were lower than adults. But no matter what the captains may have wanted to purchase, they took an ever increasing number of children, especially in the nineteenth century. But it also seems that children were more prized than adult males in the internal slave trade and that, at least before the nineteenth century, they may not have appeared on the coast in as great a number as the Europeans may have been willing to purchase.

For those Africans who survived the capture, shipment to the coast, and the Middle Passage, their arrival in America had a profound impact on the evolution of New World societies from the sixteenth to the twentieth century. The 10 million slaves who arrived before the late 1860s represented a classic migratory population of mostly healthy young males with a relatively smaller share of young adult women and fewer children. This demographic composition of the arriving African slaves would have a profound impact on the demographic and social evolution of American societies.

The 33 females per 100 arriving slaves did not permit the overall population to reproduce itself for a variety of reasons, among which was the obvious one of the high rates of masculinity among the Africans in America reducing the number of family units. These African women after arriving usually maintained the African spacing pattern of three years between children due to longer lactation periods. Their newborn in America also experienced the normal high infant mortality of a premodern population. It was common for adult women, who usually represented three-quarters of all females in most periods, to arrive without their infant or young children, most of whom had been left behind in Africa. This loss of the first children in many cases and the fact that later children are always spaced further apart than the first births, also weighed in the reproductive effort of these arriving African women. While this was not the case with the young girls under fifteen years of age, they only represented a quarter of the total female group. Together, all of these negative factors prevented these arriving women from reproducing the total cohort of their fellow Africans in the next generation. In most areas of America these 33 arriving African women could not reproduce their cohort of 100 African immigrant slaves in the second generation.

Populations subject to heavy migration flows of Africans thus experienced negative population growth. This was the case of the North American colonies in the seventeenth and early eighteenth centuries, as it was in Brazil and the West Indian plantation islands of France, England, and Spain. There was growth of a creole (native-born) slave population everywhere, and these populations had positive growth rates with the usual 105 males per 100 females per birth, with subsequent sexually balanced populations overall. But initially their positive growth rate was masked by the inability of African-born women to reproduce their arriving cohorts, and their positive rates would only become manifest and influence total slave population growth when the volume and ratio of African immigrants declined significantly. Until 1700 all plantation colonies experienced a negative growth rate of their resident slave population that was only obviated by continued arrivals of African slaves.

These negative rates varied from region to region, but reached a high of close to 5 percent per annum in Jamaica in the eighteenth century, though they moved toward a stable rate of population maintenance by the first decade of the nineteenth century. This same pattern was experienced in the other West Indian islands and in Brazil.

In those societies in which Africans made up a majority of the population, the sexual balance was heavily biased toward men and the reproductive rates of the African women were insufficient to replace their original migrating cohort. The inability of the African slave migrants who arrived in America to reproduce themselves in the short run was perceived by all the master classes in America and their respective governments, and this had a profound effect on the evolution of the Atlantic slave trade. Those American regions which experienced a heavy and constant stream of African slaves would thus find it difficult to maintain their slave populations, let alone increase their size, without the resort to more migrants. Therefore, the pressure to maintain the trade was constant and planters everywhere except in North America were totally opposed to its abolition. This factor explains the tenacious opposition of the Spanish, Portuguese, and Brazilian governments to the British anti-slave-trade campaigns of the nineteenth century.

Of course, there were positive rates of growth achieved by the creole populations. But this growth was initially insufficient to offset the factors making for decline. Once the trade ended and the ratio of Africans to native-born slaves declined, the population stopped declining and positive growth rates were experienced. Moreover, there were many marginal or interior areas that experienced positive growth rates for their slave populations well before the abolition of the Atlantic trade in the 1860s. This was the case in the provinces of Paraná and Minas Gerais in nineteenth-century Brazil, and of course it was the norm for the slave populations of North America, which from the middle of the eighteenth century began to achieve positive growth rates that went from 1.5 percent per annum by the last half of the century to over 2 percent per annum in the decade before slavery was abolished in the nineteenth century. These were zones that either experienced very moderate imports of African slaves over a long period and in which the ratio of native-born to African-born reached a dominant position relatively early on (the case of the Brazilian provinces), or in which the growth of the native-born slave population was so rapid that late massive immigration of Africans could not dampen that growth (the experience of the United States). In general, it would appear that slaves

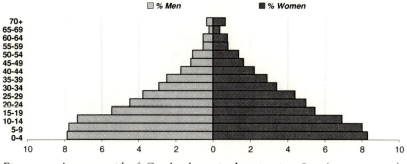

Figure 7.1. Age pyramid of Creole slaves in Jamaica in 1817 (n = 219,174). *Source:* Higman (1984), p. 464, table S4.1.

in the temperate zones were able to achieve positive growth rates more rapidly than slaves in the tropical zones.

The age and sex biases of the slaves of different origin can be seen in the age pyramids for the creole slaves and the African-born ones in three select regions of America at the time of the slave trade. Looking at the Jamaica slave population in 1817, the age pyramid for the 219,174 creole slaves (Figure 7.1) shows a virtually normal premodern population in terms of the normal pyramid shape of ages from earliest childhood to old age, with the single largest group being in the 0–4 age cohort. This was a population with a positive rate of growth. In contrast, the 126,839 African slaves then resident in Jamaica were primarily male (with 120 men per 100 women) and showed a very biased age structure (Figure 7.2) with the largest contingent in the 35–39 age category. Though their children were included in the creole population and thus are not included here, even returning these children to the African category

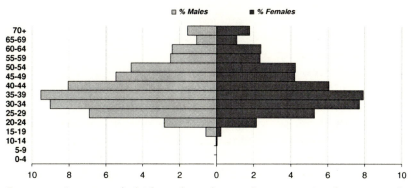

Figure 7.2. Age pyramid of African-born slaves in Jamaica in 1817 (n = 126,839). *Source:* Higman (1984), p. 464, table S4.1.

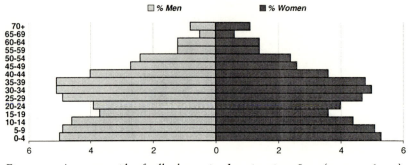

Figure 7.3. Age pyramid of all slaves in Jamaica in 1817 (n = 346,013). *Source:* Higman (1984), p. 464, table S4.1.

would not lead to a positive birthrate. The combination of these two groups in the total slave population (Figure 7.3) shows the negative influence the Africans had on overall rates of reproduction.

A similar pattern emerged in the southeastern province of São Paulo in the late 1820s. This was the most rapidly expanding zone of Brazil, with sugar and above all coffee production absorbing ever growing numbers of African slaves. Whereas African-born slaves constituted 37 percent of all the resident slave population in Jamaica in 1817, in São Paulo they represented an extraordinary 57 percent of all resident slaves whose age and origin were known in the late 1820s. Here too, in an even more pronounced fashion, we can see the same pattern similar to the one found among the slaves of Jamaica. African-born slaves were heavily male, to the extent that there were 2 men for every woman, for a sex ratio of 215 males per 100 females. The African born slave population was also primarily grouped in the age cohorts of the working age population (see Figure 7.4). In contrast, the creoles – the American born slaves – had a classic premodern age structure with children being the largest group (see Figure 7.5). In turn, when the African and Creole populations are combined, the slave population of São Paulo showed a higher incidence of males and a bias toward working-age adults and a low ratio of children, all of which suggest a population that was experiencing negative natural growth rates (see Figures 7.6).

Jamaica and São Paulo can be contrasted with the U.S. slave population in the mid-nineteenth century (Figure 7.7). This was an overwhelmingly creole slave population, the small slave trade to North America having ended in 1808. It was also a slave population that had a positive rate of natural growth, increasing over 2 percent per annum in this period. The data are for the decade before the abolition of slavery,

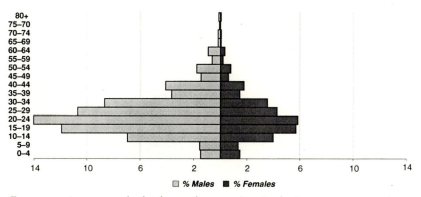

Figure 7.4. Age pyramid of African slaves in São Paulo Province in 1829 (n = 29,989). *Source:* Arquivo Público do Estado de São Paulo, mapas de população.

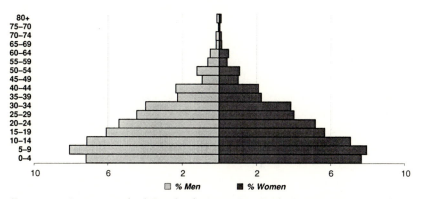

Figure 7.5. Age pyramid of Creole slaves in São Paulo Province in 1829 (n = 22,554). *Source:* Arquivo Público do Estado de São Paulo, mapas de população.

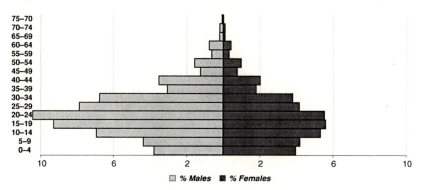

Figure 7.6. Age pyramid of all slaves in São Paulo Province in 1829–31 (n = 75,072, including 22,529 slaves of unknown origin). *Source: e:* Arquivo Público do Estado de São Paulo, mapas de população.

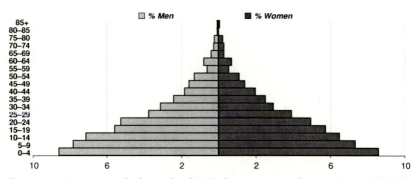

Figure 7.7. Age pyramid of sample of U.S. slaves, census of 1850. *Source:* IPUMS USA Slave Sample 1850.

the first census that provided reasonable age breakdowns for this slave population.

Once African migration stopped influencing the age and sex divisions of the resident population, it was possible for the slave populations to begin to rise through natural growth. This could occur, of course, so long as there was no heavy out-migration through manumission. In this respect, the Brazilian case is an example of how positive growth rates in the main regional slave populations could be wiped out by very high rates of manumission, which led to the positive growth being absorbed by the free colored population.

This consistently negative growth of the first generation of African slaves explains the growing intensity of the slave trade to America in the eighteenth and nineteenth centuries. As the demand for American products grew on European markets because of the increasingly popular consumption of tobacco, cotton, coffee, and, above all, sugar, the need for workers increased and this could only be met by bringing in more Africans. Though some 2.2 million slaves had been shipped before 1700, it was in the eighteenth and the first half of the nineteenth century that four-fifths of all slaves ever crossing the Atlantic were transported to America.

But the impact of the slave trade on the growth of the American population was not uniform across all colonies or republics. The United States stands out as a relatively unique case because its slave population grew at unusually high positive natural rates from the mid-eighteenth century onward. While the originally minor flow of North American exports to European markets explains the relatively low volume of migration of African slaves, and the consequent earlier domination of native-born slaves in the workforce, the ultimate population explosion can only be explained by more complex demographic variables. The U.S. slave growth rate even exceeded the rate that would be achieved in the nineteenth century by other slave societies that finally found themselves with a large creole or native-born slave population.

Initial claims by North American historians for better "treatment" of U.S. slaves have been rejected by demographic historians. It is evident that the period of potential fertility of slave women in all America was approximately the same. Since the length of fertility (determined by the ages of menarche and menopause) is directly related to health conditions, food supplies, and work experience, a lack of difference leads to a rejection of the better-treatment argument. Recent scholars have argued that the primary difference is to be explained by shorter periods of lactation, with the U.S. slaves adopting the northern European scheme of breast-feeding children for only one year, and the slaves of the rest of the Americas maintaining traditional African practices of breast feeding for two years. The contraceptive aspects of on-demand breast feeding in turn explain the longer child spacing of the non-U.S. slaves. This spacing in turn explains the higher number of children born to fecund slave women in the United States.

The differential treatment argument is also based on the fact that all life tables produced for slaves in nineteenth-century America show that U.S. slaves lived longer than their counterparts in the rest of the Americas. The average life expectancy of slave males was in the upper twenties in Brazil, for example, and in the mid-thirties for the United States. Discounting for the high rates of infant mortality, the comparable life expectancies of those reaching five years of age, was in the mid-thirties for the Brazilians and the lower forties for the U.S. slaves. At first glance this would appear to support the "better-treatment" argument. But in fact, it would appear that the same differences could be found for free coloreds and whites in all American societies. That is, white Brazilians lived comparatively shorter lives than white North Americans. Thus, the general differences in overall health conditions explain the comparative differences in life expectancies, and not any special treatment afforded slaves.

To contemporaries, the negative growth of the resident slave population seemed to be due to high mortality. Thus, a popular myth developed of high mortality due to "seasoning" or the acclimation of slaves to local climates and disease environments and new work regimes. Though no hard numbers exist for these deaths in the first year or two, sometimes it has been estimated that 25 percent of the Africans died in their first eighteen months in America. But even if this figure is true, the average life expectancy of slaves is still quite high. In no case were any American slaves in any slave society to experience the so-called "average seven years" of life that the contemporary eighteenth- and nineteenth-century literature in all languages constantly alluded to. This myth of a short-lived labor force was related to the observed reality of slave population decline under the impact of heavy immigration of African slaves. Observers did not recognize the age and sexual imbalance of these Africans as a causal factor for the negative population growth of the slave labor force. Rather, they saw this decline as related to a very high mortality and a low life expectancy. Yet all recent studies suggest both a positive rate of population growth among native-born slaves, and a life expectancy well beyond the so-called average seven working years in all American societies.

One study of African slaves brought to Cuba suggests that even with a very high mortality schedule (including a 10 percent "seasoning" mortality in the first year), a newly arriving African of twenty years of age still would have a life expectancy of twenty more years. Moreover, with each year of residence on the island, the African's life expectancy approached that of the native-born slaves, finally equaling their life expectancy. Thus, the "seven-year" survival rate, which can be found in both contemporary documents and standard historical texts, is a myth. At a minimum, at least half of the arriving slaves, some 80 percent of whom had passed beyond the high infant and child mortality years, could expect to reach their mid forties or fifties, thus completing a full life in America.

The slaves who arrived in America were mostly illiterate, spoke a multitude of different languages, and often had few common ties among themselves. Though recently it has been argued that western Africans shared more common language and cultural features than previously thought, and that the trade itself was not as divisive in breaking cultural ties as earlier studies suggested, it nevertheless did not foster a coherent transfer of either languages or cultural traits to the New World. Moreover, even this revisionist school largely accepts the idea that final sale in America did systematically break apart coherent African cultural groups. Even in those cases where planters did not divide their slaves by language or cultural background, the simple demands of the market meant that, even in the most supportive environment, Africans from quite different regions would be found on any given plantation. Though many Africans may have been able to continue to speak their native languages with fellow members of their "nations" in America, and have married and maintained friends from these groups, they were ultimately forced to adopt the language of the master class if they were to survive even in their slave communities since this was the only lingua franca that could tie all slaves together. Even in the heavily African slave population of the city of Rio de Janeiro in the early part of the nineteenth century, advertisements for Africans listed their fluency in Portuguese as a common trait, even after only a few months in the city. This was especially evident among the African children who arrived, who quickly adopted Portuguese, even as elders continued to be bilingual in Portuguese and their native language. Even in areas where one group might predominate, such as on the plantations of Jamaica, the practice of using Akan day names for slave children was a cultural norm of an earlier group of migrants but became common for the majority of slaves, most of whom came from Angola.

However much the young Africans might fight to retain their native languages and cultures, they were slowly incorporated into a larger Afro-American culture in which their own origins only partly helped define the cultural norms and patterns of behavior. Moreover, their color and special status in these New World societies slowly bound them together and forged them into a more coherent American community and culture in which many of their more distinctive original traits were lost or amalgamated. The culture that they and the nativeborn slaves created derived from African, American, and European sources, and it was partly shared by the white elite who kept them in bondage. This outcome could be the only expected one given the multiplicity of often conflicting backgrounds these slaves came from and the power that the whites held over their lives. Planters tried to mix their slaves from as many different African cultures as possible – that possibility always being limited by the constraints of the Atlantic slave trade to their local region – both to divide them politically and to force them to deal with each other in the common language of the whites. No matter how much a patois or creole a slave language became, it was still intelligible to the white masters.

This does not mean that the amalgamated culture that emerged did not have African elements in it or that it did not take on a vitality of its own. It simply means that the culture had to make selective adaptations of those African traits best suited to survival in the dominant culture of the white master class, and to those which fitted the new

economic, social, and political roles of Afro-Americans. In contrast
to usual African arrangements, for example, most African men in the
New World engaged in full-time agricultural labor and gave up hunting
and warfare. Nor were there any special male associations or other
living arrangements that might have existed in Africa. Africans on
large plantations lived either in barracks of one type or another if they
were single, and in barracks or huts in family units common to the
western European model.

As for religious beliefs, Africans in America had no state apparatus,
no political classes, and their clan organizations were destroyed. Thus,
African beliefs associated with all these activities were abandoned by
those who arrived in America. What often remained were beliefs and
deities related to health and daily life experiences and generalized attitudes of the relationship of the individual to the cosmos. These in
turn could influence such attitudes among the creole slaves and become
part of a generalized belief system that included formal Christianity
as well as African beliefs often mixed from different African religious
systems. Given the heterogeneity of the African origins, the existence
of large numbers of American-born slaves and the total imbalance of
power between slaves and free, it was inevitable that large elements
of the emerging Afro-American cultures were influenced by European
beliefs. Variants of European Christianity became the dominant religion, even if they were syncretized with important elements of African
beliefs and deities. The hierarchy of status in terms of occupations and
even skin colors was imposed on the slave population, though internal
slave divisions often did not replicate the white standards. Even in their
ultimate adaptation to peasant agricultural practices, the Africans and
their descendants often adopted European tools, technologies, and ways
of life. In many of their habits of work, friendships, beliefs about the
world order, and especially the language in which they came to express
themselves to others, the slaves of America were forced to accommodate
to the dominant culture of the master class.

But there were norms of behavior and beliefs that were unique to
slaves and helped to fortify an alternative version of that dominant
culture. Some of these were brought with them from Africa, others
were created to make their lives more meaningful in the context of
slavery, and others were deliberately oppositionist to the culture that
justified and rationalized their bondage. To unravel all of these strands
is a difficult task, made more difficult by the limited knowledge available
on contemporaneous African cultures, and of free lower-class culture in
general within America during the time of slavery.

Certain features of this slave culture were common to all slave societies in America and others were more especially developed in the Latin American context. It is now generally accepted that in the slave periods in Cuba, Haiti, and Brazil, powerful movements of proscribed religious practices developed that were most heavily influenced by a syncretic arrangement of African religious deities. These movements came to light in the postabolition period in these Catholic countries, but never arose to any significant extent in the Protestant societies. These essentially non-Christian religions were among the more significant features that distinguished Latin Afro-American cultures from the others. Many of these Afro-American cults and religions were often themselves syncretized from several different African sources. This, of course, was inevitable, given the deliberate master attempts to keep African groups apart or the fact that these practices became embedded with the first group of Africans to which all later groups had to adapt.

They also survived because the formalized structure of Catholicism permitted a dual folk and elite practice to emerge within the confines of a formal Christianity. Popular folk beliefs were already part of Spanish, Portuguese, and even French Catholicism. It was therefore often difficult for the elite to perceive African cults as they were masked by folk practices that included special emphasis on particular saints and their ritualized support and adoration. When the elite did recognize such syncretisim, they were as adamant at expunging this "idolatry" from the slaves as were the Protestant clerics. But the postemancipation survival of these cults and religions suggests that the Africans and their followers were mostly successful in their efforts to hide their more radical beliefs under a Christian mantle.

The most important of these cults in the era of slavery were candomblé, voudou, and santería. Each appeared in various guises throughout Latin America, though in the end only one would predominate in any given area. Which one would predominate often had to do more with the history of local acculturation than the weight of numbers. Thus a small initial group often established the basic cults, which later massive migrations from entirely different areas in Africa adopted in their new environments. Even where many national candombles existed, as in Bahia for example, the Nago (Yoruba) candomble provided the basis for the theology, ritual, and festival activity of all other candombles, even those named for Dahomean, Angolan, and Congolese tribes or nations. In Saint Domingue, where many cults (or mysteries) were established by groups from all over Africa, the Dahomean religious ritual of the Fon peoples eventually dominated voodoun practice and belief. Among the Bush Negroes in Surinam and Cayenne, the Fanti-Asanti culture predominated even though many Bantu peoples were well represented among these escaped slaves. Thus a process of acculturation went on among the slaves themselves, even in terms of the proscribed African cults and practices.

This process of syncretization and acculturation among the African religions helps to explain in turn why these cults found it relatively easy to accept and integrate parts of Christian religious belief and practice into the local cult activity. Initially, this integration was purely functional, providing a cover of legitimacy for religions that were severely proscribed by white masters. But after a few generations, a real syncretism became part of the duality of belief of the slaves themselves, who soon found it possible to accommodate both religious systems. In the Protestant societies this involved the selective acceptance of parts of orthodox religion. The stress on Moses and the liberation of the Israelites from Egyptian slavery, for example, were beliefs that fit in with the needs and aspirations of blacks, just as evangelical conversion experiences could be adapted to African rites. In the Catholic societies, dogma of the elite church was not affected, but a rich tradition of folk Catholicism with its saints and local cults provided a good medium for syncretization of African deities. Also, the elaborate structure of lay religious societies and local community saint days was extended to the slaves and free colored by the white authorities in their desire to integrate and control slave beliefs. They also hoped these associations, many of which in the early days were based on African tribal origins, would guarantee internal divisions among the slaves and prevent a coherent racial or class identity from developing. Though moderately successful in this aim, these associations and local festival activity proved of vital importance in both legitimating and spreading African religious practices and giving blacks and mulattoes important communal organizations.

Aside from formal religious beliefs and practices, there was a whole range of cultural elements that defined the slave communities of America. The creation of a coherent belief system that would provide the slave with a sense of self, of community, and of his or her place in the larger cosmological order was fundamental to the survival and adjustment of the arriving African slaves who had to acculturate to the New World in which they found themselves. Given the fact that the Africans came from a multiplicity of backgrounds of belief, and were forced to accept large parts of a cultural system alien to most of the systems known to Africa, this growth of a belief system would be a hard and slow task. One of the first areas where this evolved beyond the family level was in those practices that bound the community together. As in any peasant village, there were inevitable interpersonal conflicts among the slaves over resources. Sometimes these involved garden lots, personal effects, conflicts over potential spouses, sexual fidelity, or just personality clashes. These, plus the common problems of curing and divination, all led to the emergence of part-time specialists in witchcraft and curing. Given the importance these crafts had within Africa and the lack of such a clearly defined role within the white society, it was inevitable that African influence predominated. Usually, older and single African males and females provided the white or black magic that was an indispensable part of any community structure. Such individuals prepared herbs for curing and for influencing desired emotional or physical states in given subjects. They also provided recourse to a system of rough justice, which guaranteed a limit to the amount of personal violence that the community could afford in these fights over resources. Aggrieved adults who could not directly confront their opponents often had recourse to witchcraft to harm their rivals. This use of witchcraft and the knowledge that it was effective kept conflict within acceptable limits in a community that had no policing powers of its own or any type of communal self-government.

These beliefs and uses of witchcraft, while largely African in origin, did not evolve from any single African source or completely elaborated set of known rituals. Rather they tended to be an ad hoc mixture made up of many strands of different African beliefs. This was to be expected in a society in which such knowledge was not available in the highly coherent and structured form in which such specialists had developed it in Africa. There was no priestly class within the slave quarters, for such was destroyed with the migration. In such an ad hoc development of admixtures of beliefs, it was not accidental that much American influence was also present, especially in areas were there was access to the knowledge of local Amerindian and mestizo populations, as in Brazil and mainland South American colonies. In most of the slave societies these part-time specialists slowly faded away in importance as the African element within the slave population died out.

Although a belief system was fundamental to the definition of Afro-American slave society, whether influenced by African or European norms, the prime influence on slave society was work and legal status. Though whites viewed all slaves as equal before the law, the differential prices paid for skilled slaves as opposed to field hands clearly suggest that whites recognized important variations in aptitudes, abilities, and other individual traits. While it might be assumed that Africans would find themselves at a disadvantage in access to such skills, it is surprising to find them well represented in all the formal European skills that were taught to the slaves. In all slave societies where statistics on origins are available, it appears that Africans were represented in the skilled occupations in numbers equal to their share of the overall population. They became carpenters, stonemasons, blacksmiths, and even artists in as equal a ratio to their numbers, as did the creole slaves. They were even well distributed between urban and rural residence. Thus, as far as the white master class was concerned, there seems to have been little bias against Africans in terms of their access to what the whites perceived as better working and living conditions.

As for the slaves themselves, their perceptions of what constituted status often differed from that of the master class. Positions with control over resources or over other persons were not necessarily those which guaranteed higher status within the community of slaves, or even those recognized by the price differentials given by whites. Autonomy and knowledge often played an equally important role. Autonomy was clearly related to independence from the control and supervision of whites, whatever the job, just as knowledge could be both of the African culture of the past or of the white culture of the present. Work dominated the life of the slave more than others in the society and questions of work autonomy or dependency were of vital concern to the slaves. Supervision of the strictest kind was the lot of the majority of slaves, but relative control over one's time was available to a surprising number. On a typical sugar or coffee plantation, gang labor only involved half of the slaves. Another third or so were craftsmen or had occupations giving them freedom from direct white or overseer direction. In the half of the rural slave populations who were not on plantations, there was equally a distribution of jobs under close supervision on family farms as well as relatively independent families of slaves tilling lands on their own, or skilled artisans or muleteers who could escape direct white control. In the urban setting, domestics made up a large share of the labor force, and these came into close contact with whites and were most tightly controlled. But those who worked on a self-hire basis or as independent craftsmen tended to have the most free time for themselves outside the normally controlled work environment.

The control over their time and labor permitted some minority of slaves to achieve a fuller development of their talents and abilities.

Short of total freedom, this was considered a highly desirable situation, and slaves who held these jobs had a higher status within the slave community. It was no accident that many of the leaders of slave rebellions and other political and social movements came from these more autonomous slaves. Interestingly, some of these jobs were highly regarded by the whites as reflected in price potential, and some were not. Commentators on slave occupations noted that these jobs created an independence not found among the field hands or even the domestic slaves. In the coffee plantations of eighteenth-century Saint Domingue and those in early nineteenth-century Brazil, for example, the muleteers who carried the crop to market were considered a particularly lively group and were thought to be the "kings" of the slave force, as the French literature defined them.

Knowledge was also an important granter of status in the slave community. This could be an ability to read and write the local European language, or even Arabic and a reading knowledge of the Koran, just as it could be an understanding of the dynamics of the master class and the socioeconomic realities of the free world. These types of knowledge would often be associated with either skilled occupations, those possessing autonomy, or domestic service that entailed contact on a frequent basis with the master class and other nonslave groups. It was also more commonly found in urban settings and could be discovered even at the lowest level of the occupational skills ladder. But knowledge of African ways and customs or even, in some rare instances, of noble or elite status transferred directly from Africa gave some slaves a leverage in their community in contrast with their official status. Thus, in one of the more extreme examples, the leader of one of the Bahian slave rebellions of the 1830s was an African nobleman who in Brazil was the lowest type of unskilled worker. The same occurred with many of the male and female Africans who were part-time religious, health, and witchcraft specialists, most of whom had a status inside the community completely unrecognized by the master class.

To the surprise of most researchers, Africans were to be found not only in the ranks of the skilled American slave occupations, but also among the free colored in all societies in America in numbers roughly proportional to their weight within the slave society. In fact, in some cases they even exceeded their share of the total population. Thus, in a major study of the slaves of Lima, it was found that, in 1650, 87 of the 121 highly skilled slaves found in the city were of African birth, compared with just over a quarter of whom were native-born to the American colonies. Nor was this unique. In Brazil in the early nineteenth century, Africans could be found already as free landowners, who in turn owned slaves. In the newly developing farming district of Campanha in Minas Gerais in 1831, which then had 407 free African residents (along with 4,618 Africans who were enslaved), some 16 were heads of households who owned slaves and another 117 headed households without slaves. In each case they represented a much higher ratio within their free class than did the creole free colored. The same ratio existed in the old mining town of Sabará, also in Minas Gerais, in 1831, which had a total of 292 free Africans (and 3,769 African slaves). The 4 Africans heading households with slaves and the 66 heading free households both represented higher ratios in these categories than the native-born free colored. Though, as the numbers suggest, Africans were not the largest group within the free colored, and freedom was not their norm (being 8 and 7 percent, respectively, of the total class of Africans), once achieving freedom they did well.

Even in processes of emancipation, Africans did reasonably well. Though only 109 out of the 3,408 Africans in the town of São José d'El Rey in Minas were manumitted in the year 1795, they represented some 17 percent of the colored population that had been freed in their lifetime, and 17 of them owned slaves. Also 29 of the 55 slaves listed as *quartados*, or in the process of purchasing themselves from their masters, were Africans. But as could be expected given their initial incorporation into American society and their age at arrival, they were on average older than the native-born emancipated slaves. Unlike the creole slaves, these Africans were rarely freed in youth, and in fact 91 percent of them were forty-one years of age or older before obtaining their freedom, compared to only 46 percent of the native-born who were in this category.

In the urban areas, Africans did even better. Among the 950 slaves who were manumitted in the city of Salvador de Bahia from 1684 to 1745, the 292 Africans represented close to a third of all persons freed. The same age patterns were, of course, also evident here as well. Whereas 82 percent of the native-born slaves had been freed before the age of fourteen, only 4 percent of the Africans whose age was known fall into this category. Nor was this any different in the nineteenth century. Of some 657 manumissions recorded in the same city from 1813 to 1853, 48 percent were Africans. Other cities and periods were similar. Of 1,319 slaves freed in the city of Rio de Janeiro between 1807 and 1831, 42 percent were Africans. In all these cases the ratio of Africans who had obtained their freedom was roughly the same or even greater than their relative importance in the resident slave population. Thus Africans, despite all the impediments of language and culture, were able to achieve relatively quickly a solid place in the labor market of the American republics, and even achieve rates of manumission on a par with those of the creole slaves. They were more likely to purchase their freedom than were the native-born and were consistently older when they obtained their freedom.

That the Europeans brought millions of Africans to America against their will is undeniable and the basic fact about the slave trade. Nor were the Africans brought to America to better their lives. On the contrary, they lost their lands, their savings, and their freedom when they were forced to cross the Atlantic. Nor did Europeans reward them for creating the enormous wealth that helped to build America and which enriched their owners alone. But the resilient African immigrants were still able, despite everything, to forge their culture and to create a working class that fought to create a viable life for itself in America, even given the most limited of resources with which to create that life. Thus the unintended result of the Atlantic slave trade was to create a viable and vibrant working-class Afro-American population, which would slowly emerge as a vital element within almost every major society in the Americas.

CHAPTER 8

THE END OF THE SLAVE TRADE

If the slave trade was profitable and the Africans were put to productive use in the Americas, then why did Europeans begin to attack the trade at the end of the eighteenth century and systematically terminate the participation of every European metropolis and American colony or republic in the nineteenth century? Most economists now seem to agree that the organization of American plantation slave labor guaranteed that this system of labor was profitable to the planters and slave owners. Moreover, prices of slave-produced American goods fell over the course of the late eighteenth and early nineteenth centuries, with the result that consumption of those products was expanding at a rapid rate. The elastic demand for sugar, coffee, and cotton, the three major slave-produced crops of America, produced profits for the planter class. Nor could any free workers, except for some indentured Chinese or part-time peasants, be found who would work under these plantation systems. The question then remains as to why the trade was finally abolished if it was still profitable and important to the American economy.

It is now believed that the campaign to abolish the Atlantic slave trade, which began in the last quarter of the eighteenth century, was the first peaceful mass political movement based on modern types of political propaganda in English history. The early literature viewed this campaign as a moral crusade that was achieved at the cost of profits and trade. Once having abolished the slave trade to the English colonies in 1808, the British then attempted to force all the other major European slaving countries to cease their trades and to force African states and rulers to stop exporting people. This campaign was seen as a costly one in terms of lost trade, the alienation of traditional allies, and the high costs of a naval blockade.

The anti-slave-trade campaign had its origin in the intellectual questioning of the legitimacy of slavery and of the slave trade, which began in the context of Enlightenment thought in the eighteenth century and became a moral crusade of a small group of Protestant sects in the later decades of this century. Previously there had been a few abolitionist thinkers and people who held the slave trade to be immoral, but these were isolated voices with no serious impact on European ideology. But in the late eighteenth century, writer after writer began to view slavery as antithetical to a modern market economy, or considered it a fundamental challenge to the newly emerging concept of the equality of all men, or held it to be basically anti-Christian, no matter what the Bible had decreed.

Early eighteenth-century writers such as Montesquieu and Francis Hutcheson condemned the institution and were followed by such seminal thinkers as Adam Smith and Rousseau. Along with the philosophical debates came the attacks of Quakers and Protestant evangelicals, which added a special religious component to the increasing negative opinion about slavery and particularly African slavery and its accompanying slave trade. The French and Haitian revolutions of 1789 and 1791 further reinforced these new and challenging ideas. For the first time in western European thought, there now emerged a widely disseminated set of beliefs that held slavery, and even more so the slave trade, to be a morally, politically, and philosophically unacceptable institution for western Europeans. By the end of the century, in Europe, there were no longer any major defenders of slavery on any but pragmatic grounds.

Although the philosophical origins of the antislavery movement are fairly clear, the fact that this became a significant movement in England in the 1790s and the first decade of the nineteenth century is not as easily explained. Though English statesmen and writers portrayed their campaign as a moral one, there were many who attacked their motives. Cubans, Spaniards, and Brazilians, the objects of most of the post-1808 attacks by the British abolitionists, argued that the nineteenth-century campaign was motivated by fears of competition, especially after the British abolition of slavery in 1834 when sugar became a free-labor crop in the British West Indies. The Latins argued that it was the desire to keep their more efficiently produced slave products off the European market by driving up their labor costs that motivated these anti-slave trade campaigns. This argument was taken up by later historians of the West Indian economy who argued that even the preemancipation slave plantation system in the British islands was inefficient and in serious economic trouble. Eric Williams and other West Indian historians in the twentieth century believed that economic motivations explained the wellsprings of the British abolition campaign against the foreign slave traders, because the British West Indian plantations from as early as the late eighteenth century could not compete with the French, Spanish, and Brazilian planters.

In contrast to arguments based upon economic decline, recent scholars have argued that the late eighteenth- and early nineteenth-century economy of the British West Indies was a thriving one. Even after abolition of the slave trade, both the older and newer islands were competitive on the English and European markets, and it was only ending the slave trade and more importantly the emancipation of the slaves that weakened the British West Indian economies. In fact, the newer plantation colonies within the British Caribbean zone made significant gains in the world sugar market despite the increasing labor costs, which were exacerbated by the British refusal to permit postabolition internal slave trading among the colonies. If competition and fear for their declining sugar islands did not drive the British abolition campaign, was it just a moral crusade as earlier scholars argued?

Though abolition had a profound appeal because of its moral component and was clearly detrimental to British planter interests, the morality of its leaders, the so-called Saints, was not based on a pro-African stance or belief in the inherent equality of blacks. In fact, racism sometimes tinged some of the positions of these leaders. The anti-slave-trade campaign was based fundamentally on a belief in free labor as one of the most crucial underpinnings of modern society and the institution that guaranteed mankind's progress out of its medieval past. Such a position appealed not only to those wedded to free trade and laissez-faire, but also to workers being integrated into the urban and increasing industrial world of nineteenth-century England. To the workers of England facing the full impact of a wage system and selfdetermination in modern urban society, slavery was seen as antithetical to all the values of a modern society and a basic threat to their own security, even if it was only in distant lands. While the arguments against the slave trade may have had a moral origin, they were also based on the interests of European workers and capitalists and not on any concern with the African slaves themselves. The institution and its trade might be unacceptable, but at least in the English campaign it was not fought in the name of equality for blacks.

Of all parts of the institution of African slavery, the Atlantic slave trade itself was initially held to be both the most contemptible part of the institution as well as the one easiest to attack. It began in the 1750s among the 90,000 English-speaking Quakers on both sides of the Atlantic who started forcing members to abandon both slave ownership and participation in the slave trade. This was achieved as basic policy by the American Friends as early as the 1770s. The English Quakers followed a decade later and by the 1780s were exhorting their members to desist from participation in the slave trade as well. Then, in 1787, they helped start the national campaign to abolish the slave trade, which quickly moved beyond the Quakers to Methodists, and a large number of both radical and traditional Protestant churches. Between 1787 and 1792, popular antislavery clubs were established and a mass campaign of petitions to Parliament was organized. This led first to amelioration laws specifying conditions for carrying slaves. In 1788, Parliament passed the Dolben's Act, which established for England the first limits on the manner of carrying slaves aboard English slavers. This act in turn was further modified in 1799 giving greater space for each slave on English vessels.

But this was only the beginning. After several failed attempts at passing a definitive prohibition of the trade, the abolitionists in Parliament, under the leadership of William Wilberforce, moved toward partial restrictions by closing down parts of the trade. In 1805 the government banned the importation of slaves into the recently acquired territories of British Guiana and Trinidad. Then, in May 1806, legislation that prohibited British subjects from engaging in the slave trade with foreign colonies was passed. Finally, in March 1807 came the definitive abolition of the British slave trade itself, which was forced to end by the first day of 1808.

The next major campaign in the anti-slave-trade movement was the obvious one of trying to get all other nations to desist in their participation. This became a major theme of the British abolitionist movement in the 1810s, after the end of the Napoleonic Wars. Responding to a potential reopening of the French slave trade, the English abolitionists organized another mass petition campaign in 1814, which in one month sent over 700 petitions signed by close to 1 million persons to Parliament demanding universal abolition. Under this pressure, the British government negotiated a treaty with Portugal in January 1815 that immediately prohibited slave trading above the equator and promised to begin progressive abolition of the rest of the trade to Brazil. This was in addition to a treaty of 1810 that restricted Portuguese slave trading to its own possessions. At the Congress of Vienna in 1815 the major continental powers agreed to abolish the trade, but France and the Iberian states refused to go along. Then after Waterloo in November 1815, France was forced into the abolitionist camp. This left only Portugal and Spain as active slave-trading nations, and even Portugal had abolished the trade north of the equator.

From this period onward, British foreign policy in regard to Portugal and its colony Brazil and Spain and its American colonies of Cuba and Puerto Rico was consistently to oppose the trade and demand its abolition. At the same time the abolitionist movement finally turned on slavery in America, and not just the trade, and a series of acts pushing toward emancipation within the British islands finally got underway. First came a slave registration act in 1816; then in the 1820s and 1830s campaigns for total emancipation led to the formal abolition of slavery and the creation of an apprenticeship system whereby the former slaves were to work for their old masters for a specified period of time. This in turn ended in 1838 with the abandonment of apprenticeship and the freeing of all ex-slaves from any obligations to their masters.

Having carried the campaign so successfully against the British slave trade, and against slavery itself within the British Empire, the over 1,000 antislavery committees within the British islands kept up constant pressure on the British government throughout the nineteenth century to terminate the slave trade of all other nations. This campaign defined much of the relationship between England and the two Iberian states, and the newly established Empire of Brazil when it separated from Portugal in 1822, for the first half of the nineteenth century. In this campaign, Brazil would remain defiant until the end, disagreeing with concessions made by Portugal and demanding the maintenance of the trade south of the equator. This defiant attitude finally would bring direct naval attacks on Brazilian ports in 1850. In contrast, Spain tried to placate British demands while it procrastinated as long as possible. With the loss of the bulk of its American empire in 1825, Spain became ever more dependent on the expanding sugar plantation slave economy of Cuba as a major source of funding for itself and its merchants and was loath to abandon the slave trade. Thus it was able to play a constant game of duplicity, which enabled it to maintain the trade until the late 1860s.

Given Portugal's close dependence on Britain because of the protected markets for its port wine, and on its political support in continental affairs going back to the eighteenth century and its struggles against Napoleonic invasion, the Portuguese proved to be the most sensitive to British pressure. In July 1817, there was signed a "right to search" agreement with Portugal that allowed British war vessels to stop and search on the high seas any Portuguese vessel on suspicion of carrying their slaves north of the equator. This was the first such "right to search" treaty and became the model for others signed in later years. With success seemingly assured, the British later in 1817 drafted a major treaty with Spain that immediately abolished the trade north of the equator, allowed for British search of Spanish vessels, and finally promised total abolition of the Spanish slave trade in 1820.

To enforce these treaties, Britain established an independent African naval squadron in November 1819, which took up residence off the African coast and was to be a major presence until the end of the century. But this was only the beginning. France and the United States, though agreeing to terminate their slave trades, consistently refused the right of search to the British navy. Spain itself was less sensitive to British pressure than the Portuguese. The original treaty of 1817 was negotiated with a desperate Spanish regime, which was in the midst of an intense international conflict to prevent the loss of its American colonies. England had obtained a treaty by providing a cash payment to Spain, which in turn was used to finance the purchase of Russian vessels needed to ship a Spanish army to the Americas to suppress the independence rebellions then in progress in South America. But this whole scheme eventually failed and Spain was left with only Cuba and Puerto Rico as its American colonies. Fearful of losing these colonies, which were then in a phase of major expansion based on the export of slave-produced goods, Spain never enforced the total prohibition of 1820.

But the British did not desist. In the early 1820s they signed new treaties with Portugal and Spain that expanded the search provisions to allow the British to examine ships that had the equipment used in the slave trade even if not carrying slaves. They also got agreement from Portugal in this period to accept that the slave trade was now illegal for all its subjects – though this, of course, had little impact on newly independent Brazil. But British pressure on the new American empire was intense and finally in 1826 an Anglo-Brazilian anti-slave trade treaty was signed in Rio de Janeiro that forced the Brazilians to abandon the slave trade as of March 1830. Thus, for Cuba after 1820 and for Brazil after 1830, the slave trade was officially illegal.

Though the trade to Cuba and Brazil temporarily stopped in the first months of these two dates, in fact the local governments made no attempt to halt the trade. Brazilian newspapers no longer published ship arrivals after March 1830 and otherwise no longer provided any formal information on the trade. But the ships kept coming. In 1831 and 1832 the Brazilian government passed enabling legislation that supposedly carried the official prohibition into practice by criminalizing slaving and providing for police inspection of all arriving vessels. But even this new legislation was ignored and the trade was carried on openly until direct British intervention in 1850.

But the British did not stop their efforts on closing down these trades even when the local governments resisted. After much pressure they finally forced the French in 1833 to accept a very complete search-and-seizure treaty for vessels flying the French colors and carrying slaves or slave-trading equipment. They also obtained significant French naval support for African blockades after 1845. The flight to the Spanish flag of convenience was stopped with a complete search-and-seizure treaty signed in 1836. Then, in 1839, England unilaterally declared the right to seize all suspected Portuguese slaving vessels and judge them in its own vice-admiralty courts. In late 1840 came the first landings on African soil (at Gallinas near Sierra Leone) to liberate slaves being held in pens for shipment. This new British policy of direct intervention on the African coast in turn led in the 1840s to the signing of numerous treaties with local African governments along the entire western coast in which the British obtained the right to land and search for slavers. By 1847 the West African Squadron consisted of thirty-two ships, of which half a dozen were steam-driven vessels, and was actively engaged in intervention at sea and now on land as well.

Aside from maintaining a naval squadron off the coast and signing ever more complete treaties with African, European, and American governments, the British also established mixed judicial commissions with most nations to condemn slave vessels seized by the British or other cooperating navies. The most important of such commissions were the ones established in Freetown, Sierra Leone, in 1819, which had three such courts: Anglo-Dutch, Anglo-Spanish, and Anglo- Portuguese. In the same year, an Anglo-Spanish court was established in Havana, an Anglo-Dutch one in Surinam, and an Anglo-Portuguese one in Rio de Janeiro. Though these courts were often rent with dissension and the British had difficulty in getting convictions in the early years, by the time most of them were abolished in the mid-1840s, the non-British judges agreed with the decisions of the British navy, so that condemnation became the norm.

The final phase began against Brazil in 1845 when the Brazilians terminated their treaty with Britain, which had given the Royal Navy the right to search Brazilian vessels. In retaliation the British abolished the mixed commissions and ordered the seizure of all Brazilian ships caught with equipment or slaves on the high seas and their automatic condemnation before exclusive British vice-admiralty courts. At this point the British were also financing Brazilian abolitionist newspapers and had the Brazilian captain of the port of Rio de Janeiro (a mulatto named Leopoldo de Câmara) on its payroll. There also seemed to be a large body of popular opinion building in Brazil against the trade, which the British also supported. But the British decided that this was still too slow a process. In 1849, the stabilization of relations between Britain and the Argentine government of Manuel Rosas permitted the Admiralty to finally move its South American squadron to operate exclusively off the Brazilian coast where it concentrated on trade intervention, including a partial blockade of Santos. This fleet contained the latest in warships and proceeded to enter Brazilian waters with impunity. Though Great Britain was actively violating international law, no nation would support Brazil on this issue and it saw itself helpless to defend its shipping or citizens. In June 1850 came the final campaign as British ships entered Brazilian ports directly and seized suspected slavers, which resulted in British seamen and marines engaging in battle with Brazilian troops. Brazil's coastal shipping was disrupted, lives were lost, and the government was faced with a virtual blockade. As no one would defend the trade internally, and no one would support the government internationally, the Brazilians finally agreed to total and effective abolition of the trade in an act of 4 September 1850. The trade was declared piracy and all slaves seized were to be reshipped to Africa at government expense. A now more powerful Brazilian government carried out the terms of its decree fully, and in alliance with the British navy the trade was brought to a virtual halt by the end of that year, with only a few isolated ships arriving in 1851. Thus, after some 400 years ended the longest and largest African slave trade in history. An immediate result of the closure of the trade was the collapse of slave prices in Africa and the rise of slave prices in Brazil.

The last trade to be terminated was the forced African migration to the Spanish colony of Cuba. Whereas defiant attitudes of Brazilian officials had led to direct confrontation, the numerous Spanish governments at Madrid constantly promised to terminate the trade and thus effectively held off more aggressive British intervention. Though condemning the trade, the Spanish Crown refused to prosecute it. But it conceded the right to search for equipment for the trade on the high seas in 1835, which forced Cuban traders to adopt Portuguese colors. In 1842, the U.S. government sent a squadron to West Africa as a response to Cuban slavers using the American flag.

The fears of U.S. annexationist plans for Cuba restrained the British government from more direct intervention. But the abolition of slavery in the British islands freed British abolitionists to concentrate on the slave trade from the late 1830s onward, and the British government came under increasing pressure to move against Spain. As in Brazil, there was also a growing abolitionist sentiment developing within Cuba and Puerto Rico – Spain's other major slave colony. These movements were supported by Britain. In one such incident, the British consul in Havana was accused of fomenting a revolution by free colored intellectuals on the island. This was the so-called Escalera conspiracy of 1844 in which David Turnbull, the British consul in Havana and an active member of the British anti-slave-trade movement, was accused of direct involvement. Some 3,000 free colored and slaves were tried for the conspiracy, many were executed, and hundreds were deported. The free colored militia was disbanded and the consul expelled.

Although the abolition of the Brazilian trade in 1850 brought renewed vigor to the Cuban campaign, the distractions of the Crimean War in the 1850s and the increasing pressure of southern U.S. leaders to expand the slave system overseas to Cuba through annexation damp-ened Britain's ability and interest in maintaining pressure against Spain. Nor would England retaliate against Cuban sugar after it had abandoned all protective tariffs for the sugar produced in its own sugar islands in 1846 and became increasingly dependent on Cuban imports to supply its market. But the growing conflict between the southern and northern states in the United States finally provided the incentive needed to terminate the trade. In 1859, the U.S. Navy joined the British patrols in the Caribbean, though initially they could only seize ships carrying slaves. British sources believed that a new boom was on in the Cuban slave trade in the three years from 1859 to 1861. But the outbreak of the Civil War in the United States finally pushed the U.S. government into signing a treaty with Great Britain in 1862 that allowed free search of all its vessels. Also, all northern ports were closed to Cuban slave trade outfitters, an important provisioning source for Cuban traders, and even southern officials agreed to oppose the slave trade. Here, as with the

Brazilian trade, U.S.-built vessels and supplies had been a major factor in the nineteenth-century Atlantic slave trade. Thus, with the American flag of convenience denied to them, there was no legal protection anywhere for slavers. The British and U.S. naval forces now caused the volume of the trade to decline precipitously to only a few ships per annum after 1862. With the United States and Great Britain, the two previously opposing forces, now in agreement, Spain seriously feared the loss of its colony to foreign powers and finally conceded total defeat. In 1866 came an effective Spanish anti-slave trade act, and the last slave ship is supposed to have landed some unknown number of slaves in Cuba in 1867. Thus ended the Atlantic slave trade.

In examining the evolution of the slave trade in this last century of its existence, the most obvious factor determining its organization was its transition from a legal to an illegal trade. This direct government intervention was to have a major impact on how the trade was conducted and was to lead to certain fundamental changes in the last decades that marked this late trade as different from what had preceded it. The nineteenth-century Atlantic slave trade can be divided into roughly three periods: the legal trade that continued until 1817 for all the African coast; the period of legal trading south of the equator from 1817 to 1830, in which the Spanish colonies and Brazil carried on a traditional pattern of trading; and then the post-1830 period to 1867, when it was officially illegal everywhere. In many ways the pre-1830 trade followed the patterns of the eighteenth-century trade in terms of its shipping, carrying of slaves, and commercial organization. But the post-1830 era was to experience new developments in all aspects of the trade, from the initial purchase of the slaves on the African coast to the financing of the voyages, and the final sale of the slaves. All these new strategies were designed to handle either the direct military intervention by the British and/or the necessity to bribe American officials so as to land their slaves in the Americas. These activities raised the cost of shipping considerably and, with it, the subsequent prices of Africans sold in the Americas in the last thirty years of the trade.

Despite the rising costs of slaves and the increasing risk of the business due to the British naval intervention on the high seas, the actual volume of forced African slave migrations to the Americas tended to follow the pattern of growth and decline in American labor demand. This labor demand, as always, was related to European demand for slave-produced sugar, coffee, and cotton, which remained strong and growing throughout the nineteenth century. Although there was a steady decline of prices for these goods after the 1780s, they remained profitable as the demand for them kept expanding. Some 3 million Africans were shipped across the Atlantic in the nineteenth century, or about 30 percent of all those who were forced to enter the Atlantic slave trade, and the slave traders were able to keep the Cuban sugar fields and Brazilian coffee plantations supplied with sufficient workers until the end. That the supply of slaves kept pace with the demand for workers can be seen in the fact that slave prices, though rising during the nineteenth century, were more influenced by levels of slave owner profitability and some inflationary pressures than by the increasing costs of illegal trading. Only after 1850 in Cuba and Brazil did prices steeply rise in response to the end of the trade in Brazil and serious threats to end it in Cuba. Moreover, this trade was so intense, even despite the British intervention, that the number of Africans crossing the Atlantic remained greater than those of the free European migrants now crossing the Atlantic in large numbers until the 1840s.

The volume of the transatlantic trade had reached its peak in the decade of the 1780s, when close to 80,000 slaves per annum were crossing the Atlantic to America. The shock of the Haitian rebellion and the destruction of the economy in the New World's premier slave agricultural colony of Saint Domingue in the last decade of the century, combined with the disruption of transatlantic trade due to the imperial and Napoleonic Wars, which lasted until the early 1810s, caused a drop in the volume of African forced migrations to some 61,000 per annum in the first decade of the new century and just 53,000 per annum in the worst of the war years in the second decade of the century. By the 1820s the trade revived to close to 60,000 per annum. But after 1830, when the trade became illegal in most places, volume declined to 55,000 per annum in the 1830s and 43,000 per annum in the following decade. The elimination of Brazil as a market after 1850 dropped the volume to less than half the previous rate. Cuba absorbed only 14,000 per annum on average in the 1850s and by the early 1860s the rate was down to less than 4,000 per year.

As several commentators have noted, this decline was not due so much to the direct naval blockade as to the declining American demand. In almost all slave zones in the Americas in the nineteenth century native slave populations began to experience positive rates of growth. The United States, of course, had the highest such rates and had seen a major growth of its slave population well before the abolition of the slave trade in 1808. But the slowing of the heavy African immigration to other American regions permitted positive or stabilizing rates of growth among resident slaves by the middle of the nineteenth century. Thus, the decline in slave imports was not initially reflected in rising slave prices in America, since native American-born slaves could replace the imported Africans or else slaves could be moved out of less productive areas and moved into more advanced centers. Shifts in local economies, with Cuba, the United States, and Brazil developing new export products, all saw major movements of slaves from declining industries to new expanding ones. In the United States, tobacco and rice were progressively being replaced by cotton, while in Brazil sugar and cattle product exports were ceding the place of prominence to coffee. Only Cuba was developing all of its exports at the same time, but even here there were shifts of slaves out of coffee to sugar, as the former production went into decline after the 1830s.

Along with changing volume in the trade, there were also fundamental shifts in the sources of slaves along the African coast. Many traditional West African zones either went out of the trade or no longer produced large numbers of slaves, just as several new East African zones came into the market. The Gold Coast, which had shipped over 640,000 slaves in the eighteenth century, no longer participated in the trade in the nineteenth century. The Windward Coast to the east and north went into decline and essentially dropped out of the trade by the 1840s. Whereas it had accounted for 11 percent of all African slaves entering the Atlantic in the eighteenth century, it now sent only 1 percent of the slaves leaving Africa in the nineteenth century. In the Upper Guinea, or Senegambia region, only the zone of Gallinas was a major producer of slaves in the nineteenth century. It averaged some 5,000 slaves per annum until the middle decades and accounted for 8 percent of the slaves shipped from Africa until the end of the trade. In the Bight of Benin, exports were centered at Lagos, which along with Ouidah, made up 60 percent of the total volume of slaves leaving this region. Benin was a major source of slaves in the eighteenth century and continued to be a major origin zone in the nineteenth century. These two ports had a large cachement area and slaves were brought long distances from the interior. The region usually shipped around 10,000 slaves per annum until the 1850s. In this decade, shipments dropped to some 2,000 slaves per annum and became insignificant in the following decade. By African standards, a relatively low proportion of children left from Benin and Biafra, in sharp contrast to the ports to the south.

Overall, this region accounted for 15 percent of the slaves shipped in the nineteenth century.

The ports of the neighboring Bight of Biafra serviced the most densely populated region along the West African coast and obtained their slaves from sources close to the shore. Here the two leading zones were Bonny and the two Calabars. Local slave prices remained high even when the volume of transatlantic migrations declined because of the competitive use of slaves in local palm oil production, which in the first decades of the nineteenth century became a major export from this African area to the world market. Like the Benin region, Biafra was a solid producer of slaves in the eighteenth century and shipped a comparable number of slaves until 1840. It averaged between 9,000 and 12,000 slaves per annum until then, when its shipments declined more precipitously than in neighboring Benin. Despite this early decline, Biafra in the nineteenth century still accounted for 13 percent of the slaves shipped west and together the two regions of Benin and Biafra shipped almost 30 percent of all forced migrants leaving Africa in this century.

This precipitous decline of the Biafran ports had much to do with local political developments, but also reflected the growth of alternative exports. In the early nineteenth century, as it had for most of the eighteenth century, some 90 percent of the value of African exports were slaves. But the relative importance of slaves in the total African economy would change profoundly in the nineteenth century. In the second and third decades of the century, while slave exports were still high, Africans began finding an overseas market for peanuts and palm oil. Thus, well before final abolition of the slave trade, most of the densely populated regions of West Africa were exporting commodities that soon became more valuable than slaves. Sometimes slaves were retained in Africa to produce these new export goods, as in the case of the Biafra region, and sometimes they were produced by free peasant farmers. But everywhere African traders now engaged in multiple exports, among which slaves now were only one part. The African economic ties to the world economy were becoming more complex just as the slave trade was coming to face its most determined opposition.

The Congo and Angolan regions remained the single largest producers of slaves in the nineteenth century, as they had been throughout the whole history of the slave trade. Accounting for an estimated 37 percent of slaves shipped from the beginning to 1809, they now accounted for an even higher 48 percent of all slaves leaving Africa in the nineteenth century. Loango, Cabinda, and Ambriz (the so-called Congo North or

Loango coastal zone) was a traditional zone of extraction for French, British, and Portuguese traders, and continued to service the American markets in the nineteenth century. Congo North, or Loango, was supplying from 5,000 to 11,000 slaves per annum throughout the nineteenth century until the late 1860s. Given the lesser density of the local coastal population, slaves were brought long distances from the interior. This region, the neighboring Angolan region to the south, and East Africa were unique by African standards in the high ratio of children being shipped in the nineteenth century, who in general accounted for over half the migrant population. The export of agricultural commodities produced on farms and plantations was not a major factor here, even though a commodity trade developed before the end of slavery. This local alternative trade, however, came later than in the northern regions, but by the 1850s there were important exports of such products as ivory and wax and, to a much smaller extent than elsewhere, some palm oil exports as well.

The Angolan region, with Luanda and Benguela being the major ports, remained a major producer of slaves in this century, as it had been in the centuries before. With a strong resident Portuguese presence on shore, and close contacts with both Brazil and India, this was a zone that averaged close to 20,000 slaves per annum for most decades until the late 1840s, when it went into a severe and more rapid decline than the Loango region to the north. The abolition of the slave trade to Brazil in 1850 ended its premier role and it went into steep decline in the 1850s, sending less than 1,000 slaves per annum to America in the next decades. Nevertheless, Angola was Africa's single most important exporting region in the nineteenth century and accounted for 30 percent of all African slaves.

The newest area to enter the trade was Southeast Africa, essentially Portuguese-controlled Mozambique, which had begun sending slaves to America at the end of the previous century. The ports of Quilemane and Mozambique were the two leading centers for Atlantic shipping, and produced some 9,000 to 10,000 slaves per annum in the 1820s and 1830s. This dropped to some 8,000 slaves per annum in the next decade (though still accounting for roughly 15 percent of the trade), and it quickly declined as a major exporter after that. But here too, as the slave trade slowed, ivory and cloves quickly came to be exported from this region.

Just as the origin of slaves shifted in the nineteenth century, so did their place of destination. Whereas the United States and the

British islands were absorbing 35 percent of the slaves in the last decade of the eighteenth century, and Brazil absorbed some 30 percent, the slowly developing island of Cuba took only 9 percent of the 771,000 Africans who came to America. With the trade terminated to the British islands and with Brazilian slave immigrant absorption rising steadily each decade from 181,000 in the 1780s to 431,000 in the 1820s, it was inevitable that the direction of slaves would dramatically shift as well. Although the French islands of Martinique and Guadeloupe took some 5 to 10 percent of all Africans in the first few decades of the century, the nineteenth century after 1808 can be defined as the century when the Iberian colonies and nations dominated the trade. In the first decade of the nineteenth century, Cuba and Brazil took only 42 percent of the slaves, but in the next decade this ratio rose to over 90 percent of the Africans arriving in America and this figure rarely declined after that date. By the end of the trade period, Brazil had absorbed over 1.1 million Africans, and Cuba some 600,000 in the nineteenth century.

Of the two, it was obviously Brazil that was the dominant arrival zone in the nineteenth century as it had been from the seventeenth century onward, though Cuba by the end had become a major importer in its own right. In the first decade of the nineteenth century, Cuba received only 74,000 slaves, but this rose to 169,000 the next decade. This figure was only half of the volume of slaves then entering Brazil. Nor did Cuba maintain this high rate, for the economy could as yet not absorb so many slaves. In the 1820s, this temporary saturation of the Cuban market was reflected in the migration stream being reduced to half this figure. The 1830s saw a revival of market demand in Cuba with 182,000 Africans arriving in Havana and Santiago de Cuba and other minor ports. But this rate was just half the numbers brought to Brazil, which was then taking between 60 and 70 percent of all slaves arriving in the Americas. The 1840s saw another temporary decline of importations into Cuba, which took in only some 51,000 slaves, again because of overabundance of slaves. Brazil brought in 378,000 in this final decade, or 87 percent of the total coming to America. After 1850, Cuba alone imported slaves, and increasing demand led traders to bring in some 121,000 Africans in this decade.

The only major zone of importation in the nineteenth century outside these two Iberian colonies was the French West Indies. Though the French had lost Saint Domingue definitively in 1804, and had their slave trade temporarily closed during the Napoleonic Wars, they retained the islands of Martinique and Guadeloupe. These islands, along with French Guiana, were still major sugar-producing zones and continued to attract slaves until 1830. On average, these regions were bringing in some 4,000 slaves per annum with the peak period being in the early 1820s. Of these colonies, Guadeloupe was the center of such imports, absorbing a total of 38,000 slaves between 1814 and 1830; Martinique took another 24,000 and Guiana some 14,000. All this was a minor trade by the standards of the century, but it was an unusual trade in that French merchants from Nantes continued to dominate the trade to the end and were the only Europeans still active in the trade after 1808.

Not only did the volume shift among American countries, it also significantly shifted within regions. First, the expansion of sugar into Rio de Janeiro and part of São Paulo in the first years of the nineteenth century and then the rapid expansion of coffee after 1830 all shifted the slave trade toward the southern Brazilian ports as the century progressed. Whereas the region of Rio de Janeiro absorbed some 40 percent of the African arrivals to Brazil in the late eighteenth century, this share rose steadily to two-thirds by the 1820s and close to 80 percent by the 1840s. In fact, so rapid was the expansion of the coffee zones of Rio de Janeiro, São Paulo, and Minas Gerais that their appetite for new slave laborers could only be satisfied by a large internal slave trade once the British closed the Atlantic to Brazilian traders. In the two decades after 1850, slaves were shipped from the less remunerative sugar zones of the northeastern regions and the cattle and hide exporters of the far south and shipped to Santos and Rio de Janeiro. The end result was that the majority of slaves were found in Brazil's three central plantation agricultural states when slavery ended in 1888.

In the case of Cuba, slaves were most concentrated in the sugar and coffee zones, but an unusually large percentage were working in the urban sector for most of the nineteenth century. But even here there were basic shifts. As of 1846 only a third of Cuba's slaves worked on the sugar estates, over a quarter worked in its cities, and another quarter worked in coffee and the rest in rural activities of all kinds. But the increasing pace of sugar expansion in the 1850s brought arrivals of slaves to 12,000 per annum and even saw the importation of 6,000 Chinese coolie contract laborers per annum beginning in 1853. By 1862 the proportion of the island's 386,000 slaves working in sugar had risen to 47 percent of the total, those in coffee had declined to 5 percent, and even the urban slave populations were down to 21 percent of the total. The progressive expansion of sugar estates across the western part of the island drew ever higher numbers of slaves into the *ingenios*, or sugar mills, especially as local slave prices began a dramatic rise after the effective close of the slave trade in the late 1860s.

That the slave trade continued to function despite all the efforts of the British is due to the insatiable demands of Europeans for American plantation crops and of American producers for African slaves. Though the British expended large sums, they could not stop this trade. The British blockades that began in the 1810s and lasted in many regions to the 1860s did succeed in seizing 160,000 Africans on the high seas and in taking 1 out of every 5 slavers (or some 1,600 slave ships) operating in the period of illegal activity. All this naval intervention is estimated to have prevented about 10 percent of the potential slaves from crossing the Atlantic and clearly had an impact in raising some slave prices in the American republics and colonies that used slave labor. But the British naval intervention's major impact was to force American governments to honor their treaty commitments. The costs of evading the blockade were less than the costs of bribing Cuban officials. It was only when Brazil and Cuba agreed to terminate the trade in a definitive manner that the Atlantic slave trade formally and effectively ended.

Until that time, the increasing illegal trade adopted ever newer techniques to compensate for British intervention. In all cases local African "factors" – either Africans or direct representatives of American firms – became more important as turnaround time along the African coast was reduced. Faced with a naval blockade and even direct British coastal landings to seize their boats, slavers attempted to reduce the usual several months of time required to purchase and load their slaves on the coast. This led to the necessity of maintaining full-time representatives whose job it was to gather large groups of slaves over a long period of time so as to be ready for rapid loadings when the American slavers arrived. African traders or resident American business representatives now remained on the coast over many years and developed full-time facilities to accumulate slaves in large permanent pens so that their slave ships could be loaded rapidly and leave the African coast in days instead of the traditional months that was the norm in previous years.

Because of fears of capture on the high seas, there also developed after 1830 a new type of trading vessel. Increasing use was now made of supply ships as distinct from slavers, which brought the merchandise used to purchase slaves to Africa directly from America, Europe, or Asia and returned with commodity products such as peanuts or palm oil, but which never carried slaves. Though the voyages after 1830 began in America, most of their supplies and even much of their credit was arranged through England and the United States. It should also be recalled that the British and North Americans never stopped their subjects from engaging in African trading – if not the trade in humans – and so English credit and manufactured goods were used by the slave trades, and North American- or European-built ships were purchased for use in the slave trade, both during its legal and illegal periods.

Given the increasing risks of capture and loss of slaves and ships to British warships, there also developed new forms of financing of the trade. True joint-stock companies were now established to spread the risks and to concentrate the large blocks of capital needed to maintain an African presence. Previously, joint-stock voyages were common in the trade, but these multiowner voyages were usually organized for only one trip, and individual merchants tended to spread their risks over several voyages with several different groups. Now companies were formed among partners willing to subsidize many ships and voyages as a stable multiowner company.

Finally, control of the trade passed exclusively to Cubans and Brazilians, or Europeans resident in these countries, as European criminal law made slaving a capital crime for its own citizens. Though English credit and English and North American goods continued to fuel the trade of Brazil and Cuba, British, North American, and French merchants no longer took any direct role in the trade. By the 1820s over four-fifths of the ships arriving in Cuba with slaves were of Cuban origin, and this was a trade that had begun the century as the most open of the Atlantic slave trades in terms of foreign participation. Brazilian trade had always been controlled by Portuguese or Brazilians, but in the nineteenth century there was even more pronounced local control over the trade. Thus Bahian-owned ships made up over 90 percent of the slavers arriving in that port and over 80 percent of the ships arriving in Rio de Janeiro were outfitted by Rio de Janeiro merchants. Thus, American traders now dominated the trade as never before and, though credit and goods still came from Europe and North America, the ownership of the trade was confined to the countries that still imported slaves, a distinct change from the pre-nineteenth-century period when the Europeans had played such a prominent role.

Though shipping and carrying of slaves remained relatively unchanged from earlier periods, with a ratio of two slaves per ton and a relatively small tonnage ship being the norm, the last two decades of the trade saw some experimentation. In the 1840s in Brazil and the 1850s in Cuba there was the introduction of a few steamships to transport slaves across the Atlantic. But time of crossing changed little over the course of the century, except in the case of these few steamers.

All of these changes undertaken in the period of the illegal trade had the effect of keeping the majority of the slaves and slave ships out of the hands of the English. But they had little impact in changing the types of ships used to move the slaves, or the regions from which the slaves came. Small ships by world merchant fleet standards continued to be the norm. Mortality in the pre-1830 period still hovered in the 6 to 13 percent range, not much different from the late eighteenth century. Though it rose slightly in the next decade, it was not until the last two decades of the trade that it rose to the 15 to 17 percent range, levels not seen since the mid-eighteenth century. Africans were still carried under roughly the same conditions as they had been in the eighteenth-century trade. In general, technology introduced well before the midcentury when a large part of the trade was still legal did reduce sailing time to America, but little changed within the nineteenth century. Given the increasing costs and risks of trading, however, profits did rise on individual voyages and the relative cost factors shifted. Shipping costs rose from approximately 15 percent of the sale price when moving slaves across the Atlantic was legal, to close to 50 percent in the illegal trade period.

Thus the slave traders effectively responded to the increasing Atlantic blockade of the British with new techniques and new trading practices, and American buyers and African sellers continued to participate in the movement of Africans to America. But if the naval blockade was only a minor deterrent to the Atlantic trade, the political power behind that blockade was not. Not only did the British keep the diplomatic pressure constant, but they now began to find support not only throughout all of Europe but also within the American nations themselves. From the northern states of the United States to the southern provinces of Brazil, more and more leaders began to accept the end of the trade as inevitable and a first step in the eventual abolition of slavery itself. This progressive reversal of world opinion left Brazil and Spain with no alternatives but to accept the inevitable decision effectively to end forced African immigration to America. Even those leaders who wanted to maintain slavery in America realized that the trade itself was a hopeless cause and many slave owners even became abolitionists in terms of the Atlantic trade. Thus, it was not force of arms in the end so much as a profound change in world opinion that effectively ended the Atlantic slave trade. To one and all, this was now considered an immoral trade in human life that could not be sustained on any grounds, including even the limited justification of necessity or the defense of American production. Some slave owners hoped that they could redistribute their slave populations or promote natural growth to defend their institutions of forced labor. But many thought that without the trade slavery might die out. Yet, even the defenders of slavery who feared the end of the trade would end their way of life finally refused to defend the universally condemned institution. Thus, a generation before the end of slavery in America, the Atlantic slave trade was finally destroyed.

The fact that planters and slave owners in the United States, Brazil, and Cuba were still purchasing slaves just months before final abolition of slavery itself occurred clearly indicated that both the trade and slavery could have survived well into the twentieth century. In 1859, 1887, and 1889, slave owners were still buying slaves and willing to pay extra for women who were in their childbearing years. This so-called positive price for unborn children indicated that they expected slavery to last at least another full generation.

But however much slave owners fought to retain slavery, the abolition of the trade by the 1860s marked a clear turning point. In every region but the United States, the total number of slaves declined. Moreover, the pressure that led to the abolition of the trade now shifted to attacking the institution of slavery itself. Most educated elites of Europe and America began to view slavery as a retrograde institution that could no longer be tolerated. In countries like Brazil and Cuba, the pressure for manumission grew steadily and the number of slaves freed began to match the numbers born, so that not only did the resident populations still experience negative growth rates from the continued presence of Africans, but part of the positive reproduction of the creole slave population was being siphoned off to the free colored class. By the 1880s, free colored persons outnumbered slaves in these two societies. Only in the United States did the rate of manumissions actually go in the opposite direction in the nineteenth century. This trend, plus ever higher reproduction rates, meant that the slave population of the United States was the only one that was growing in the nineteenth century.

But even as that servile population grew, the United States was beginning to resolve its never ending labor problem by turning toward European immigrants. Though migrants had been coming to North America in ever increasing numbers in the eighteenth century, the nineteenth century was the great age of immigration. By the 1820s, some 14,000 European immigrants were arriving per annum; this flow to the

United States alone increased to 58,000 per annum in the 1830s and was over 250,000 per annum by the middle decades of the century. For the Americas as a whole, already by the 1840s free European immigrants were more numerous than the slaves and reached some 220,000 per annum in this decade.

A combination of factors suddenly made this free labor available, first to North America and then to Brazil and the other American republics. The single most important factor was the sudden growth of the European population to historic levels due to the so-called demographic transition. Beginning in the last decades of the eighteenth century, western Europe began to experience a stable or declining death rate for the first time in world history. The high birthrates that compensated for earlier fluctuating death rates initially did not come down – in many regions not for a century. This created growing population pressure, first, within western Europe and then spreading to the Mediterranean world and eastern Europe by the end of the nineteenth century. Governments faced by increasing demands for services and with already well saturated labor markets were ever more willing to open their frontiers to residents who wished to emigrate. The result was the freest labor market the world has ever known, and this lasted from roughly the early 1800s until the 1920s.

With the tremendous growth of the American economies, there came the increasing exploitation of previously uninhabited lands. The settlement of the U.S. West and the Argentine Conquest of the Desert were all early and late nineteenth-century movements that saw the slaughter of the resisting native American Indian populations and their replacement by immigrant farmers. Not only did America become Europe's breadbasket and supplier of coffee, cotton, and tobacco, but in the case of the United States it also began to ship manufactured goods in ever larger numbers.

The introduction of steam shipping and its usage on a steady basis by the 1840s and 1850s finally completed the picture. Transport costs quickly dropped and the time of the transatlantic voyage went from months to days as the steamships kept increasing in size and the trade in immigrants grew at an ever faster pace. In the 1821–25 period, some 39,000 Europeans arrived in the United States, 97,000 came the next quinqennium, and by the early 1830s another 244,000 reached the Americas. Canada, Brazil, and even Argentina and Uruguay were beginning to bring in Europeans by the 1850s and 1860s. Already by the decade of the 1840s, over 2 million immigrants reached the Americas.

Between 1821 and the time the Civil War brought slavery down in the United States, some 5 million Europeans had voluntarily migrated to the United States, a number larger than its slave population. In the period before slavery ended in Brazil, that is up to 1886, some 590,000 free and subsidized European immigrants had arrived in Brazil, the majority of whom were working on coffee plantations, but rarely alongside the slaves. Constant strikes and revolts of these free coffee workers convinced planters that the two groups should never work in the same units.

For those American plantation colonies and republics that could not attract free workers because they could not raise wages sufficiently high or offered no possibility of land purchases – a major attraction for those arriving to North America and Argentina – there remained only two possibilities. Either they had to subsidize immigration, which was the choice selected by the coffee planters of Brazil, or they turned toward Asian indentured laborers, which occurred everywhere but was especially important in the West Indies colonies and Cuba. Thus, from the 1830s to the 1860s, the British colonies of the West Indies imported some 39,000 African indentured workers, and the French brought in some 18,000 in just the two decades of the 1850s and 1860s. Before protests that this was a form of enslavement since the indentured workers never went home, this migration was finally stopped after close to 58,000 Africans were brought to the islands. But no protest occurred when the British and French resorted to East Indian indentured workers. From the 1830s to 1890, some 289,000 Indian workers arrived in the British islands and from the 1850s to the 1880s, the French American colonies imported another 79,000 for a total of close to 383,000. In the 1870s and 1880s, Dutch Guiana (Surinam) brought in 15,000 such contract workers, this time from Java. Chinese coolies were also brought as indentured laborers to replace the slaves who had been emancipated or because slave labor was becoming increasingly scarce. From the 1850s into the 1880s, Cuba obtained 122,000 Chinese workers and Peru another 100,000, for a total of 222,000. Thus in the regions where slavery had been important, some 663,000 workers were brought in from 1831 to 1890 to maintain labor on the plantations. In the case of Cuba and even Peru, these workers often worked alongside the slaves.

Nor were these the only semiservile labor brought into the plantation area. In the northeast of Brazil, Indian-white mestizos known as *caboclos* worked alongside the slaves in the sugar plantations, and in Cuba, Yucatan Indians taken in Indian rebellions and sold as indentured workers were also put to work in sugar along with Chinese coolies and

African and creole slaves. By the early 1860s there were over 1,000 on the island. Finally, in Puerto Rico, local subsistence peasants known as *jíbaros* also worked on the same sugar plantations as the slaves. Everywhere planters tried to maintain the same plantation gang labor regime with any dependent labor force available and had little trouble mixing these types of contract or poor free workers and slaves.

But where free European immigrants were used to supplement or replace slaves, an alternative work system had to be organized. The Brazilian coffee planters of São Paulo began experimenting with free immigrant coffee workers even before the end of slavery. But any attempt to put these workers alongside slaves failed, and they totally refused to work in gangs under supervision. Thus, when total emancipation occurred and the planters of São Paulo, Minas Gerais, and Rio de Janeiro resorted to free immigrant workers as their ex-slaves abandoned the coffee estates for access to their own private lands, they moved from supervised gang labor to fields divided among the immigrant families. Piecework replaced the factory in the field and labor costs consequently rose. But though this was a far more costly labor system, emancipation occurred at the height of the coffee boom and the planters were able to maintain profits, and also force the local state and national governments to underwrite the costs of subsidization

Thus everywhere in the Americas but the United States slave owners began experimenting with semiservile contract workers, subsidized European families, or subsistence peasants even before total emancipation occurred. In northern Brazilian and Puerto Rican sugar plantations creole peasants worked alongside slaves and in Cuba contract laborers from Asia first worked in the same fields as the slaves. In many of these areas, the slaves abandoned the plantations after emancipation and were replaced by contract or immigrant workers. But in the United States, the defeat of the planter class in the Civil War prevented it from using the state to subsidize immigrants and creating a regime like that developed in the south-central Brazilian coffee plantations. At the same time, however, the mass European immigration to the north closed off land and opportunities for the ex-slaves, who were eventually forced to remain on the old cotton plantations. But even here, sharecropping on the individual family farms replaced the plantations with gangs working on routinized tasks under supervision – the universal system of the slave plantation.

Thus, the ending of the slave trade, if it did not immediately end slavery in America, marked a dramatic change for the system and clearly indicated its future demise. The steady rise of slave prices after the abolition of the slave trade was followed by universal attempts at alternative labor arrangements, mostly with indentured contract labor. Though planters were buying slaves until the last months of the slave regimes in Brazil, Cuba, and the United States, all regimes but the North American one were already experiencing sharp declines in the number of slaves because of negative growth rates and increasing manumissions. Although direct political action by the individual states was needed to end slavery, just as it had been needed to end the slave trade, slave owners had already begun to anticipate the final ending of this historic institution. The slave trade gave way to an indentured and subsidized immigrant trade, and its demise spelled the end of slavery in the Western Hemisphere.

Appendix

Table A.1. *Estimates of Regional Distribution of Slave Embarkation from Africa, 1501–1866*

	Senegambia[a]	Sierra Leone	Windward Coast	Gold Coast	Bight of Benin	Bight of Biafra	West-Central Africa[b]	Southeast Africa[c]	Totals
1501–1510	1,900					0	0		1,900
1511–1520	8,807					0	637		9,444
1521–1530	10,990					0	0		10,990
1531–1540	12,229					719	1,453		14,402
1541–1550	23,257					1,361	2,771		27,390
1551–1560	4,796					282	664		5,742
1561–1570	32,277	1,168				1,867	5,412		40,725
1571–1580	22,206					1,883	5,367		29,456
1581–1590	25,448	237				0	31,206		56,891
1591–1600	5,370		2,482			2,346	70,368		80,566
1601–1610	9,991					0	81,936		91,926
1611–1620	8,541			68	1,873	1,142	137,308		148,932
1621–1630	6,652				1,655	2,247	172,595	345	183,494
1631–1640	4,562				1,988	1,630	112,020		120,199
1641–1650	24,476	1,372		2,429	4,092	31,442	59,530		123,342
1651–1660	17,723	752	351	1,437	12,163	24,791	95,382	3,088	155,687
1661–1670	6,407	154		19,193	29,926	37,668	126,758	9,432	229,539
1671–1680	13,267			28,835	29,813	34,394	108,966	7,116	222,391
1681–1690	21,927	1,894		16,274	79,890	21,709	109,373	9,497	260,564
1691–1700	22,558	2,671	999	40,443	108,412	31,299	130,939	2,237	339,557
1701–1710	16,344	1,217	3,059	81,144	136,943	21,979	133,434	120	394,241
1711–1720	22,669	3,114	4,365	97,287	149,463	34,615	131,867	10,029	453,408
1721–1730	34,933	9,419	4,532	113,877	194,430	41,830	145,437	3,934	548,392

214

Period									
1731–1740	44,816	1,468	9,392	106,723	145,805	56,583	231,989	1,226	598,003
1741–1750	24,210	8,004	25,202	61,626	108,220	93,891	245,436		566,589
1751–1760	50,555	17,419	44,083	88,174	122,566	93,294	223,830	3,036	642,958
1761–1770	52,405	42,296	76,521	108,658	110,383	146,542	280,240	1,916	818,960
1771–1780	51,267	36,551	65,186	112,562	109,887	109,997	267,293	2,924	755,667
1781–1790	37,944	31,378	36,067	135,036	113,692	151,242	333,888	28,746	867,993
1791–1800	28,043	51,119	21,176	109,441	93,197	154,642	371,789	19,000	848,407
1801–1810	53,702	42,627	25,241	75,746	95,428	140,385	339,975	50,450	823,554
1811–1820	29,166	22,624	7,190	1,712	74,093	65,870	407,491	77,697	685,843
1821–1830	13,073	43,543	7,867	5,362	59,250	163,525	441,968	121,158	855,747
1831–1840	4,626	43,926	3,155	3,293	73,081	97,829	343,464	116,910	686,284
1841–1850	8,375	21,023			108,943	27,554	387,008	43,640	596,542
1851–1860		4,795			22,528	2	113,927	30,167	171,418
1861–1866					11,339		42,852		54,191
TOTALS	755,513	388,771	336,868	1,209,321	1,999,060	1,594,560	5,694,574	542,668	12,521,336

a Senegambia includes off-shore Atlantic islands.

b West-Central Africa includes slaves shipped from St. Helena.

c Southeast Africa includes Indian Ocean islands.

Source: Accessed on September 14, 2009 from the Estimates series of the Transatlantic Slave Trade Database: Voyages, Wilson Library, Emory University, http://wilson.library.emory.edu:9090/tast/assessment/estimates.faces.

Table A.2. *Estimates of African Slave Arrivals by Region, 1451–1870*

	Europe	Mainland North America	British Caribbean	French Caribbean	Dutch Americas	Danish West Indies	Spanish America	Brazil	Africa	Totals
1501–1510							1,340			1,340
1511–1520	452						6,170			6,622
1521–1530							7,693			7,693
1531–1540							10,083			10,083
1541–1550							19,171			19,171
1551–1560							4,021			4,021
1561–1570							27,380	1,365		28,745
1571–1580							18,310	2,782		21,092
1581–1590							33,338	7,814		41,152
1591–1600	188						41,864	17,314		59,366
1601–1610			567				35,460	34,279		70,306
1611–1620	85						44,190	72,759		117,034
1621–1630		100					50,638	95,199		145,937
1631–1640							35,455	59,181		94,636
1641–1650			26,639				13,448	58,989	172	99,793
1651–1660		1,064	17,490	2,278	8,661		22,088	73,493	1,970	127,043
1661–1670	916	2,289	47,350	11,430	24,308		8,866	93,544	206	188,909
1671–1680	1,503	2,455	53,884	6,476	34,420	196	4,788	78,738	281	182,740
1681–1690		2,554	84,733	10,242	33,532	2,152	3,868	75,956	0	213,037
1691–1700	477	6,684	79,814	7,715	23,237	15,798	6,703	142,320	493	283,242
1701–1710		13,131	107,133	13,771	24,835	4,061	15,371	156,445	0	334,747
1711–1720		12,679	116,400	42,390	16,359	1,941	14,618	178,650	0	383,038
1721–1730	1,081	36,838	147,068	55,954	25,491	2,887	12,260	184,380	259	466,218

Period										
1731–1740	2,640	62,181	141,323	82,239	25,943	1,013	6,548	180,846	166	502,899
1741–1750	405	21,144	125,696	100,117	33,836	2,672	6,495	191,530	90	481,986
1751–1760	1,090	42,947	169,393	99,271	36,230	7,921	1,549	192,785	308	551,495
1761–1770		46,691	244,461	133,249	54,166	7,180	19,005	191,979	92	696,825
1771–1780		31,185	238,163	146,987	42,702	6,513	679	193,583	29	659,841
1781–1790	23	14,298	223,303	243,947	15,381	12,301	21,212	237,078	281	767,823
1791–1800		14,388	300,383	77,207	20,271	22,118	47,797	281,740	1,093	764,997
1801–1810		72,978	177,440	17,523	21,012	14,185	76,930	341,149	6,254	727,471
1811–1820		4,635	5,983	21,604	812	0	116,779	451,078	13,809	614,700
1821–1830		91	1,356	46,497	3,532	7,782	142,448	524,300	38,216	764,222
1831–1840		0	9,166	774		277	197,148	338,182	32,054	577,601
1841–1850		0	507				55,252	400,016	41,800	497,574
1851–1860		413					126,823	6,899	8,987	143,122
1861–1866							37,124		9,011	46,135
TOTALS	8,860	388,747	2,318,252	1,120,216	444,728	108,998	1,292,912	4,864,374	155,569	10,702,656

Source: Accessed on September 14, 2009 from the Estimates series of the Transatlantic Slave Trade Database: Voyages, Wilson Library, Emory University, http://wilson.library.emory.edu:9090/tast/assessment/estimates.faces.

BIBLIOGRAPHIC ESSAY

The Atlantic slave trade remained one of the least studied areas in modern Western historiography until the past quarter century. This late start was not due to any lack of sources, for the materials available for its study were abundant in both printed and manuscript form from the very beginning. Rather, as I have suggested in the text, it was ignored because of its close association with European imperialism, which resulted in a lack of interest in a morally difficult problem and to a lack of methodological tools by which to analyze the complex quantitative data.

The first studies of the Atlantic slave trade began in the 1780s at the very height of its momentum, when some 79,000 slaves were arriving in the ports of America each year. In an attempt to build a case against slavery and the forced migration of African slaves, English abolitionists began an attack on the trade by trying to determine its basic dimensions, the patterns of mortality of slaves and crew, and the relative economic impact of the trade on the African and American economies. Among the major abolitionists who dealt with aspects of the trade in a series of famous pamphlets were James Ramsay, a Jamaican-based cleric and medical doctor; Thomas Clarkson; and, above all, William Wilberforce. A complete listing of their works can be found in Peter C. Hogg, *The African Slave Trade and Its Suppression: A Classified and Annotated Bibliography of Books, Pamphlets and Periodical Articles* (London, 1973). Though their aim was to provide useful propaganda for their campaign, the abolitionists nevertheless did engage in some serious research. When the English Parliament began to impose the first formal constraints on its traders in the 1780s and 1790s, it initiated the systematic collection of statistical materials on the trade by British government agencies, a service that the government would continue until the middle of the nineteenth century. The final work of analysis on the trade provided by the abolitionists was the influential study of Thomas Fowell Buxton, *The African Slave Trade and Its Remedy* (London, 1838).

After the 1830s, there was little interest in analyzing the trade since all agreed on its evils, and the termination of the Atlantic slave trade in the middle decades of the nineteenth century coincided with the growing dominance of imperialist and racist ideology in metropolitan thought, which preceded the European conquest and colonization of Africa in the late nineteenth century. In this context, there was little interest in discussing the trade. It was not until the crisis of World War I that European intellectuals began to question the basic assumptions behind imperialism. In this debate, the Atlantic slave trade became one of the "crimes" of Western imperialism and could only be denigrated. It was from this perspective that writers began to restudy European contact with the rest of the world. The result was a narrative filled with stories of violence, exploitation, and passive natives, based on a minimum of research and an ignorance of the archival sources. This literature created a series of myths about the costs of the trade, the pattern of shipping slaves across the Atlantic, the mortality they suffered, and the ultimate gains and benefits to the Europeans. "Tight packing," mortality rates of 50 percent or more, "cheap slaves" bought for supposedly worthless beads and costless rum – all were added to the crimes list. Popular modern summaries of these ideas are found in the works of D. P. Mannix and M. Cowley, *Black Cargoes: History of the Atlantic Slave Trade, 1518–1865* (New York, 1962); James Pope-Hennessy, *Sins of the Fathers: A Study of the Atlantic Slave Traders, 1441–1807* (London, 1967); and most recently, Robert E. Conrad, *World of Sorrow: The African Slave Trade to Brazil* (Baton Rouge, LA., 1986).

Despite the dominance of this uncritical literature, which still survives in many of the history texts for secondary- and university-level courses, critical studies began to appear as early as the second decade of the twentieth century. The first modern scholarly studies were the work of a small group of dedicated French and North American scholars. Gaston-Martin and Padre Rinchon in France and Elizabeth Donnan in the United States initiated the systematic study of the trade, gathering together much of the archival material available in French and English archives. These works of reconstruction included the publication of systematic listings of voyages by Dieudonné Rinchon, *La traite et l'esclavage des Congolais par les européens* (Brussels, 1929); Elizabeth Donnan, *Documents Illustrative of the History of the Slave Trade to America*, 4 vols. (Washington, D.C., 1930); and Gaston-Martin, *Négriers et bois d'ébène* (Grenoble, 1934).

But, without question, the one book that can be said to have created the modern study of the slave trade was the work of synthesis and analysis published in 1931 by Gaston-Martin, *Nantes au xviiie siècle. L'ère des négriers (1714–1774)* (Paris, 1931). This is the first dispassionate and modern interpretation of the trade and would define most of the basic issues examined by all later historians. Everything from slave mortality in the Middle Passage to provisioning and, above all, financing the trade in this central French slaving port was examined. Though there were issues he did not fully understand and areas not fully explored, the work was a model of coherent analysis and interpretation. Unfortunately, the crisis of European society in the 1930s and 1940s and the general lack of interest in the theme outside Europe meant that little systematic work was added in the following decades. It was only after World War II that interest again revived among Europeans. Initially, an interest in overseas trading companies led to a series of studies of the early history of the trade as a European business activity. This defines the works of Abdoulaye Ly, *La Compagnie du Sénégal* (Paris, 1958), and K. G. Davies, *The Royal African Company* (London, 1951), as well as the much earlier studies of George Frederick Zook, *The Company of Royal Adventurers Trading into Africa* (1919; reprinted, New York, 1969), and Waldemar Westergaard, *The Danish West Indies under Company Rule (1671–1754)* (New York, 1917).

The main thrust for the modern study of the trade came, however, from basic political and intellectual changes within Europe and North America in the decades of the 1950s and 1960s. Without doubt the single most important development was the breakup of Europe's African empires and the rise of independent African republics. This led to the rise of the modern study of Africa and the creation of the subfield of precolonial African history, of which the slave trade was an important part. The civil rights movement in the United States created an explosive growth in Afro-American studies. Finally, the emergence of the field of demographic history and the application of modern quantitative methodologies to historical research opened up the modern era in slave trade studies. By the early 1960s, numerous articles began to appear as well as several important books. Though many scholars were beginning to work on various aspects of the trade from the African, European, and American perspective, it was a book by Philip Curtin that provided a major new impetus to slave trade studies. In 1969, he published *The Atlantic Slave Trade: A Census* (Madison, Wisc.), which was an attempt to estimate the volume of the trade from the available secondary and published primary literature. As important to slave trade studies as the work three decades earlier of Gaston-Martin, it was an original contribution to historical methodology. It involved a careful scrutiny of all the published estimates and a reconstruction of the numbers by zone and period based on explicit demographic and economic models. Though concentrating on the theme of the numbers of Africans shipped, Curtin was required to survey all of the issues that would eventually become basic themes in this latest period of research. The demographic evolution of the American slave populations was a fundamental concern of Curtin, as was the mortality suffered in the Atlantic crossing, since these were the primary factors that permitted estimates of the numbers of Africans transported when no known figures were available. He also touched on the problems of African population growth and European economic interests in the trade.

But it was his estimate of a total of 8 to 11 million Africans transported over the course of the trade that caused the most immediate response among scholars. The resulting debate generated a major search among the unpublished sources for new numbers and new sources to challenge or refine the numbers he provided. It was this international search of the European, American, and African archives for all the extant data on slave ship crossings that led to a major new period of research and analysis of the Atlantic slave trade. Among the first efforts was the attempt to build on the work of Donnan, Rinchon, and Gaston-Martin and publish the extant manuscript materials. Recent publications of new archival materials have included the monumental catalog of the French slave trade by Jean Mettas, *Répertoire des expéditions négrières françaises au xviiie siècle*, 2 vols. (Paris, 1978–84); supplemented by the compilation of Serge Daget, *Répertoire des expéditions négrières françaises à la traite illégale (1814–1850)* (Nantes, 1988); a more complete listing for Virginia by Walter Minchinton, Celia King, and Peter Waite, eds. *Virginia Slave Trade Statistics, 1698–1775* (Richmond, Va., 1984); and the publication of the Bristol shipping lists by David Richardson, *Bristol, Africa, and the Eighteenth-Century Slave Trade to America*, 4 vols. (Gloucester, 1986–96). Some work has been done on individual English trades, among which are Herbert S. Klein, "The English Slave Trade to Jamaica, 1782–1808," *Economic History Review* 31, no. 1 (Feb. 1978): 25–45; Darrold Wax, "Negro Imports into Pennsylvania, 1720–1766," *Pennsylvania History* 32 (1965): 255–87, and "Black Immigrants: The Slave Trade in Colonial Maryland," *Maryland Historical Magazine* 73 (1978): 30–45; David Richardson and Maurice M. Schofield, "Whitehaven and the Eighteenth Century British Slave Trade," *Transactions of the Cumberland and Westmorland Antiquarian and Archeological Society* 92 (1992): 183–204. Other lists were published in the books of Elena F. S. Studer, *La trata de negros en el Rio de la Plata durante el siglo xviii* (Buenos Aires, 1958), on the trade to the Rio de la Plata; Johannes Postma, *The Dutch in the Atlantic Slave Trade, 1600–1815* (Cambridge, 1990), on the Dutch trade; and Pierre Verger, *Flux et reflux de la traite de nègres entre le golfe de Benin et Bahia de Todos os Santos, du dix-septième au dix-neuvième siècle* (Paris, 1968); Antonio Carreira, *As Companhias Pombalinas de navegação, comercio e tráfico de escravos* . . . (Porto, 1969); Herbert S. Klein, *The Middle Passage: Comparative Studies in the Atlantic Slave Trade* (Princeton, 1978); and Joseph Miller, *The Way of Death: Merchant Capitalism and the Angolan Slave Trade, 1730–1830* (Madison, Wisc., 1988); Manolo Garcia Florentino, *Em coastas negras: Uma história do tráfico atlántico de escravos entre a Africa e o Rio de Janeiro, séculos XVIII e XIX* (Rio de Janeiro, 1995), Luiz Felipe de Alencastro, *O trato dos viventes: formação do Brasil no Atlântico Sul* (São Paulo, 2000) and most recently the two volumes of Jaime Rodrigues, *O infame comércio, propostas e experiências no final do tráfico de africanos para o Brasil (1800–1850)* (Campinas, 2000) and his more complete *De costa a costa, escravos, marinheiros e intermediários do trafico negreiro de Angola ao Rio de Janeiro (1750–1860)* (São Paulo, 2005) on the Portuguese trade to Brazil; and Roger Anstey, *The Atlantic Slave Trade and British Abolition, 1760–1810* (London, 1975), on the English trade. On the Danish trade, see Svend E. Green-Pedersen, "The Scope and Structure of the Danish Negro Slave Trade," *Scandinavian Economic History Review* 19 (1971): 186–93. All of these materials, along with new sources on the slave trade to Latin America, were brought together in a first compilation of some 27,000 voyages published in David Eltis, Stephan D. Behrendt, David Richardson, and Herbert S. Klein, *The Transatlantic Slave Trade, 1562–1867: A Database CD-ROM* (Cambridge, 1998). Since then Eltis has led a team to further develop the listing. Some of the preliminary findings of this new research group are found in David Eltis and David Richardson, eds., *Extending the Frontiers: Essays on the New Transatlantic Slave Trade Database* (New Haven, 2008), and in Daniel B. Domingues da Silva, "The Atlantic Slave Trade to Maranhão, 1680–1846: Volume, Routes, and Organisation," *Slavery and Abolition* 29, no. 4 (Dec. 2008): 477–501. The results of this new research, given as both actual voyages and estimates, can be downloaded from the constantly updated Web site "Transatlantic Slave Trade Database: Voyages," which is currently found at the Wilson Library Web site of Emory University, located at http://wilson.library.emory.edu:9090/tast/.

Once this new body of materials was made available, many older debates could be directly addressed and new and more sophisticated questions raised about the economic, social, and even political history of this major transoceanic human migration. This new scholarship resulted in a surprisingly large international output of publications, which has made this field one of the more active and productive in modern historical scholarship. Most of these studies were informed by a comparative perspective, and several works were explicitly comparative across several trades. My own studies on Middle Passage mortality in the various American trades were gathered together in Klein, *The Middle Passage*. Equally comparative in nature is the major study of the nineteenth-century trade by David Eltis, *Economic Growth and the Ending of the Transatlantic Slave Trade* (New York, 1987). The comparative work also appeared in a constant flow of conferences and volumes of collected essays on this subject. These began with Stanley L. Engerman and Eugene Genovese, eds., *Race and Slavery in the Western Hemisphere: Quantitative Studies* (Princeton, 1975); and included the volumes of Henry A. Gemery and Jan S. Hogendorn, *The Uncommon Market: Essays on the Economic History of the Transatlantic Slave Trade* (New York, 1979); the special issues dedicated to the trade of the *Revue Française d'Histoire de Outre-Mer* nos. 226–7 (1975) and no. 336–7 (2éme semestre 2002); Roger Anstey and P. E. H. Hair, eds., *Liverpool, the African Slave Trade and Abolition* (Liverpool, 1976); David Eltis and James Walvin, eds., *The Abolition of the Atlantic Slave Trade* (Madison, Wisc, 1981); J. E. Inikori, ed., *Forced Migration: The Impact of the Export Slave Trade on African Societies* (London, 1982); Barbara L. Solow and Stanley L. Engerman, eds., *British Capitalism and Caribbean Slavery* (Cambridge, 1987); Serge Daget, ed., *Actes du colloque international sur la traite des noirs*, 3 vols. (Nantes, 1989); Barbara Solow, ed., *Slavery and the Rise of the Atlantic System* (Cambridge, 1991); Joseph E. Inikori and Stanley L. Engerman, eds.,

The Atlantic Slave Trade: Effects on Economies, Societies, and Peoples in Africa, the Americas, and Europe (Durham, N.C., 1992); and, most recently, David Eltis and David Richardson, eds., *Routes to Slavery: Direction, Ethnicity and Mortality in the Transatlantic Slave Trade* (London, 1997).

Along with constant cross-national studies, there now appeared as well very detailed studies on individual trades or national traders, all informed by the new debates and themes. For the largest of the trades, that of Brazil, there is a good study of the unusual eighteenth-century monopoly trade to northeastern Brazil, examined by Carreira, *As Companhias Pombalinas* (1969). The trade to Bahia is studied in a classic work by Verger, *Flux et reflux* (1968), while the trade to Rio de Janeiro is examined in Manoel dos Angos da Silva Rebelo, *Relações entre Angola e Brasil, 1808–1830* (Lisbon, 1970); Klein, *The Middle Passage* (1978); Miller, *The Way of Death* (1988); and most recently by Garcia Florentino, *Em coastas negras* (1995); Roquinaldo Amaral Ferreira, "Dos sertões ao Atlântico: trafico ilegal de escravos e comércio lícito em Angola, 1830–1860," (M.A. thesis, UFRJ, Rio de Janeiro, 1996); and several recent collections of essays: Selma Pantoja and José Flávio Sombra Saraiva, eds.; *Angola e Brasil nas rotas do Atlântico Sul* (Rio de Janeiro, 1999); Linda M Heywood, ed., *Central Africans and Cultural Transformation in the American Diaspora* (Cambridge, 2002); Manolo Florentin, ed., *Tráfico, cativeiro e liberdade, Rio de Janeiro, séculos XVIII-XIX* (Rio de Janeiro, 2005) and Mariza de Carvalho Soares, ed., *Rotas atlânticas da diáspora africana: da Baía do Benim ao Rio de Janeiro* (Niterói, 2007).

The trade to mainland Spanish America has been partially examined. For the trade to Río de la Plata, see Studer, *La trata de negros* (1958); for the trade to northeastern South America, see Jorge Palacios Preciado, *La trata de negros por Cartagena de Indias* (Tunja, Colombia, 1973); Nicolás del Castillo Mathieu, *Esclavos negros en Cartagena y sus aportes léxicos* (Bogotá, 1982); and Colin Palmer, *Human Cargoes: The British Slave Trade to Spanish America, 1700–1739* (Urbana, IL., 1981). The complex trade arrangements of the closed asiento Spanish trade are discussed in Bibiano Torres Ramírez, *La compañía gaditana de negros* (Seville, 1983); Enriqueta Vila Vilar, *Hispanoamérica y el comercio de esclavos. Los asientos portugeses* (Seville, 1977); and María Vega Franco, *El tráfico de esclavos con América . . . 1663–1674* (Seville, 1984). I have recently examined in detailed subsets of the trade, see Herbert S. Klein "The Atlantic Slave Trade to 1650," in Stuart B. Schwartz, ed., *Tropical Babylons: Sugar and the Making of the Atlantic World, 1450–1680* (2004) pp. 201–236; "El comercio atlantico de esclavos en el siglo xix y el suministro de mano de obra a Cuba y Brasil," José A, Piqueras ed. *Azúcar y esclavitude en el final del trabajo forzado* (2002), pp. 37–49; and the "The Structure of the Atlantic Slave Trade in the 19th century: An Assessment," *Revue Française d'Histoire d'Outre-mer* (2éme semestre 2002), pp. 63–77.

The buying and selling of slaves is a subject that just recently has become a major theme of study with the issue of prices the most advanced of the areas examined, while the mechanism of credit, purchases, and internal shipment must be pieced together from a whole range of works and is still better studied from the African and European side than from the American viewpoint. The best current price information on the cost of African slaves on the western African coast has been gathered together and analyzed by David Richardson, "Prices of Slaves in West and West Central Africa: Toward an Annual Series, 1698–1807," *Bulletin of Economic Research* 43, no. 1 (1991): 21–56; and the most complete set of American prices is found in Laird Bergad, Fe Iglesias, and María del Carmen Barcia, *The Cuban Slave Market, 1790–1880* (Cambridge, 1995), and Laird Bergad, *Slavery in the Demographic and Economic History of Minas Gerais, Brazil, 1720–1888* (Cambridge, 1999). For a comparative analysis of prices in the Americas, see Manuel Moreno Fraginals, Herbert S. Klein, and Stanley L. Engerman, "Nineteenth Century Cuban Slave Prices in Comparative Perspective," *American Historical Review* 88, no. 4 (Dec. 1983): 1201–18. Useful on the pricing and selling of slaves in the West Indies is David W. Galenson, *Traders, Planters and Slaves: Market Behavior in Early English America* (Cambridge, 1986). On the special economy of cowrie shells, see Jan Hogendorn and Marion Johnson, *The Shell Money of the Slave Trade* (Cambridge, 1986).

The economic organization of the French trade, the best one studied in terms of its European organization, was examined by Dieudonné Rinchon, *Les armements négriers au xviiie siècle* (Brussels, 1956); Jean Meyer, *L'armement nantais dans le deuxième moitié du xviiie siècle* (Paris, 1969); Robert Louis Stein, *The French Slave Trade in the Eighteenth Century: An Old Regime Business* (Madison, Wisc., 1979) and most recently by Olivier Pétré-Grenouilleau, *Nantes au temps de la traite des Noirs* (Paris, 1998), and Guillaume Daudin, "Le rôle du commerce dans la croissance: une réflexion à partir de la France du XVIIIe siècle." Doctorat thesis, Université Paris-I, 2001. The Dutch trade in both its monopoly and free-trade periods is masterfully analyzed by Postma, in *The Dutch in the Atlantic Slave Trade* (1990).

The definitive study of the profitability of the slave trade is the recent work of the modern economic historian Guillaume Daudin, "Profitability of Slave and Long-Distance Trading in Context: The Case of Eighteenth-Century France," *Journal of Economic History* 64, no. 1 (Mar. 2004): 144–171; "The Quality of Slave Trade Investment in Eighteenth Century France," Documents de Travail No. 2002–06, Observatoire Français des Conjonctures Economiques (OFCE), and more elaborately presented in his thesis "Le role du commerce." This is complemented by alternative sources that come to the same basic conclusions in the essay by C. S. McWatters, "Investment Returns and *la traite négrière*: Evidence from Eighteenth-Century France," *Accounting, Business and Financial History* 18, no. 2 (July 2008): 161–85. On the accounting rationality of the eighteenth-century French commercial text that discussed the business accounting of the trade, see Cheryl S. McWatters and Yannick Lemarchand,

"Accounting for Triangular Trade," *Accounting, Business and Financial History* 19, no. 2 (July 2009): 189–212, and their earlier essay, "Accounting Representation and the Slave Trade: The Guide du Commerce of Gaignat de L'Aulnais," *Accounting Historians Journal* 33, no. 2 (Dec. 2006): 1–37.

The organization of the British trade has generated a series of studies and debates. A good general summary of the English trade can be found in Anstey, *The Atlantic Slave Trade and British Abolition* (1975). A debate about the nature of the companies operating in this trade is found in a set of articles by J. E. Inikori, R. P. Thomas, and R. N. Bean, among others. See Joseph E. Inikori, "Market Structure and the Profits of the British African Trade in the Late 18th Century," *Journal of Economic History* 41 (1981): 745–75; the critique of this position is found in two articles by B. L. Anderson and David Richardson, "Market Structure and Profits of the British African Slave Trade in the Late 18th Century," *Journal of Economic History* 43 (1983): 713–21, and "Reply" in 45 (1985): 705–7. The North American commercial organization is examined in Jay Coughtry, *The Notorious Triangle: Rhode Island and the African Slave Trade, 1700–1807* (Philadelphia, 1981). Recent overall assessments of the trade can be found in David Richardson, Suzanne Schwarz, and Anthony Tibbles, eds., *Liverpool and Transatlantic Slavery* (Liverpool, 2007).

The role of the trade within the European economy has been subject to intense debate. It began on a systematic basis with the publication of Eric Williams's *Capitalism and Slavery* (Chapel Hill, N.C., 1944). The so-called Williams thesis has been challenged by Stanley L. Engerman, "The Slave Trade and British Capital Formation in the Eighteenth Century: A Comment on the Williams Thesis," *Business History Review* 46 (1972): 430–43. It has also gotten some support from Pierre Boulle, "Slave Trade, Commercial Organization and Industrial Growth in Eighteenth Century Nantes," and "Merchandises de traite et développement industriel dans la France et l'Angleterre du xviiie siècle," both in *Revue Française d'Histoire de Outre-Mer* 59, no. 214 (1972): 70–112, and 62, nos. 226–7 (1975): 309–30. A recent discussion is also to be found in David Richardson, "The Slave Trade, Sugar and British Economic Growth, 1748–1776," *Journal of Interdisciplinary History* 17 (Spring 1987): 739–69, and the essays in Solow and Engerman, *British Capitalism* (1987). There is also considerable debate in relationship to the distribution of relative costs and benefits in the slave trade. The most systematic work in this area is that of David Eltis, "Trade between Western Africa and the Atlantic World before 1870: Estimates of Trends in Value, Composition and Direction," *Research in Economic History* 12 (1989): 197–239; and David Eltis and Lawrence C. Jennings, "Trade between Western Africa and the Atlantic World in the Pre-Colonial Era," *American Historical Review* 93 (1988): 936–59. There is also a recent debate about the value of slaves in total trade before 1700 in Ernst van den Boogart, "The Trade between Western Africa and the Atlantic World, 1600–90," *Journal of African History* 33, no. 3 (1992): 369–85; and the reply of David Eltis, "The Relative Importance of Slaves and Commodities in the Atlantic Slave Trade of Seventeenth-Century Africa," *Journal of African History* 35, no. 2 (1994): 337–49.

Detailed issues within the trade have now also been examined with some care. The ships themselves have been studied in Charles Garland and Herbert S. Klein, "The Allotment of Space for African Slaves Aboard Eighteenth Century British Slave Ships," *William and Mary Quarterly* 42, no. 2 (Apr. 1985): 238–48, and Patrick Villiers, *Traite des noirs et navires négriers au xviiie siècle* (Paris, 1987). An excellent analysis of the construction of a typical eighteenth-century slave ship is found in Jean Boudriot, *Traite et navire négrier* (Paris, 1984). Useful information is found in Walter E. Minchinton, "Characteristics of British Slaving Vessels, 1698–1775," *Journal of Interdisciplinary History* 30, no. 1 (Summer 1989): 53–81. An older study on this subject is George F. Dow, *Slave Ships and Slaving*, 2nd ed. (Port Washington, NY, 1969).

The sex and age division of the departing Africans is treated in the articles of Paul E. Lovejoy, "The Impact of the Atlantic Slave Trade on Africa: A Review of the Literature," *Journal of African History* 30 (1989): 365–94; David Geggus, "Sex Ratio, Age and Ethnicity in the Atlantic Slave Trade: Data from French Shipping and Plantation Records," *Journal of African History* 30 (1989): 23–44; David Eltis, "The Volume, Age/Sex Ratios and African Impact of the Slave Trade: Some Refinements of Paul Lovejoy's Review of the Literature," *Journal of African History* 31 (1990): 485–92; David Eltis and Stanley Engerman, "Was the Slave Trade Dominated by Men?" *Journal of Interdisciplinary History* 23, no. 2 (Autumn 1992): 237–57; David Eltis and Stanley Engerman, "Fluctuations in Sex and Age Ratios in the Transatlantic Slave Trade, 1663–1864," *Economic History Review* 46, no. 2 (1993): 308–23; and Herbert S. Klein, "African Women in the Atlantic Slave Trade," in Claire Robinson and Martin A. Klein, eds., *Women and Slavery in Africa* (Madison, WI, 1983).

Questions related to death in the Middle Passage can be found in Klein, *The Middle Passage* (1978); Richard L. Cohn and Richard A. Jensen, "The Determinants of Slave Mortality Rates on the Middle Passage," *Explorations in Economic History* 19 (1982): 269–82; David Eltis, "Mortality and Voyage Length in the Middle Passage: New Evidence from the Nineteenth Century," *Journal of Economic History* 44 (1984): 301–18; Raymond L. Cohn, "Deaths of Slaves in the Middle Passage," *Journal of Economic History* 45 (1985): 685–92; Richard H. Steckel and Richard A. Jensen, "New Evidence on the Causes of Slave and Crew Mortality in the Atlantic Slave Trade," *Journal of Economic History* 46, no. 1 (1986): 57–77; Herbert S. Klein and Stanley L. Engerman, "Long-Term Trends in African Mortality in the Transatlantic Slave Trade," in Eltis and Richardson, *Routes to Slavery* (1997); and most recently Herbert S. Klein, Stanley Engerman, Robin Haines, and Ralph Schlomowitz, "Transoceanic Mortality: The Slave Trade in Comparative Perspective," *William and Mary Quarterly* 58, no. 1 (January 2001): 93–118.

The issues of disease transmission and the slave trade are discussed in Kenneth F. Kiple and Virginia H. King, *Another Dimension to the Black Diaspora: Diet, Disease and Racism* (Cambridge, 1981); Kenneth F. Kiple, *The Caribbean Slave: A Biological History* (Cambridge, 1984); and Frantz Tardo-Dino, *Le collier de servitude: La condition sanitaire des esclaves aux antilles françaises du XVIIe au XIXe siècle* (Paris, 1985). The demographic impact of the trade was first examined in an original essay by Jack E. Eblen, "On the Natural Increase of Slave Populations: The Example of the Cuban Black Population, 1775–1900," in Engerman and Genovese, *Race and Slavery* (1975); Herbert S. Klein and Stanley L. Engerman, "Fertility Differentials between Slaves in the United States and the British West Indies: A Note on Lactation Practices and Their Implications," *William and Mary Quarterly* 35, no. 2 (1978): 357–74; Barry W. Higman, *Slave Population and Economy in Jamaica, 1807–1834* (Cambridge, 1976), and his general survey on *Slave Populations of the British Caribbean, 1807–1834* (Baltimore, 1984).

For the unusual contacts of Afro-Americans with Africa, see Manuela C. da Cunha, *Negros, estrangeiros. Os escravos libertos e sua volta a Africa* (São Paulo, 1985). The origins of the Africans in the trade have been studied in Gabriel Debien, *Les esclaves aux antilles françaises* (Basse-Terre and Fort-de-France, 1974); Arlette Gautier, "Les origenes ethniques des esclaves de Saint-Domingue d'apres les sources notariales," paper presented at the Neuvième Colloque International de Démographie Historique (June 1987); Castilla Mathieu, *Esclaves negros* (1982); the old classic by Fernando Ortiz, *Hampa afro-cubana. Los negros esclavos; estudio sociológico y de derecho público* (Havana, 1916); and in a host of works on slavery in Latin America that are cited in Herbert S. Klein and Ben Vinson III, *African Slavery in Latin America and the Caribbean*, 2nd rev. ed. (New York, 2007).

There are few recorded experiences of the slave trade itself; the best is by Olaudah Equiano, *The Interesting Narrative of the Life of Olaudah Equiano, Written by Himself*, ed. Robert J. Allison (1789; reprint, Boston, 1995). On the other hand, we have detailed accounts by slave captains of their experiences in the trade. The single most important source will be found in Great Britain, House of Commons, *Sessional Papers of the Eighteenth Century*, ed. Sheila Lambert (Wilmington, DL, 1974), vols. 67–76 and 82, covering the testimony given to Parliament in 1788 to 1790, and in 1791–92. Useful studies of individual captains or firsthand accounts of voyages are Dieudonné Rinchon, *Pierre-Ignace-Liévin van Alstein, capitaine négrier, Gand 1733–Nantes 1793*, 2nd ed. (Dakar, 1964); Alexander Falconbridge, *An Account of the Slave Trade on the Coast of Africa* (1788; reprint, New York, 1973); *The Journal of a Slave Trade (John Newton) 1750–1754*, ed. Bernard Martin and Mark Spurrel (London, 1962); plus numerous others, which are cited in Hogg, *The African Slave Trade* (1973). Mention here should also be made of the ongoing bibliography on slavery, including material on the slave trade organized by Joseph Miller and others, which appears with some frequency in the English journal *Slavery and Abolition*.

Given this ever growing body of studies on the slave trade, it was inevitable that Curtin's estimates of the volume, direction, and timing of the trade would be challenged. This has come from reestimating all the trades through the analysis of the new archival sources, which has often resulted in revising upward or downward given regional trades. Many of these new estimates were first summarized in Paul E. Lovejoy, "The Volume of the Atlantic Slave Trade: A Synthesis," *Journal of African History* 22, no. 4 (1982): 473–501; *Transformations in Slavery: A History of Slavery in Africa* (Cambridge, 1983), and his essay "The Impact of the Atlantic Slave Trade: A Review of the Literature," *Journal of African History* 30 (1989): 365–94. They are now being revised once again on the basis of the recently collected voyages database created by Eltis et al., *The Transatlantic Slave Trade* (1998); and the latest version of this updated dataset is found in the Wilson Library at Emory University and the estimated numbers can be found at http://wilson.library.emory.edu:9090/tast/assessment/estimates.faces. See also David Eltis and David Richardson, "West Africa and the Transatlantic Slave Trade: New Evidence of Long-Run Trends," in Eltis and Richardson, *Routes to Slavery* (1977), and David Eltis, "The Volume and Structure of the Transatlantic Slave Trade: A Reassessment," *William and Mary Quarterly*, 3rd ser., 58, no. 1, (Jan. 2001), 17–46.

Given time periods and regional trades have also been recalculated. See, for example, Ivana Elbl, "The Volume of the Early Atlantic Slave Trade, 1450–1521," *Journal of African History* 38, no. 1 (1997): 31–75; David Richardson, "Slave Exports from West and West-Central Africa, 1700–1810: New Estimates of Volume and Distribution," *Journal of African History* 30 (1989): 1–22; and David Eltis, "The Nineteenth Century Transatlantic Slave Trade: An Annual Time Series of Imports into the Americas Broken Down by Region," *Hispanic American Historical Review* 67, no. 1 (1987): 109–38. The volume of the English trade has been carefully examined by David Richardson, "The Eighteenth-Century British Slave Trade: Estimates of Its Volume and Coastal Distribution in Africa," *Research in Economic History* 12 (1989): 151–95; David Eltis, "The Volume and African Origins of the British Slave Trade before 1714," *Cahiers d'Études Africaines* 35, nos. 2–3 (1995); some of these numbers were challenged by Joseph E. Inikori, "The Volume of the British Slave Trade, 1655–1807," *Cahiers d'Études Africaines* 32, no. 4 (1992): 643–88, and were debated by David Richardson and Stephan D. Behrendt, "Inikori's Odyssey: Measuring the British Slave Trade, 1655–1807," *Cahiers d'Études Africaines* 35, nos. 2–3 (1995): 599–615, and most recently reanalyzed by Stephen D. Berhrendt, "The Annual Volume and Regional Distribution of the British Slave Trade, 1780–1807," *Journal of African History* 38, no. 2 (1997): 187–211. The French trade has been reexamined by Charles Becker, "Note sur les chiffres de la traite atlantique française au XVIIIe siècle," *Cahiers d'Études Africaines* 26, no. 4 (1986): 633–79. Although numbers are changed in given periods or regions, surprisingly, all these revisions to date do not seriously challenge the total figures generated by Curtin.

To examine slavery in Africa and the African organization of the trade, there is now a very impressive international literature. The problem with defining the limits of slavery, a fundamental issue when examining the institution in Africa, is best examined in Orlando Patterson, *Slavery and Social Death: A Comparative Study* (New York, 1982). Also see Claude Meillassoux, ed., *L'esclavage en Afrique précoloniale* (Paris, 1975). On the organization of the trade in relationship to Africa, a good place to begin is with the general surveys of Lovejoy, *Transformations in Slavery*; John Thornton, *Africa and Africans in the Making of the Atlantic World, 1400–1680* (Cambridge, 1992); and Patrick Manning, *Slavery and African Life: Occidental, Oriental and African Slave Trades* (Cambridge, 1990). Also useful for the context of the trade are A. G. Hopkins, *An Economic History of Africa* (London, 1973). Detailed studies devoted to the trade include Walter Rodney, *A History of the Upper Guinea Coast, 1545–1800* (Oxford, 1970); Philip D. Curtin, *Economic Change in Precolonial Africa: Senegambia in the Era of the Slave Trade*, 2 vols. (Madison, WI, 1975); John Vogt, *The Portuguese Rule on the Gold Coast, 1469–1682* (Athens, Ga., 1979); K. Y. Daaku, *Trade and Politics on the Gold Coast, 1600–1720* (Oxford, 1970); Albert van Dantzig, *Les Hollandais sur la côte de Guinée à l'époque de l'essor de l'Ashanti et du Dahomey, 1680–1740* (Paris, 1980); Robin Law, *The Slave Coast of West Africa, 1550–1750: The Impact of the Atlantic Slave Trade on an African Society* (Oxford, 1991); Larry W. Yarak, *Asante and the Dutch, 1744–1873* (Oxford, 1990); David Northrup, *Trade without Rulers: Pre- Colonial Economic Development in South-Eastern Nigeria* (Oxford, 1978); A. J. H. Latham, *Old Calabar, 1600–1891: The Impact of the International Economy upon a Traditional Society* (Oxford, 1973); A. F. C. Ryder, *Benin and the Europeans, 1485–1897* (London, 1969); and Phyllis M. Martin, *The External Trade of the Loango Coast, 1576–1870: The Effects of Changing Commercial Relations on the Vili Kingdom of Loango* (Oxford, 1972). Good studies of individual nations in the period of the trade are Malyn Newitt, *A History of Mozambique* (London, 1995); Tony Hodges and Malyn Newitt, *São Tomé and Príncipe: From Plantation Colony to Microstate* (Boulder, Colo., 1988); and David Birmingham, *Central Africa to 1870: Zambezia, Zaire and the South Atlantic* (Cambridge, 1981).

The abolition of the trade is most definitively studied in the work of Eltis, *Economic Growth* (1987). L. Phillip LeVeen, *British Slave Trade Suppression Policies, 1821–1865* (New York, 1977), examines the economic costs of this effort. For detailed recent analyses of the complex maneuverings of the Brazilian and Spanish governments to defend their trades, see David R. Murray, *Odious Commerce: Britain, Spain and the Abolition of the Cuban Slave Trade* (Cambridge, 1980); Arturo Morales Carrion, *Auge y decadencia de la trata negrera en Puerto Rico (1820–1860)* (Rio Piedras, 1978); and Leslie Bethell, *The Abolition of the Brazilian Slave Trade* (Cambridge, 1970); and most recently João Pedro Marques, *Os sonos do silêncio: o Portugal de oitocentos e a abolição do tráfico de escravos* (Lisbon, 1999) and Alencastro, *O trato dos viventes* (2000). On the British campaign, see F. J. Klingberg, *The Anti-Slavery Movement in England* (New Haven, 1926), and R. Coupland, *The British Anti-Slavery Movement* (London, 1933). The debate about the economic motivation behind the campaign and the supposed crisis in the West Indian economy can be seen in L. J. Ragatz, *The Fall of the Planter Class in the British Caribbean, 1763–1833* (New York, 1928); Anstey, *The Atlantic Slave Trade* (1975); and three works by Seymour Drescher, *Econocide: British Slavery in the Era of Abolition* (Pittsburgh, 1977), *Capitalism and Anti-Slavery: British Mobilization in Comparative Perspective* (New York, 1986), and *The Mighty Experiment: Free Labor versus Slavery in British Emancipation* (New York, 2002). For information on the European migrations to the Americas in the 19th century, see Imre Ferenczi and Walter F. Willcox, *International Migrations* Vol I (1929).

On the internal slave trades, which developed after the end of the Atlantic slave trade, see among others Herman Freudenberger and Jonathan B. Pritchett, "The Domestic United States Slave Trade: New Evidence," *Journal of Interdisciplinary History* 21, no. 3 (Winter 1991), 447–77, and Michael Tadman, *Speculators and Slaves: Masters, Traders and Slaves in the Old South* (Madison, Wisc., 1989) and the old classic Frederick Bancroft, *Slave Trading in the Old South*... For the Brazilian post-1850 trade, see Herbert S. Klein, "The Internal Slave Trade in Nineteenth Century Brazil: A Study of Slave Importations into Rio de Janeiro in 1852," *Hispanic American Historical Review* 51, no. 4 (Nov. 1971): 567–8; Alexandre Vieira Ribeiro, "E lá se vão para as minas: perfil do comércio de escravos despachados da Bahia para as Gerais na segunda metade do século XVIII," *XII Seminario sobre a economia mineira* (Diamantina, Minas Gerais, 2006); Maria do Carmo Salazar Martins and Helenice Carvalho Cruz da Silva, "VIA BAHIA: a importação de escravos para Minas Gerais pelo Caminho do Sertão, 1759–1772," *XII Seminario sobre a economia mineira* (Diamantina, Minas Gerais, 2006); Gabriel Santos Berute, "Dos escravos que partem para os portos do sul: características do tráfico negreiro do Rio Grande de São Pedro do Sul, c.1790-c.1825," M.A. thesis, UFRGS Porto Alegre, 2006; and Fábio W. A. Pinheiro, "O tráfico atlântico de escravos na formação dos plantéis mineiros, Zona da Mata c.1809-c.1830," M.A. thesis, UFRJ, Rio de Janeiro, 2007.

Finally, it is worth noting that some recent general surveys of the trade have begun to incorporate this new scholarly research into their findings. See Hubert Deschamps, *Histoire de la traite des noirs* (Paris, 1971); Pierre Pluchon, *La route des esclaves, négriers et bois d'ébène au xviiie siècle* (Paris, 1981); James A. Rawley, *The Trans-Atlantic Slave Trade* (New York, 1981); Françoise Renault and Serge Daget, *Les traites négrières en Afrique* (Paris, 1985); Hugh Thomas, *The Slave Trade: The Story of the Atlantic Slave Trade, 1440–1870* (London, 1997); and most recently Olivier Pétré-Grenouilleau, *Les traits négriéres. Essai d'histoire globale* (Paris, 2004).

Index

233